Suggestive Accelerative Learning Techniques

Suggestive Accelerative Learning Techniques

by
Donald H. Schuster
Iowa State University
Ames
and
Charles E. Gritton
Des Moines Public Schools
Des Moines

GORDON AND BREACH SCIENCE PUBLISHERS
New York • London • Paris • Montreux • Tokyo

Gordon and Breach Science Publishers

P.O. Box 786
Cooper Station
New York, New York, 10276
United States of America

P.O. Box 197
London WC2E 9PX
England

58, rue Lhomond
75005 Paris
France

P.O. Box 161
1820 Montreux 2
Switzerland

14–9 Okubo 3-chome,
Shinjuku-ku,
Tokyo 160
Japan

Library of Congress Cataloging in Publication Data
Schuster, Donald H.
　Suggestive accelerative learning techniques.

　Bibliography: p.
　Includes indexes.
　1. Educational acceleration.　2. Learning, Psychology
of. I. Gritton, Charles E., 1930–　.　II. Title.
LB1029.A22S38　1986　370.15'23　85-30487
ISBN 2-88124-055-0 (Switzerland)
ISBN 2-88124-054-2 (Switzerland: soft)

Illustrations by Locky Schuster

CONTENTS

We want to dedicate this book to the children of the world: may they have fun learning easily and well!

List of Figures

List of Tables

Acknowledgments

We would like to take this opportunity to express our appreciation to many people for their help and support in making this work possible.

First and foremost, we owe a huge debt of thanks over the last 10 years to our wives, Locky Schuster and Hazel Gritton, for their encouragement and support for what turned out to be a very large job indeed: researching, developing and writing about SALT.

Since the ideas and concepts behind SALT come basically from Suggestopedia, we owe a special debt of appreciation to Dr. George Lozanov.

The Society for Accelerative Learning and Teaching has been helpful and supportive over the last 10 years. We want to express our appreciation to the past presidents of SALT: Owen Caskey, Allyn Prichard, Jon Edwards, Jane Bancroft, Charles Schmid, Kay Herr, and Bob Prall. We also want to express our appreciation to these other former SALT officers for their help: Pat and Marge Mankins, and Charles and Anne Connolly.

I.

INTRODUCTION

In this chapter we're going to look at the basics: What is SALT? Suggestopedia? SuperLearning? Suggestology? First we will take a look at definitions, then an example of what SALT can do. Then we'll peek at research results, theory and a typical lesson.

A. DEFINITION

The Suggestive-Accelerative Learning Techniques (SALT) method uses aspects of suggestion similar to advertising and unusual styles of presenting material to accelerate classroom learning. The essence of this technique is using an unusual combination of physical relaxation exercises, mental concentration and suggestive principles to strengthen a person's ego and expand his or her memory capabilities while material to be learned is presented dynamically with relaxing music. Many of the independent elements have been known here in the Western World, but Dr. George Lozanov at the Research Institute of Suggestology in Sofia, Bulgaria apparently has been the first to put all of these component elements together in an integrated and highly effective learning procedure.

Several other terms need definition. "Suggestology": Suggestology is a term coined by Lozanov (1978) for the study of suggestion in its theoretical and practical aspects. "Suggestopedia": Suggestopedia is a term also first used by Lozanov to mean the application of suggestion to education and learning, especially improving them. In this book we will use SALT and Suggestopedia interchangeably, although there are minor differences as discussed later. In the early 1970's we developed SALT as an American synthesis of Suggestopedia as we had only

1

fragmentary reports from Lozanov at that time. "SuperLearning": Superlearning is a trade-marked term by Ostrander and Schroeder (1979) to refer to their book and accelerative learning methods such as SALT and Suggestopedia. As a final caution, please note that SALT as used in this book is not the same thing as the SALT Society, the Society for Accelerative Learning and Teaching.

B. BRIEF RESEARCH RESULTS

This humanistic teaching method has been evaluated in several field experiments in US public school classrooms, and the component elements evaluated in analytic laboratory studies with college students. The classroom studies rather consistently show that students trained with the SALT method showed significantly higher achievement scores than the controls, sometimes with significantly better attitudes than controls. Classroom subject matter in these studies has ranged from reading, spelling, mathematics, science, art, ag education to beginning German and Spanish. Grade levels have ranged from first grade in elementary school to college freshmen. The lab studies have provided significant support for the major component features of the method. Many of these studies have been published in the *Journal of the Society for Accelerative Learning and Teaching*.

Lozanov (1971, 1978) presents the results of many of his pilot studies in evaluating the various components of the method. Combined, the components of his method have produced results that have speeded up language learning by factors of 5 to 1 or more. Pilot projects in this country (Bordon and Schuster, 1972) and Schuster (1972) provide limited corroboration of these results; language learning has been speeded up by a factor of 3 to 1 in this U.S. research. Refer to the Research Results section of this book for further details.

To give the reader a feel for what happens with this method, we present here an account of a 4 day tutoring session by one of us (CEG) in 1975. We had 2 eighth grade students recommended by their parents as learning disability students, students who had difficulty in math. The students themselves asked for some help in spelling. These 2 students were ideal for experimenting, trying to see whether or not we could get some of the results that Lozanov had reported. I (CEG) worked with the students in the living room of their own home with comfortable chairs and good stereo equipment. The students took their pretest on spelling words quite willingly, but refused even to try on mathematics because it was way beyond their expectations. The Lozanov method of presentation to these students was different than with a regular class. No objections were expressed by either the students or their families in doing this.

We took one day to give the students some background, another day to start preparing them, to give them a pretest and to try to establish the basic beginning conditions. The second day we started with the Lozanov presentation of 50 spelling words and preparation to present fractions as an arithmetic lesson. After presenting the 50 words from the list of 200 spelling demons, I asked the kids for verification. Now with only 2 students we did not ask or try to score the papers, but watched while they corrected their own papers. They did fantastically well. At the end they were surprised and expressed amazement at their ease and pleasure. They had such comments as, "It's fun to learn, it's easy to learn, there's nothing to learning."

Having let them converse for a few minutes I decided we should start with the arithmetic lesson, and there's where I failed. At least I didn't get to do my lesson. I said that we should review the rules for the addition of fractions, the problems they could not work and which on the previous day they refused to have anything to do with. The young gentleman involved immediately started through a discussion of the need for a lowest common denominator, so that when you had achieved the common denominator you could add the numerators, or the numbers "on top" as he called them. The young lady chimed right in with him; they went through the complete addition set, reducing their answers to the lowest possible ratio with no comments made by the teacher. When I tried to introduce subtractions, they took off again, until the only 2 things they let me talk about were the rules. Their learning barriers had broken down, their acceptance of themselves was very high, they were excited and pleased about learning. They could work all problems given to them with ease regardless of the complexities of the denominators; they had no problems or difficulties at all.

We started again the next day with another 50 words from the 200 demons. They mixed the order up, checked their own answers, were thrilled and overjoyed. The girl was still working at 100%, but the boy kept erasing correct words and changing the spelling words so they were wrong. He certainly was fixed in his mind that he could not spell even though he did know how to spell the words correctly after they were presented in the Lozanov style with music as a background.

I started the next day again to introduce an arithmetic lesson by saying that we were going to talk about multiplication and division. The students presented and discussed the rules between themselves. I watched in amazement because these 2 students who 2 days earlier could not, and would not do any fraction problems were quoting the rules as well as any teacher could. The only area of difficulty was that the girl had learned a different set of division rules than had the boy. I personally favored the side of the young man; we convinced the girl our rules were much simpler, less involved and less complicated. She enjoyed hearing that they could work any fraction problem we could present to them in addition, subtraction, multiplication and division.

On our fourth day they did another 50 words for a total of 150 of the 200 spelling demons given to the kids. They could spell correctly right up and down the line, with the exception of the boy's continuing to erase and change the words so they were wrong. We then talked about percentages, the next area of arithmetic. The ratio or proportion method was new to them. After a very few minutes they said, "We're just doing our fractions over again; it's very simple." They took off again and could work the percentage problems without any difficulty.

The participating students showed a completely reversed attitude about themselves now as compared with 4 days earlier. The students were quite eager to continue with the program. Their folks had said they only wanted to review math because they were going on to algebra. We stopped after I had this chance to apply and see the amazing effect the Lozanov approach can have when you desuggest the student, encourage him/her and raise their expectation level. They remembered and recalled rules the other teachers had told them before with amazing ease. They simply were a pleasure and joy to work with, because there was nothing you could say that they were not anticipating, that they could not and did not go ahead and take the initiative on. Students who had come by their parents' recommendation as uninterested in school, unable to work fractions, unable to work percentage problems, and unable to spell, had a completely reversed attitude in 4 days of class, including the introduction and explanation of the things we were going to try to do. As far as they were concerned, we had accomplished the goal we had set, so we stopped the workshop. This experience increased the desire on my part to apply the method to classroom situations, because every trial of the Lozanov approach worked beyond any expectation I had had.

To lend an objective note to the above subjective account of Lozanov style tutoring, here are the verification test data over the course of the 4 days, starting with pretests:

	Spelling	Fractions
Jane	30, 90, 100, 100%;	0, 90, 100, 80%.
Joe	20, 90, 60, 60%;	0, 90, 90, 90%.

That was in 1975. These 2 pupils had been diagnosed as learning disabled by the school psychologist, and due to their inferior academic achievement at the end of the eighth grade, were simply "passed on" to the ninth grade. Their parents objected to their lack of achievement as written above. Normally, these 2 children would have been predicted to drop out or flunk out of high school. That did not happen. Both Jane and Joe finished high school, and in the top half of their class. The following year, both started college at a local community college, and finished their first year there satisfactorily. Recently Joe graduated from a 4 year college in Iowa with a BS. At last contact, Jane was enrolled in a 4-year nursing program. Their performance has been impressive, and certainly far beyond what one would expect for learning disabled children.

Case histories such as this one about Jane and Joe are interesting, but they only lead to suggestions about how to accelerate teaching, not prove it. For classroom and laboratory studies that collectively do prove this method works, refer to the Research Review section of this book. And refer to Figure 1-1, which epitomizes our feeling about SALT/Suggestopedia.

C. OVERVIEW OF METHOD

The basic theory behind the Lozanov method is:

1. Learning should be characterized by joy and the absence of tension.

2. As humans we operate with conscious and paraconcious levels.

3. Suggestion is the means to use the normally unused reserves of the mind for increased learning.

Fig. 1-1.   There Must Be A Better Way

There are three basic phases to the Lozanov method, preliminary preparations, presentation of material and practice of material. These are given in detail in the next chapters in this book, as well as outlined here. It should be pointed out here that this sequence is based on teaching foreign language; another sequence might be appropriate for other subjects.

In the preliminary activities the teacher creates an initially favorable atmosphere prior to presenting the didactic material to be learned. He or she does this by his/her composure, expectations and statements with a totally positive attitude. S/he provides waking state suggestions as to the effectiveness of previous desuggestive barriers by which people have lowered their learning ability to the so-called norm or average for society. The teacher is authoritative but honest in his/her presentation; s/he knows. The instructor states that they will be expected to improve their learning dramatically and that they will have a series of control quizzes ungraded by the teacher to prove to themselves that this indeed happens. The instructor communicates an integrated, consistent message at conscious/subconscious levels and verbal/non-verbal levels. This takes training and practice to achieve.

The students prepare themselves prior to the presentation of didactic material by several types of exercises, physical relaxing exercises, mind-calming exercises and restimulation of previous pleasant learning experiences. Examples of how to do this are given in the next chapters.

In the presentation phase the material to be learned is given in several consecutive passes the same day: review of previous material, dynamic presentation of new material, and repetition of new material to be learned in a passive, but receptive, state. Previous material is reviewed and integrated with the material to be presented in today's session. Then the new material to be learned is first presented in a dynamic, dramatic style by the instructor. Typically, the teacher picks everyday material that is positive and of interest to the students. The instructor uses imagery, as well as drama, to get the point across and may suggest word images to the students to facilitate remembering the material. Students are also given instruction to experience the material in a sensory way as much as possible.

These presentational techniques facilitate learning with the whole brain. Typical classroom verbal material is learned primarily by the left brain hemisphere for right-handed persons. The Lozanov techniques present non-verbal (paraconscious) material simultaneously with the verbal (conscious) to stimulate both brain hemispheres in an integrated way. (Note: Lozanov use "paraconscious" to refer to things beyond our normal conscious awareness, e.g., subconscious.)

The new material to be learned is repeated later in a second phase with the students in a passive, but alert, state as if they were going to attend a favorite music concert. The students first calm their minds with a technique such as watching their breathing. Then material may be presented in synchronization with the students' breathing, or merely read monotonously with frequent pauses. Several ways to do this will be covered later. The material to be learned also may be presented in a fashion orchestrated with the background music and synchronized breathing. Music is selected that has a definite rhythm, and played for this passive review at a volume level approximately equal to the instructor's speaking voice. After the material has been presented for the second time in this passive pseudo-concert style, several minutes of mind-calming are given again to fix the material in the students' minds, and to prevent mental distractions from interfering with the acquisition and retention of the material.

In the practice phase the material just presented is practiced in something approaching conventional laboratory discussion sessions. These are held in alternate sessions or preferably on alternate days. As an example of this activity, students may look initially at the book or printed material for practice as they are requested to make up words and sentences using the material just presented. Students may pair off by 2's and 3's for this conversational practice in a language class. Near the end of a SALT class, students are expected to make up a play that has direct relevance for them and then perform this play with the entire class participating. The students obviously have to utilize most of the material that they have learned in this psychodrama.

The instructor also grades the students individually on how well they perform during this final play or psychodrama. Control or check quizzes have been given near the end of these practice sessions. These quizzes are graded by the students themselves, and are not seen by the instructor unless so requested by the students. However, comprehensive exams may be given by the instructor at various times throughout the course for the purpose of determining grades in addition to using the psychodrama for this purpose. Of course, these tests are announced in advance, and the students are prepared suggestopedically for them beforehand.

D. OVERALL SEQUENCING

In our opinion, the Lozanov method is so remarkably effective because the individual components in the method have been combined together in an overall, integrated fashion which increases the effectiveness of the individual elements in a cumulative way. This sequence and explanation follow.

In the preparatory phase there is a suggestive, positive atmosphere which is highly permissive regarding learning and quite different from what students expect in the usual classroom. As a result, students are willing to go along with the preliminary and preparatory exercises. Students go through stretching exercises which leave them physically relaxed. This in turn makes it possible for students to calm their minds with an exercise such as watching your breathing. Research very clearly points to the fact that suggestion is more effective when a person's mind is calm, such as after watching your breathing or having one's mind in a relaxed state. Further, research also indicates that suggestion itself is much more effective when it is indirect and permissive rather than direct and peremptory.

The presentation phase also is carefully sequenced in that the active phase has the material first presented in a dynamic, dramatic fashion by the teacher. The students are requested to experience the material sensorially as completely as possible and to go along with whatever suggestions for word images the instructor may make. Next the material is repeated during the passive, pseudo-concert phase where the students are requested mentally to reenact the images and scenes from the previous active phase. This passive phase utilizes both hemispheres of the brain in learning due to the relaxation, music and free flowing imagery reviewed along with the verbal material. This is an additional advantage for the method, being able to use most of the mind in learning rather than just the verbal hemisphere as is typical in conventional classroom presentation.

The practice and use phase of the material just presented has both conventional and unconventional aspects. It has been fairly well demonstrated that practicing material just presented does indeed help in learning. However, Lozanov has taken the pressure off of the practice in several ways. Students are given fictitious names, personalities and biographies so that when they make a mistake, "they" did not make the mistake; this helps to eliminate embarrassment and fear of failure. In addition, students tend to identify with this new personality, and use it a context in learning the language itself. Secondly, the control or check quizzes are given on an ungraded basis, that is, they are scored and graded by the students and are not seen by the instructor. Thus again fear of failure is eliminated. Grades are given only on the basis of the final tests.

A snowball effect is very much in evidence from the first class on. By means of the unusual techniques and suggestions, students do indeed learn in the first lesson more effectively and easily than they had in the past. Once the students see this happening to themselves, the snowball starts rolling. Very soon the students are learning with something approaching perfection, and with a very high degree of average retention. Many students in fact have a nearly perfect memory for the classroom material presented in the Lozanov method.

SUMMARY

In this chapter we have defined terms important to the concept of accelerative learning, given an example of what SALT can do, listed the relevant theoretical concepts, and looked at a typical sequence of activities in a SALT class.

We defined SALT as Suggestive-Accelerative Learning Techniques, a generally superior method of classroom instruction. The method uses relaxation, advertising-like suggestion, dramatic presentation of classroom material with students' generating imagery to help learn, quiet review of material with music, a fun-and-games elaboration of class material, and finally an ungraded quiz. The American synthesis called SALT is essentially the same thing that George Lozanov in Europe called Suggestopedia, the systematic study of suggestion designed to improve education. Suggestology is the study of suggestion in its own right. SuperLearning (TM) is a popular term referring to accelerative learning in general and specifically to a book with that title by Ostrander and Schroeder (1979), but it is different than SALT or Suggestopedia.

A typical SALT lesson has 3 major phases: preliminary activities, presentation of material in several ways, and practice using the material. A SALT class has a relaxed, fun atmosphere. This is based on the theory that learning should be joyful and free of tension. Theory also states that we as human beings always operate with unity of our conscious and subconscious minds, and that suggestion is the key to using our mental reserves to accelerate learning.

QUESTIONS

1. Now you'll be able to recall these definitions and how they differ. Define: accelerative learning, SALT, Suggestopedia, suggestology, superlearning, learning barriers, restimulation.
2. Give several roughly synonymous terms for accelerative learning. How do they differ?
3. What is a typical ratio of SALT acceleration compared with conventional teaching for beginning teachers? For advanced?
4. What are the three theoretical principles of SALT and Suggestopedia that come from psychotherapy?
5. What is a typical sequence of activities in a SALT class?

II.

THEORETICAL WORKING PRINCIPLES

Have you ever considered teaching as communication? It is that, among other things. Our first step in this chapter is to consider teaching as communication, with the transmission of information (didactic material) from the speaker (teacher) via a medium (e.g., lecturing) to the listener (students). This communicative process can be helped or hindered by personal barriers, noise, restimulation and feedback. These concepts are important because the teacher has to recognize barriers to learning in students and know how to circumvent them, how to minimize noise and restimulation, and how to improve communication with feedback.

What makes SALT or Suggestopedia work? The theory says we always operate as the sum or total of our conscious and subconscious functioning. Paying attention to this can improve our communication. Furthermore, the subconscious is trainable. So here is a good place to introduce the George Concept, a way to integrate our conscious and subconscious functioning.

Theory also says that suggestion is a key concept to let us get at the reserves of the human mind to produce accelerated learning. Appropriate suggestion when accepted by the student produces an expectancy of accelerated learning, a critical factor in the speeded-up learning itself.

Theory says further that not only should we enjoy learning in a relaxed way, but that we should also learn more and remember longer when relaxed and enjoying the process. We will conclude the chapter with a brief consideration of relaxation research and learning.

A. COMMUNICATIONS MODEL

A fundamental concept in Suggestopedia is that communication can be improved considerably both between people and within a person, that is, with his/her memory. Thus we need to present the communications model used in Suggestopedia. See Fig. 2-1. Communication between people is complex and occurs on two levels, consciously and paraconsciously (beyond conscious awareness).

1. Barriers

As the figure shows, communication (such as teaching) flows from the conscious mind of the speaker through his/her paraconscious through some transmission medium (such as the air or TV) through the paraconscious of the recipient and finally to the recipient's conscious mind. There are barriers or biases in each person's paraconscious mind that filter or modify the communication. These may be:

1. Socially or culturally accepted patterns.

2. Body language signals that are culturally instinctive.

3. Subliminal communication, as among children.

4. Verbal confusion due to images generated by the recipient in interpreting the sounds received.

Noise can enter the communications process at several points and in several forms. Probably the most familiar form of noise is in the medium or channel. We immediately think of static on a radio during a thunderstorm, or bars and lines crawling across the TV screen occasionally when an airplane goes by overhead. Noise can also occur in the human speaker or sender: "slips", when a speaker says something else than what s/he had intended, speech problems such as a foreign accent or cold that interferes with the listener's comprehension, or when the speaker gets distracted and wanders off the subject.

Noise can also occur in the listener or receiver. For example, when your mind wanders or you are distracted, your reception and comprehension of the transmitted message suffers due to this internal "noise" in your head. Similarly when you are worried about some other problem due to restimulation, you find it hard to pay attention

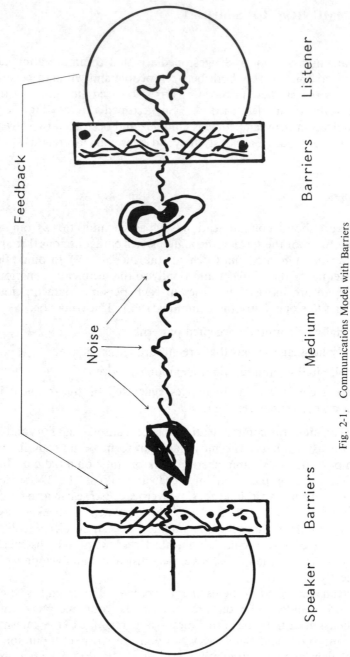

Fig. 2-1. Communications Model with Barriers

to the speaker. Finally, noise can occur in the feedback part of the communications process. This happens when the roles of speaker and listener are interchanged temporarily in the two-way communicative process. Thus the same 3 types of noise mentioned above apply also in the feedback link.

Restimulation is an important source of noise that is little recognized. Restimulation or redintegration occurs when some present stimulus triggers a long-past memory and brings up into the present the old and inappropriate reaction. Let me give you an example.

Many years ago my wife and I (DHS) were invited to dinner by an old friend of my wife's. While the women were preparing dinner, I was out in the backyard playing with our friend's two little boys. As children do, the boys got tired of playing with me, and ran off into the neighbor's yard. Their mother observed this, leaned out the kitchen window, and hollered at me, "Don, go get my kids!"

Immediately I was angry, muttering something like, "If you want your kids, go get them yourself." The very next minute I was wondering why I was so angry in the first place. I got to reflecting on why, and the answer was restimulation. It wasn't what the kids' mother had said, but the manner in which she said it. After all, asking an adult to watch over your kids for awhile is a reasonable request. The problem was her tone of voice: her demand was voiced exactly the same way and in the same tones that my mother used to order me to do things when I was a teenager. I resented my mother's unreasonable (?) demands as an adolescent, and as a young adult, I yet resented strongly demands uttered in that same tone of voice. The lady's tone of voice in present time had restimulated an adolescent reaction pattern to my mother's voice from years earlier: I had reacted the same way.

Restimulation can be good or bad, usually bad. It accounts for the lack of understanding that occurs everywhere people get together and talk. It leads to problems, arguments and fights. How can you analyze the present situation analytically when you are restimulated and reacting now the same way you did as a kid? Your reaction as a child may have been appropriate, but to react the same way now as as an adult is highly likely inappropriate.

While restimulation usually is bad, it can be used in a "good" way. A teacher can use it deliberately to rekindle an eager motivation to learn in the classroom. Refer to the chapter on Classroom Activities, and read over the "Early Pleasant Learning Restimulation" as a positive use of restimulation.

The barriers or noise or filters in Fig. 2-1 are shown operating between the conscious mind and what one says and hears; these modify our thoughts and their expression into communication such as speech. They also modify what we perceive into what we interpret without our awareness.

Lozanov (1978) lists three types of communicative barriers:

1. The moral-ethical barrier. Social and cultural patterns will stop communication that is not acceptable to a group.

2. The rational-logical barrier. Communication perceived as illogical puzzles the listener and is rejected.

3. The intuitive-emotional barrier. Something said that is not liked for whatever reason is rejected.

Let's give several examples of barriers. Starting with the moral-ethical barrier, here's an example that actually happened (to DHS). Some years ago I taught one section of beginning Spanish for one year at the university level. At the end of the fall quarter, about half of the students were able to arrange their class schedules so that they could study Spanish with me during the winter quarter also. However, a young lady, the best student in class the fall quarter, was not with me in the winter quarter for the second course in beginning Spanish. A little bit later, I happened to see her in the hall one day; to chat a bit I asked her why she wasn't taking Spanish with me, fully expecting her to say that she couldn't work it into her schedule. Surprisingly, she answered, "Learning Spanish with you was so easy it bothered me!" She was an excellent student, always studying; the thought that she had learned so easily and well didn't seem right to her — so she switched to another section of Spanish because of her ethical barrier that learning shouldn't be so easy.

The emotional-intuitive barrier is similar, but has more of an emotional tone than ethical. An example quite familiar unfortunately, is a student who says, "I hate math!" This student may be justified in this emotional expression after years of trying and not succeeding in mathematical subjects. The teacher of course counters this with SALT, possibly with some reassurance as follows, "Just leave it to me; I can help you learn math easily and well with SALT. I've been teaching this course this way now for some time, and I've worked with many students like yourself. Rely on me, I can help you; try it my way for a week and you'll see." The teacher then might use the George Concept to get the student started on learning math in a relaxed fashion.

The logical-rational barrier again is similar, but is based on solid, objective evidence for that student. An example is, "Learning for me has always been hard; I've always had to study and study just to pass my courses and get an occasional B. Then you tell me I can relax and learn easily in your class? I've never been able to learn like that!" The teacher could counter in this case by citing research studies, "Learning for you has always been hard, and you're hanging on by the skin of your teeth. However you learned to learn the hard way unnecessarily. We have a lot of research studies quoted in this book about students just like yourself who thought learning was hard. It isn't; try it my way for a few days and find out. Would you like to see for yourself just how easy it really is?"

To communicate effectively, the teacher must harmonize his/her communication with these barriers to allow the communication to pass from the conscious mind of one person to that of the other. No frontal assault will win this communicative battle. The barriers are not hammered down, but they can be bypassed readily by the suggestopedic teacher. These barriers in the student are part of the self-imposed self-image of that student, and are repositioned each time you work with that student. The teacher must plan each day to meet a new self-image with new barriers, at least until the student becomes a self-actuated person. When the reserves of the mind are activated, the student is self-actualized.

Lozanov (1978) presents three means or ways to use suggestion in the classroom to bypass student barriers:

1. Psychological. With appropriate training, the teacher organizes the lesson material psychotherapeutically, psychoprophylactically, psychophysically and emotionally. Peripherally received communication is accepted non-critically.

2. Didactic (instructional). The teacher presents the material in different ways deliberately to promote learning.

3. Artistic. For example, the teacher uses artistic posters, uses classical music as background to globalize the lesson.

Lozanov claims that suggestion is the key to unlock the reserves of the mind to make possible accelerated learning. The teacher's opening procedures then are a "suggestive ritual" that helps the students get themselves set-up to learn faster and better than before. While we will say much more about suggestion in subsequent chapters, we want to introduce one of the most important suggestive means next for training unconscious levels of the human mind.

Fig. 2-2.   George, at Your Service

2. The George Concept

The George Concept is singly the most valuable thing we could ever teach you. This is a way of getting your subconscious mind to work with you deliberately and consciously, rather than willy-nilly or haphazardly. Normally we use only a small part of our minds in thinking or any mental activity. Typically we are conditioned to think only in words. The George Concept changes this. Your subconscious mind, possibly involving only the right half of your brain, deals with non-verbal material: pictures, emotions, sounds, feelings, just to name a few of its concerns. These usually ignored aspects are attended to and used carefully when using the George Concept. See Figure 2-2.

The George Concept is a way to use your subconscious mind in helping you with your daily living and everyday problems. As you will see shortly, it involves focusing on both the verbal and nonverbal aspects of a situation in an integrated way.

Let's look at the rules first for using the George concept and then we'll consider an example. The simple rules are: 1. Visualize yourself having just accomplished your goal, or having just solved your problem. See yourself there, feel yourself there; how would it feel? Include other modalities, such as hearing, smelling and tasting as appropriate. Use your imagination freely to make the situations vivid and realistic. It is important to use present perfect timing: you have just now gotten your goal accomplished, achieved or done.

Next, distract yourself; think about something else. If you have doubts about whether you actually can accomplish your goal, your subconscious mind at this point will bring up doubts, or you may find yourself skeptically thinking about the impossibility of your goal. Don't. Talk to your subconscious mind saying something like this, "George, I don't want the doubts or the scepticism; what I want is . . . (repeat your detailed goal image with feelings.)" Then distract yourself again; think about something else deliberately again. You may have to repeat this several times, but soon your subconscious mind (George) will accept your goal image and stop pestering you consciously with doubts.

2. While the above is the nonverbal or subconscious part of getting your subconscious mind to work with you consciously in the George Concept, this second part is a complementary verbal goal setting. State the goal verbally, give yourself reasons or rationalizations why you want the goal, and finally tell yourself what you can do once you have achieved your goal.

As an example, tell yourself, "I want goal X so I can make more money (or be happy, etc.) I can use the additional money to live a little better, help other people, or travel.''

3. The above two points get your subconscious and conscious parts of your mind working together. This last point deals with how to get logically from here and now to your goal. Work out a schedule of necessary steps or events that will lead you one by one to your goal. What do I have to do first? What do I do second? Next? Then? Last? Once this sequence is worked out, then start doing the necessary things in order.

Let's take an overall example of using the George Concept. Suppose you want to buy tickets to go see your favorite entertainer this coming weekend. Assuming the ticket office will be open, visualize yourself stopping by the ticket office on the way home from work. See yourself driving to the building instead of taking your usual route home. Imagine yourself parking the car, walking up to the ticket window, asking about and buying the tickets you want. In addition to seeing yourself do this, use your imagination also to hear yourself talking to the ticket seller, and feel yourself driving the car in a different route than usual, parking the car, getting out of it and walking up to the ticket window. If there would be smells or other perceptions involved, include them in your goal imagery. Then put this imagery out of your mind by thinking about the verbal aspect, such as, ''I want to enjoy a concert or performance by my favorite star, and take along my wife (or husband, friend, whatever.) That will be a great evening for us both.'' Last is the sequence of steps to get to your goal. Ask yourself, ''Do I have enough money to pay for the tickets? If not, do I have to stop at the bank, or bring along a blank check?'' ''On the way home, where do I have to leave my usual route and turn differently?'' Figure this out and then see yourself doing it on the way home.

Having completed these three steps in the George Concept, you can relax and put the thought of buying tickets out of your mind. On the way home, your subconscious mind (George) will guide you to do the appropriate things at the right times to buy your tickets just as if this were an old habit and you did it every day. However, you could cancel this, say by mentally drawing an ''X'' through your goal image, and saying to yourself, ''No, I don't want that any more.'' You could also water down the effect by being skeptical or doubtful about its working. Your subconscious mind averages these goal images for a given goal. If you want George to do something, leave a clear, unambiguous image of that goal. If you have conflicting images for a given goal, George will work this conflict into the goal itself; you may or may not get your goal!

Do you have to call your subsconscious "George"? Of course not! We have taught the George Concept to many people — it works. Some men will pick another name for their subconscious mind; many women will pick a feminine name, possibly "George Anne". But some women use "George". The important thing is to think about this intimate, silent part of your being and pick a name. Use this name to talk to yourself in using the George Concept to set and get goals. Be sure to pat yourself on the back mentally when you do achieve your goal, "Thanks George" or something similar. This reinforcement helps George get in the groove to help you next time.

Using the George Concept and talking silently to yourself this way sounds schizophrenic. People would think you're crazy if you did this out loud. The reverse is true: rather than being schizy, using George promotes your mental health. You will be using your conscious and subconscious minds in an integrated way to achieve goals, rather than having them working at cross purposes. And this is definitely healthy for you!

Uses for the George Concept are many. The obvious use in this book is for students to use the George Concept to help them learn fast, easily and efficiently. Instructions to do this are straightforward and should be obvious. Also, George can help you find lost objects, get parking spots, learn efficiently, help you out of tough spots, aid you in accomplishing life goals — to name just a few possibilities. Uses range from the trivial to the sublime. Some people think of George as their guardian angel. The George Concept is a door-opener into the little used non-specific mental reserves of our human being.

Here is a short example of how a teacher can use the George Concept in the classroom. Suppose you are teaching a lesson on English grammar in high school. Before you start, here is what you might tell your students: "Imagine that we have come to the end of today's lesson and you are now taking the short quiz over the material. See yourself looking at the quiz questions; they are easy, you know all the answers! Feel yourself smiling as you write down the answers quickly to all the easy questions. Hear yourself talking to your friends later about how easy learning is in this class.... Then give yourself a reason for wanting to learn grammar today, such as 'It can help me get a job when I get out of school.' ... Finally, realize that you do have to stay awake, listen, and do the fun things I ask you to do to help you learn today."

B. SUGGESTOPEDIC PRINCIPLES

1. Unity of the conscious and paraconscious

According to Lozanov (1978), our being is always integrated, our conscious and paraconscious minds always act as one, like it or not. We cannot act as split personalities; we can merely act differently at different times. But whatever behavior we do, we do so in a unified way at that particular moment.

This has immediate application in the classroom. The lesson must be globalized and presented as an integrated package with artistic, didactic and psychological means. These will be detailed later.

2. Joy and the absence of tension

People just do not learn very well when unhappy, depressed, confused, angry, sad, etc. Such negative emotions are accompanied by psychological tension which hinders learning. Correspondingly the teacher needs to relax the students prior to learning and during learning, and to make the learning process enjoyable. Stop and ask yourself, "Is this the usual classroom?" Obviously not! If you find yourself wondering, "How do I make my class fun, interesting and relaxed?", read on.

Here is some research data to support our contention about relaxation in learning. Schuster and Martin (1980) had college students learn vocabulary words under different conditions of tension and relaxation. Previously, these students had been trained to control the level of tension in their foreheads, and consequently their psychological level of relaxation. Then, they learned lists of rare English words under all possible conditions of having their foreheads tensed or relaxed prior to learning a list, while learning a list, or while taking the quiz for a vocabulary list. Initially, highly anxious students did better when tensed in the learning situation than when relaxed. The converse was true for chronically low anxious students. But overall, learning was best when students relaxed their foreheads and themselves before learning, during learning, and during the quiz.

3. Suggestion is the link to the reserves of the mind

Suggestion is used to improve memory and learning in the suggestopedic class. This really is the basis for the word "Suggestopedia": "suggesto" (suggestion) + "pedia" (learning). However here in this book, we prefer to use SALT as meaning suggestive-accelerative learning and teaching, or system of accelerative learning techniques, as being more readily understood and accepted than Suggestopedia. We will use the terms SALT and Suggestopedia as generally interchangeable here in this book.

Lozanov (1978) defines suggestion: Suggestion is a constant communication factor which chiefly through paraconscious mental activity can create conditions for tapping the functional reserve capacities of personality. He uses the adjective "constant" here to mean that it cannot be turned on or off; it's present all the time between teacher and students. He uses the term "functional reserve capacities" to mean that we all have many talents that we have not developed nor do we use normally. But they can be tapped, developed, and used in the SALT classroom.

One such reserve is improved memory which makes possible accelerated memory. Another is mental control of one's body such as reduced pain sensitivity or extraordinary strength in emergencies. Yet another is the little known ability to speed up healing of one's body; see Schuster (1975) and Muñoz (1984) for details. Refer to Table 5-4 for further listing.

The reader by now may have several questions. Is Suggestopedia (Suggestology) a form of hypnosis? Some people may think it is, but we believe it is closer to advertising in form and intent than it is to formal trance definition of hypnosis. The aim of advertising is to persuade you to do something you might normally do anyhow; the aim of hypnosis is to compel you to do something you normally wouldn't do, or couldn't do.

Is Suggestopedia a form of relaxation? Not directly, but relaxation is used extensively in Suggestopedia. However, there is much more to making Suggestopedia work than mere relaxation. For a review of learning while relaxed, and learning under hypnosis, refer to Szalontai (1980).

Is Suggestopedia a form of repetology, learning with lots of repetition? No, repeating material by itself does not result in much faster learning. Repetition is used in Suggestopedia, but while the material to be learned is repeated, it is presented or repeated in different ways and styles to enhance learning. The repetitions are few. We will consider this again later under classroom procedures.

SUMMARY

In this chapter we introduced the basic theory behind SALT or Suggestopedia. First we considered the communications model behind SALT, and then introduced the basic theoretical principles in Suggestopedia.

In the communications model, the teacher communicates the classroom information using several media to the students. Interactively the roles of speaker and listeners switch, and the students feedback information to the teacher about what they have been learning and doing.

Barriers, noise and restimulation interfere with the teaching communicative process. The teacher has barriers or psychological characteristics that interfere with teaching; so do the students. Restimulation is a frequent source of noise in interpersonal communication. It occurs quite commonly when some possibly unrecognized aspect of a current situation triggers the memory of some past situation and brings back an old behavior clearly inappropriate now. Barriers exist in several types, but they all represent reality for that person and prevent the person from achieving more optimally at a higher level.

Barriers can be bypassed readily with SALT techniques for most people. Suggestion in various forms is used to work around student barriers to accelerated learning. Barriers are not dealt with head-on. The George Concept is one example of guided imagery and suggestion to bypass barriers, and at the same time help integrate conscious and subconscious functioning.

The 3 basic theoretical principles in Suggestopedia come from the mental health field. Learning should be characterized by joy and the absence of tension. There is unity of the conscious and paraconscious for each person. Suggestion is the link to our mental reserves, such as accelerated learning.

QUESTIONS

Can you imagine yourself answering these questions right now, or do you need a quick review?
1. Define communication in your own words.
2. Sketch the communication process. Include all parts.
3. Define noise, restimulation, feedback and barriers in the communicative process of teaching.
4. Give your own examples of the different types of barriers.
5. List the 3 suggestopedic principles. What do they mean?
6. What is the George Concept? How does it fit in with SALT?
7. What are reserves of the mind? Can you give more than one example?
8. How is Suggestopedia different from other forms of accelerated learning?

III.

RESEARCH REVIEW

In this chapter we are going to review the research evidence for the effectiveness and benefits of Suggestopedia and its American derivative SALT. In sequence we are going to consider similar methods and theories, foreign language studies, non-language studies, and finally studies about learning that apply to SALT.

Other technical books have been written about accelerated learning and Suggestopedia. See for instance, Caskey (1980), Prichard and Taylor (1980).

A. SIMILAR THEORIES

When I (CEG) started thinking why SALT was so effective in teaching all subjects to all ages, I felt that my training in education was not complete. So I started asking various people, psychologists, M.D.'s, and psychotherapists about psychotherapy and what theories would be best to study. Their answer was that there are over 250 different therapies being practiced in the U.S. I changed the question to what therapies had the best track record? Who had the best method for changing people?

The same few names kept being used to answer. The same giants and fields: Milton H. Erickson, Virginia Satir, Est, and Gestalt therapy. So I have tried to compare their works with the framework of Lozanov's. These gifted individuals have built constructs that have certain ideas in common. These common ideas should be the very essence of the thinking of educators. These giants are:

Dr. Georgi Lozanov, M.D., was trained as a psychotherapist, but became interested in "hypermnesia" or super memory which led to the development of *Suggestology and Outlines of Suggestopedia*. We called this program SALT (Suggestive-Accelerative Learning and Teaching) in America as in the beginning we did not have a complete translation of his work.

Dr. Virginia Satir, Ph.D., and trained in family therapy, has been called 'larger than life'. Her *Conjoint Therapy* book published in 1967, has been used as a text to train others ever since. Simon (1985) details a recent interview with her. *Peoplemaking* is a newer book for all of those in the business of communicating with or producing people. See also Simon (1985).

Dr. Milton H. Erickson, M.D., was trained as a psychiatrist and is called the father of hypnotherapy in America. Now deceased, his work is still an important source because of his many years as an author. There are yet many ideas being written about his indirect suggestion; one of the best is Lankton and Lankton's *The Answer Within*.

Werner Erhard has developed a training program that he calls "est Training", not a therapy. Some of the people who have taken the "training" talk of its curative powers, but Erhard does not. Bry's *est, 60 Hours That Transform Your Life* shows that Erhard just uses what works.

Dr. Frederick Perls, M.D., Ph.D., developed Gestalt therapy in treating patients as a psychiatrist. Gestalt therapy makes a contribution to existential philosophy.

Some personal observations: 1. None of these individuals was trained in a College of Education. They show very little regard for the traditions of education; they are excellent communicators of a different sort and have a great deal to offer us as educators. 2. The ideas contained in this paper have been filtered from the writings of others. If there are any errors in my interpretation, I am to blame. 3. My prejudices toward Suggestopedia are built into this comparison and that may cause certain other good ideas to be left out. The work of all of these geniuses should be studied in the altogether. 4. I have tried to use the various authors' own words with just some condensations in the next table. 5. The framework of SALT brings these psychotherapeutic techniques to the classroom.

Before we start analyzing the works of Lozanov and these four others, we want to point out a problem. If you remember biology, to dissect a frog is not good for the frog. Did you ever try to put a dissected frog back together? Or make it live again? Being forewarned, we'll be forearmed to keep the sections all together as the

Table 3-1. Comparison of Effective Therapies

	SUGGESTOPEDIA *Lozanov*	CONJOINT THERAPY *Satir*	INDIRECT SUGGESTION *Erickson*	est TRAINING *Erhard*	GESTALT THERAPY *Perls*
AUTHORITY		Power's adjectives: Vigorous, Forceful, Strong, Influential, Energetic. Rules are: Overt, Up-to-date, for humans, Freedom to comment, Related to reality, Appropriate, Constructive.	Prestige, TRUISM (Simple truth) (MOST IMPORTANT!) Building an Acceptance Set, Bind & Double Binds.	Agreement/Contract: Self responsibility, Don't resist criticism, "Thanks, I got that." A "Star Trainer". Restrictions as: Not leaving room, No food, or Smoking, Rest Room breaks, Drugs or Booze during training (self-enforced), Set in hotel ballroom.	Responsibility, Take a stand, My control, Anxiety is just excitement.
INFANTILIZE		Games, Dialogues, Different names, Physical stance, Masks (Role playing), Shields hide feeling, Patience & Responses to new knowledge with joy & approval	Analogy, Puns, Allusions, Metaphors, Jokes, Confusion, Depotentiating the learned limitations, Pantomime, Non sequiturs.	Belittle all beliefs, Stop automatic patterns of living, Shock words, Hurdles: Boredom, Phys. discomfort, Sleepiness (up to 20 hrs.), Feeling of nothing happening.	Role playing, Like a small child, Release to spontaneity, Transform by projection into something we are not, Ham it up, Act it out in the present.

DOUBLE PLANE	No learning is single level! Communication factors: Directly, Clearly, Specifically, Congruent levelling.	Two level comm. Multiple levels of communication, Danger, Interspersal technique, Implied Directive, Dissociation, Distraction.	Common truth in uncons., Imagery used in Truth, Cosmic Journey, and Anatomy of the mind Processes. Communicate with absent person.	Communication is beyond words, Awareness of inner & outer worlds, Subtlety and built in messages, Fantasy to connect, Wisdom of the organism, Superego & infraego, To develop one's center.
RHYTHM	Rhythm.	Rhythm.		The timing.
INTONATION	Physical stance, Vigorous, Forceful, Strong, Influential, Energetic.	Vocal Intonation, Voice dynamics, Voice locus, Folk language, Pause with expectation.	Loud, with gestures, Roller Coaster ride during training, Declarative, Authoritate.	Voices with inflection, the silences, nuances, Movements, Posture image, Listen to the sounds not the words.
PASSIVE CONCERT	Relax-eyes closed, Aware of your: breathing, thoughts, feelings, & feelings about others. Physically move at end.	NOT DOING, NOT KNOWING (Important), Parasympathetic activation of unconscious.	(Most Ingenious is:) SIT & DO NOTHING for sixty hours! Relaxation: Stay in room, Re-experience past & look at language used, Just BE in the room.	Confusion will sort itself out by itself, Dreams, Write a script, Discovery, Attention & Awareness of the Now & How, Shuttle between 'Here' & 'There', Awareness can be curative, Meaning is always Ad Hoc.

original authors stated them in any presentation. But this dissection can not and will not be their total theory. Our intellectualizing about the work of others must allow us to reassemble the theory to make it live again. These theories are lifelong pursuits of these individuals, and it is an injustice to try to compare them in the space we have here.

The sections in the table here cannot and should not be separated from each other in their use. They are all constantly a part of the total communication between the teacher's and the student's personalities. But we do need a theoretical construct for study, and we can use this comparison as a starting point.

Are the lady and the 4 gentlemen talking about the same thing? Let's take a look:

We think the similarities in these various therapies fit the construct of SALT. These five individuals have developed their methods separately, but the similarities or common factors in each development show the consensual validity for all of them. Why? Each is trying to communicate with a human mind, to change, challenge, activate, stimulate, and/or heal a human mind.

The SALT construct or paradigm changes the way teachers should be trained, how they work, what is expected of them and their students. Hithertofore good teachers were born. That is not true any longer; with these various theories of communication, we have the theoretical constructs for a training program for anyone who wants to become a teacher. We can now plan activities to fit this construct: activities at various levels that will be accepted and remembered in a usable form.

The SALT concept of education designed by Lozanov requires positive inputs. It has mental health as its foundation. Only mentally healthy mature persons can use it, but they produce many more mentally healthy, mature students. We can create a suggestive framework for a positive school setting. SALT requires only positive inputs, not imperative rules or commands like "Shut up!" "Stop!" "Don't do that!"

The interested reader can dig deeper into the works of these 5 giants as listed in the bibliography.

Now we are briefly going to consider five learning methods with many aspects or elements common or similar to Suggestopedia. Bancroft (1983) has surveyed the yoga factors in learning. We will borrow extensively at this point from her excellent paper. The 5 similar methods are Caycedo's Sophrology, the Tomatis Method, Soviet hypnopedia, the Suzuki approach, and Machado's Emotopedia.

Alfonso Caycedo, a Columbian medical doctor, discovered that yogic relaxation techniques could produce analgesia (reduced pain sensitivity) &/or hypermnesia (heightened memory). Western European techniques were also added. Its techniques include breathing, visualization and concentration exercises for physical and mental relaxation. Caycedo has developed a memory training system which is quite similar to Lozanov's Suggestopedia, although developed completely independently of each other. (Caycedo, 1973; Bancroft, 1979).

Alfred Tomatis began his research into ear-voice relations in France and later developed his system for treating dyslexia and communication problems, as well as teaching foreign languages. Tomatis also has been influenced by yoga, and emphasizes the training of the ear to hear, and the development of memory through listening and repetition of material. Paying indirect attention to the material to be learned also is an important element. (Tomatis, 1977, 1978; Bancroft, 1982).

Soviet hypnopedia or sleep-learning is based on the hypothesis that simple learning can occur in a state of reduced awareness, if the materials are reviewed appropriately and have been presented earlier to the student while wide awake. Hypnopedia thus makes use of the light states of sleep (hypnogogic or hypnopompic) while one is going to a deeper state of sleep or waking up from it. During a hypnopedic session, already familiar material such as foreign language vocabulary is presented to the students in paired repetitive form. Rhythm and voice intonation also are used. (Bancroft, 1981; Lozanov, 1978; Svyadosch, 1965; Szalontai, 1980).

Shinichi Suzuki in Japan developed his Talent Education Method primarily for teaching music, but it also has been used to teach academic subjects such as mathematics and English as well. Suzuki based his approach on how children learn their own native language: through listening and repeating over and over words and phrases. He was quite influenced by Japanese zen. His method emphasizes training the ear and memory through listening and repetition. Indirect attention is paid to the material while the students are relaxed or in a light state of sleep. Tape recordings of music or material to be learned are presented while in this state. The piece of music to be learned is played to the pupil every day while the child is engaged in some other activity such as games or going to sleep. (Bancroft, 1981; Suzuki, 1973).

Luiz Machado (1985) in Rio de Janeiro developed the principles of Emotology and Emotopedia. His method of accelerative learning and teaching is based largely on an integrated brain theory, integrated cognitive and emotional learning. Considerable use is made of positive, pleasant affective imagery which serves as motivating goal-setting. Machado has discarded verbal suggestion from Suggestopedia because of its potential misuse in the classroom. However, his goal-setting imagery is what we would call non-verbal suggestion. He has impressive results in South America to substantiate the effectiveness of his method.

The common elements of these methods are shown in Table 3-2. Suggestopedia, Tomatis, Sophrology and Suzuki emphasize authority and a sympathetic attitude on the part of the teacher, teacher-student confidence, the role of the environment, and the untapped reserves of the learner. All 5 methods stress voice intonation and rhythm in presenting material. Suggestopedia, Tomatis and Suzuki favor classical or baroque music. Suggestopedia, Tomatis, Sophrology and Suzuki along with modern holistic education try to develop the pupil's personality in a positive learning environment.

The theory of these methods comes mostly from yoga: the teacher's authority, the confidence and passivity of the student, the pleasant positive environment, voice dynamics, and rhythmic presentation. All these methods promote indirect attention to the didactic material and/or unconscious absorption of material while the students are relaxed. Suggestopedia, Tomatis, hypnopedia and Sophrology have both an active and a passive phase wherein students first pay active attention to the material and secondly let it passively go by while in a meditative state. Sophrology and Tomatis begin with a passive phase, while Suggestopedia and hypnopedia begin with an active phase. The passive phase in the Suzuki approach occurs when the material is played to the pupil while falling asleep.

The success of these 5 methods appears to depend on a number of factors as listed in Table 3-2. Most critical perhaps is the presentation of material in 2 levels of consciousness: wide awake (beta) and relaxed or light sleep (alpha). What appears critical for accelerated learning is the alternation between these 2 levels of consciousness. The interested reader is invited to dig deeper in the original articles, or read Bancroft's excellent presentation (1983).

B. FOREIGN LANGUAGE STUDIES

The section starts by reviewing briefly the requirments of scientific research such that one can draw legitimate cause and effect

Table 3-2. Common Accelerative Learning Factors

METHODS

FACTORS	Suggestology/ Suggestopedia	Caycedo Sophrology	Tomatis Method	Soviet Hypnopedia	Suzuki Method	Machado Emotopedia
Authority/personality of teacher	x	x	x		x	x
Confidence of student	x	x	x		x	x
Positive environment	x	x	x		x	x
Learner's potential	x	x	x		x	x
Intonation/tone of voice	x	x	x		x	x
Rhythm/rhythmic presentation of materials				x		
Mind/body harmony	x	x	x	x	x	x
Relaxed alertness	x	x	x		x	x
Active/passive phases	x	x	x	x	x	
Unconscious assimilation of materials	x	x	x	x	x	
Posture(s)	x	x	x	x	x	x
Breathing techniques	x	x	x		x	
Inner speech/internal singing	x				x	
Visualization (exercises)	x	x			x	x
Memory training	x	x	x	x	x	x

* Adapted with permission from Bancroft (1983) and expanded.

conclusions from experimental studies. All the known US studies were reviewed that investigated foreign language training with suggestopedic or suggestopedic-like techniques. A number of studies were also cited that did not meet the strict requirements of cause and effect laboratory studies. The American studies that have utilized tight experimental designs have rather consistently shown that Suggestopedia, or its American derivative SALT, produces a two or three times greater foreign language achievement than students taught conventionally.

Introduction

This section* reviews the scant literature in the United States wherein foreign languages have been taught with an accelerative learning method called Suggestopedia in Europe or SALT (System of Accelerative Learning Techniques) in the United States. But before we can review the scant studies, we must review the logic of the scientific method used in research to determine causality.

Scientific studies and the logic used to infer causality can be conveniently analyzed or categorized into three types. The first type of experimental study is what one could call the "case history" type of study. The classical example of this is Sigmund Freud, who developed his well-known psychodynamic theories of human motivation and psychoanalysis based upon various extensive and in-depth studies of a few neurotic patients in Vienna around the turn of the century. Many independent variables were analyzed according to the skill of the analyst, and relationships leading to putative relationships on the criterion dependent variables were explored. In the case of psychoanalysis, many variables that possibly could have affected the sex drive or the death wish were explored and Freud developed his classical scheme of defense mechanisms on this basis. According to our subsequent definition of proof, the best that we can say is that the logic of a case history study permits speculation on a cause and effect relationship between variables, but no more.

A second general type of study is one wherein many data are

---

* This is a paper presented by DHS at the AIMAV Linguistic Conference at the University of Nijmegen in the Netherlands on September 8, 1983. Published in the November 1984 *AIMAV Conference Proceedings*, reprinted by permission, and updated slightly.

collected on many individuals, and the results are then analyzed with a correlational or multiple regressional approach. The experimenter analyzes the relationships between the independent variables or predictor variables, and uses them to predict some criteria or dependent variables. The result is the multiple regression predictor equation where one or more independent variables are used to predict the major criterion of interest, or occasionally two or three criteria of interest. A typical example here is the investigator wishing to predict how well students are going to perform academically upon arrival in college; s/he will use a number of demographic and academic variables from high school, as well as entrance test scores from college, in an effort to predict college academic grade point average (GPA). Such efforts are typically quite successful, and variables such as high school class rank and entrance aptitude test scores typically are among the best predictors of college GPA. The investigator also usually will attempt to replicate or repeat these findings by applying his/her resulting prediction equation to a second sample and again with considerable success. Typically the best single predictor of college GPA is high school rank or high school GPA. When combined with entrance test scores, however, the prediction is quantitatively better. This type of research study can be characterized as a correlational approach or multiple regression apporach. The logic involved here is that high school success along with a corresponding entrance test score can predict college academic performance quite highly for groups of students. The resulting dictum is that "immediate past performance predicts future performance in the same area quite well."

Upon examining the logic of prediction, we see that at best the logic is probabalistic and not causal; that is, we can say that high school academic performance predicts college academic performance but we cannot say that high school academic performance directly causes college academic performance, because of several other possible influential variables such as motivation for a particular curriculum, variables of size and in cultural influence in high school, and whether or not the student was engaged in part-time work to support himself/herself. The best that we can say about a correlational study is that we are probably correct when we attribute high school academic success as the cause of college success but we cannot be completely confident in this regard.

This leads us to the third and last type of study wherein we can reason from effect back to cause. In this type of study, called an experimental or manipulative study under controlled conditions, an investigator deliberately manipulates some likely independent variables or causative variable. The investigator develops two or more levels of his putative independent variables and then randomly assigns students for treatment into these particular independent variable levels. The key element here is that the students are assigned at random into these different treatment levels so that the effects of all other possible influential independent variables will be minimized and theoretically eliminated. To insure against the possibility of significant results having happened by chance, the investigator usually repeats or replicates his/her experimental procedures by taking a second group of subjects and randomly assigns them in the second study into the same levels of independent variables as the first time. Thus the investigator has experimental and statistical control over chance happening by repeating or replicating his/her experiment. When the experimenter finds significant treatment effects with this type of research design, he or she is confident that the effects obtained in the criterion variables can be attributed causally to the influence of the independent variables which were manipulated at several levels. Because of random assignment of subjects to different treatment effects before criterion measurement, and because of obtaining the same results a second time (replication), the experimenter is quite confident that s/he has shown a cause and effect relationship between the manipulated independent variables and the criteria variables.

Literature Review

In the following review of studies of foreign languages taught with Suggestopedia or its American synthesis, System of Accelerative Learning Techniques (SALT), only studies that meet the criterion of causality, that is the laboratory manipulative type of design, will be included. Occasionally, studies that come close to this will be included because of their relevance; caveats will be noted accordingly.

The first study reviewed is by Marina Kurkov (1977). She was the first one in the United States to attempt to evaluate the suggestopedic teaching method. She adapted Suggestopedia to the teaching of beginning Russian at Cleveland State University in the fall of 1971. The experimental section of Beginning Russian consisted of 14 students, with 19 comparable students in the control section. In the experimental groups, 43% had had some previous training in Russian, while in the control group, the corresponding percentage was 29%.

This difference was not significant, nor did a pretest of 60 items administered to both groups show a significant difference between the groups initially. The experimenter had made an arbitrary decision before knowing anything about enrollment in classes as to which section would be experimental and which would be the control group. Thus this study met the requirement of random assignment of students to experimental treatment to control for other possible influential variables on learning Russian. The experimental class covered two quarters' worth of material in one quarter, whereas the control was taught conventionally and covered one quarter's worth of material using the same textbook for beginning Russian. Kurkov used a standard test for evaluating Russian, the MLA Cooperative Foreign Language test, as well as end-of-course test, to evaluate effectiveness of teaching Russian.

For evaluation, the control group averaged a course grade of 2.5 (C) and the experimental group 3.0 (B). At the end of the quarter, the experimental group merged with a regular third-quarter Russian course. The experimental students who had had Russian taught suggestopedically were at no disadvantage. Kurkov reported that the results were favorable and that the experimental students accomplished 20 weeks of work in 10 weeks of work without penalty. Later the experimental group students assimilated well into a group which had had their first Russian courses conventionally. The early spurt of learning Russian during suggestopedic training was followed by nearly standard development. In summary, data from this particular course led one to reason from cause and effect: With Suggestopedia, the Russian students had learned twice as much Russian as had the students taught conventionally.

The second study reviewed is a short-term, laboratory-controlled study by Bordon and Schuster (1976) done within the setting of a Spanish course taught suggestopedically. The independent variables manipulated were: suggested positive atmosphere, background music, and word presentation synchronized with the breathing of the students and the background music. Students or subjects were 32 college students without previous formal training in Spanish ranging in age from 19 to 26; half were male, half were female. The experimental design utilized a full factorial analysis of variance statistical design. The independent variables were dichotomous, that is, a suggestive positive atmosphere was either present or absent, background music was either present or absent, and the instructor/experimenter either synchronized Spanish word presentation with the students' breathing and background music or did not. Two male and two female subjects were assigned at random to each of the eight possible treatment cells. All three independent variables significantly affected the acquisition and retention of Spanish words. A significant cumulative interaction effect also occurred in accordance with the predictions of Suggestopedia. At a practical level when all three of these independent variables were present, learning was 2–1/2 times better than when all three variables were absent. The criterion was the number of words that the students had learned out of a list of 50 Spanish words presented to them experimentally under one of the eight conditions. When all three variables were absent, students learned 8.3 words from the list of 50, whereas when all three variables were present, students learned an average of 30.5 words. The data for the main effects and two-way interactions showed intermediate effects as expected.

This experimental study done on a short term in the context of a Spanish class taught suggestopedically (or SALT actually) showed the influence of three of the important suggestopedic variables. Reasoning here can proceed effectively back to cause, that is, the three variables of suggestive-positive atmosphere or climate, baroque background music, and word presentation synchronized with students' breathing and background music produced significantly better learning and retention six weeks later of Spanish vocabulary than when these variables were absent.

The next study reviewed was conducted by Schuster (1976) in a preliminary evaluation of the suggestive accelerative Lozanov method for teaching beginning Spanish at the college level. In the fall of 1972, the author taught one section of beginning Spanish with SALT or Suggestopedia. One section of the twelve or thirteen sections of beginning Spanish was selected at random to fit the author's time schedule. Two other sections of Spanish taught by other instructors using the same textbook but utilizing a conventional method served as controls. Students in the experimental section were in Spanish class for a single two-hour class per week in contrast to the six contact hours of students taught conventionally. The instructors of the comparison sections made up the final exams for all students and the experimenter had nothing to do with making up these criterion tests. At the end of the course there were insignificant differences in achievement on the common lecture and laboratory exams between the experimental and control sections. In addition, students in the experimental section spent less time on homework on Spanish than did the conventional students. Thus the experimental method resulted in a time saving of approximately 3 to 1 in teaching beginning Spanish. Test result data are given in Table 3-1.

Table 3-1. Exam scores in Spanish study

Means and standard deviations (S.D.) of exam scores for regular Spanish students (n = 32) and experimental Spanish students (n = 19)

Exam & Section	Average	S.D.	t
Written final			
Regular sections	75.41	18.92	1.96*
Experimental section	64.21	19.54	
Spoken lab final			
Regular sections	7.63	1.83	0.33*
Experimental section	7.79	1.36	

* Insignificant difference, p > .05.

The next research study that utilized a controlled laboratory design for teaching foreign language is that of R. W. Bushman (1976a). Three instructional treatments were administered to 41 undergraduate students studying Finnish; a full suggestopedic treatment, a modified suggestopedic where music and easy chairs were deleted and a conventional classroom instructional treatments. Each of two teachers taught one class of each treatment after preliminary instruction with separate students. Students then were measured on vocabulary, grammar and pronunciation and communication. Group means were adjusted only by the Pimsleur language aptitude test battery scores, as language background and suggestibility scores were found not to be significant predictors.

The suggestopedic groups performed generally better than the control group and far better on the communication measure, but the two suggestopedic groups did not vary significantly from each other. Due to random assignment of subjects to experimental treatment conditions, the author concluded that Suggestopedia did cause better Finnish language learning.

In a second study, Bushman (1976b) evaluated Russian language learning with a suggestopedically taught group and a control group taught conventionally. It is doubtful whether this second study was a true test of Suggestopedia since the major component of Suggestopedia used was finger painting as an artistic means to enhance learning. This reviewer questions whether finger painting, which has no content relevance to Russian, could have contributed significantly, and therefore feels that Bushman's second study was not a true test of Suggestopedia, that his conclusion of the invalidity of Suggestopedia in teaching Russian is invalid.

Robinett (1975) tested and evaluated an adaptation of Suggestopedia to teaching second semester Spanish for six weeks to college students randomly assigned to one of three treatments. The first experimental group had two of their five weekly classes taught suggestopedically and the second group, four of five so taught. The control group had the traditional class and laboratory combination with five classes weekly. All labs and classes were 50 minutes each. After the introduction, background and explanation, the suggestopedic treatment consisted of deep breathing, review, dynamic presentation of new material and its subsequent review with the relaxing music. In the data analyses, there were no significant differences in previous academic achievement or first semester Spanish grades among the three treatments. Both experimental classes had significantly higher exam scores than the control group, but there was no difference between the experimental groups.

Ramirez (1982), in a controlled classroom study, evaluated the effect of Suggestopedia in teaching English vocabulary to Spanish dominant Chicano third grade children. As expected, children taught vocabulary with Suggestopedia learned significantly more words (19.78) than did the children taught conventionally in the control group (12.79). However, the children taught with Suggestopedia minus imagery also learned significantly more words than control (22.83) but there was no difference between these two experimental groups. A possible explanation for the lack of significant difference between the two experimental groups was that key word imagery may have taken some time to be learned as a strategy by the children and they may not have had sufficient time. Thus, again in this study, there is a cause and effect relationship between Suggestopedia and superior vocabulary learning.

Wagner and Tilney (1983) investigated the applicability of techniques adapted from Suggestopedia as described by Ostrander and Schroeder in the book *SuperLearning* (1979). The authors used relaxation tapes produced by SuperLearning, Inc., and an electroencephalograph (EEG) to measure brainwave activity while 21 students were taught a 300-word German vocabulary over a five-week period. They used three experimental groups: a group with baroque music, a group without baroque music, and a no-contact control group who learned the same vocabulary by a traditional method in a classroom setting. These authors reported that students taught in the traditional classroom learned significantly more German vocabulary than those taught by the SuperLearning tape and techniques. They also reported that left-hemisphere monitoring of the brain waves showed no significant change in brainwave rhythms in the experimental groups. The authors claim to have been scrupulous to preserve SuperLearning methodology in their investigation, but were unable to substantiate its claim.

This reviewer would like to make some critical comments about the Wagner and Tilney (1983) study. First, the authors concluded quite correctly that the SuperLearning tapes for learning German vocabulary are a test of the implementation of SuperLearning and not a test of Suggestopedia per se. The authors had three treatment groups: one group of students randomly assigned to the SuperLearning tape where they learned German vocabulary with just an artificially varying voice intonation and baroque music in the background. Another no-contact group heard the same tape but without the background baroque music. The contact control group, however, had the same vocabulary words presented in a traditional classroom setting. The results were that the students in a typical classroom setting learned appreciably more German vocabulary words (28.7) than did the SuperLearning experimental group (13.8 words average) or the SuperLearning tape without baroque music (12.7). In this reviewer's opinion, this is not a fair way to test the benefits of vocabulary learning tapes that are meant to be used in isolation rather than in a typical classroom. Lozanov (1978), himself, makes the point that the teacher is a critical factor, and this particular research design thus confounded completely a major variable, teacher's presence or absence, with that of language tapes designed to be used by students in isolation away from classrooms. A better no-contact control group would have had the same vocabulary words on yet a third tape, but without any variation in intonation or without any music whatsoever.

This reviewer, himself, has data to show that occasionally in some studies the intonational swing and music may not always contribute as expected suggestopedically. For instance, Schuster and Miller (1979) reported that an active dramatic presentation including voice intonation variation interacted with passive review with baroque music to the extent that these variables did not accumulate as theoretically expected towards enhancing students' learning of English words. Finally, it should be noted that Wagner and Tilney did not report any reduction of beta brain waves in favor of significantly increased alpha brainwaves (relaxation toward sleep) as theoretically indicated by Lozanov (1978). Thus, without this indication of mental relaxation, students listening to the SuperLearning tapes provided no neurological data that Lozanov's methods were in use. In summary, this study provides an example of how research methodology can be applied to compare apples and oranges with the obvious conclusion that apples and oranges are different. Nevertheless, the Wagner and Tilney (1983) study does have value in the sense that commercial advertising claims and materials do need to be evaluated empirically against relevant conventional methods of teaching.

Studies that report favorable results for Suggestopedia do not necessarily prove the validity of suggestopedic claims in enhancing foreign language learning. Two examples will be given. Philipov (1978) utilized suggestopedic techniques in the teaching of Bulgarian to six female students for her doctoral dissertation research and compared their learning with ten male students learning Russian. The Bulgarian course suggestopedically took 120 hours in comparison to 330 hours for the conventional Russian course. Two expert judges independently rated the final speaking proficiency of all Bulgarian and Russian students. The median proficiency of Bulgarian students was very high with practically complete comprehension of everything, whereas the median proficiency of the Russian students indicated about 50% comprehension and many mistakes. Thus, the experimental students learned more Bulgarian than the control students had learned Russian in about one third of the time. Now the basic error of this study was the comparison of apples and oranges. It is true that Bulgarian and Russian are highly similar languages, but nevertheless, all this study did was to show that suggestopedic techniques probably were responsible for a similar Slavic proficiency in one third of the time taken by students taught conventionally. Also subjects were not assigned randomly to Bulgarian or Russian. Thus, there was no cause and effect relationship shown here.

Prichard, Schuster and Pullen (1980) adapted Suggestopedia successfully to teaching German instruction in high school. Students taught with SALT or Suggestopedia learned significantly more German as shown by their higher achievement scores on a standard German achievement test than the controls taught conventionally. While this study shows support of SALT or Suggestopedia, it can be faulted because students were not randomly assigned to class treatment and they knew which instructor they were going to have ahead of time. So again, the logic of this study, while it supports Suggestopedia in this case, can be faulted because cause and effect cannot be shown; only that it is probable that the class taught suggestopedically learned more because of the suggestopedic techniques.

Gasner-Roberts and Brislan (1984) selected one of three sections of university students enrolled in a first year German course to be taught with Suggestopedia. The achievement of the two control groups, day and evening groups taught conventionally, was compared with that of the experimental group taught with Suggestopedia. For random assignment, the chairman of the German department drew the names of those students who were to be in the experimental group out of a box. Proficiency in German was measured with a number of tests: mid-year written, end-of-year written, an oral and an objective test. The analyses of the considerable date available from this yearlong study confirmed the superiority of Suggestopedia over conventional learning and teaching methods.

Dhority (1984) in his book "Acquisition Through Creative Teaching" gives the results of several German language course evaluations. Dhority (1984) conducted several courses with his version of accelerative learning acquisition through creative teaching in Massachusetts at the university level. Following this he worked with several Army groups at Fort Devans in teaching them beginning German. Comparison between the experimental pilot class and data from four previous German courses offered at Fort Devans, provided comparative data. The regular German language courses used an audio-lingual drill approach and totaled 360 hours versus the pilot course which lasted 108 hours and 18 days. Of regular program students, only 26% achieved the first level one mastery of German or better and only 28% achieved this first level in mastery in reading. In contrast 73% of the pilot program students taught experimentally, achieved a 1 or better on the listening test and 64% a 1 or better in reading. Thus, not only did the specially taught students have a somewhat less than 1/3 the class time but they had significantly better scores as well. Overall, the superiority of the pilot program over previous classes was quite noted.

Lemyze (1978) utilized an experimental design with a random assignment of subjects using Suggestopedia to teach beginning French at McGill University in Canada. Subjects for the experiment were 21 students chosen randomly and two other sections of beginning French served as a control group. The criterion test utilized the Cloze Procedure in which every seventh word in a final exam was deleted and the student had to supply the missing word grammatically correctly. The 17 experimental students averaged 52.85 percent correct on the Cloze test and the 29 control group students 47.89 percent correct. The experimentally taught students averaged 14.41 percent better on the Cloze test but this was not tested for significance by the author.

Lahey (1974) evaluated the possible benefits of Suggestopedia in a pilot study with teaching Japanese words to college students. He had 3 groups under different suggestopedic conditions study a list of 50 Japanese words in a paired associate paradigm for 36 minutes. One group was a control, a second was "suggestopedic" and the third was suggestopedic plus suggestion. While the details of his procedure and evaluation are not clear, he reached the puzzling conclusion that learning can be enhanced with Suggestopedia, but that suggestion does not play a major role.

Zeiss (1984) compared the affects of several superlearning techniques on the learning of English as a second language (ESL) with Saudi Arabian nationals. One of two sections of ESL was selected as the experimental group and given successively over three weeks: relaxation technique, synchronized music, and synchronized music plus relaxation in the third and last weeks. The two sections were not significantly different on a pretest measure nor on the first week (relaxation alone) nor the second week (synchronized music). However when both techniques were used at the end of the third week, there was a statistical difference favoring the experimental group. However, the author concluded that no conclusive evidence exists showing that the use of the superlearning techniques with this population was valuable.

Conclusions

What can we conclude as to the benefits of Suggestopedia or SALT in teaching foreign languages in the United States? First, it is necessary to limit results only to those studies where, in this reviewer's opinion, the investigators had used a well-controlled research design with random assignment of students to treatment so that cause and effect could be determined. In this reviewer's opinion, the following studies cited have met this criterion: Kurkov (1977), Bordon and Schuster (1976), Schuster (1976), Gasner-Roberts & Brislan (1984), Dhority (1984), Lemyze (1978), Bushman (1976a), Robinett (1975), and

Ramirez (1982). The remaining studies can be faulted for one reason or another, and consequently, their conclusions are ignored at this point as possibly invalid. Secondly, all of these studies taken collectively consistently show that when the investigator had followed the intent, theory and practice of Lozanov's Suggestopedia, students can be taught a foreign language with approximately two to three times greater speed than controls for a similar amount of language acquisition and achievement.

Whereas the previous foreign language studies just reviewed had used an accelerative method similar to, or derived from, Suggestopedia, now we are going to review other foreign language studies for their heuristic value in improving foreign language teaching.

Frydman, Dierkens, and Ables (1978) used three groups of students learning Russian under identical learning conditions except for the independent variable: listening to classical music in one group, with training for body awareness according to Feldenkreis for the other group. It was shown that listening to classical music before learning did have a positive influence on language acquisition and that body awareness also influenced foreign language learning favorably.

Asher (1969) discussed the results of 24 experiments using undergraduates wherein he employed the total physical response (TPR) technique for learning listening comprehension of a second language. It was found that (a) motor acts during retention tests were more important than learning acts in training; (b) learning was facilitated with the use of long or novel sentences rather than with single word utterances; and (c) attempts to both listen and speak simultaneously decrease skill and listening comprehension. He suggested that in the first stage of learning that only one of the four language skills be selected and that listening skills were recommended as having the most positive transfer to the other three beginning skills in learning a foreign language.

Lee (1981) investigated the combination of using both Suggestopedia and the Total Physical Response method in accelerating the learning of listening comprehension for foreign language. She used four separate groups, two of which were exposed to a combination of Suggestopedia and Total Physical Response, and the two comparison groups were exposed to the Total Physical Response method alone. She concluded that possibly the two methods supplemented one another, but that there were no significant differences between the two method training and the single method training. She concluded that neither method was superior to the other in terms of training listening comprehension.

Knibbeler (1982) compared the suggestopedic and Silent Way methods with respect to language acquisition skills and their influence upon affective behavior. There were seven teachers teaching French either with the Silent Way or Suggestopedia. Three teachers taught both a section of Silent Way and Suggestopedia. Students were assigned randomly to either type of class and students had no previous acquaintance with either method. There were no significant differences between the two treatment classes on listening comprehension, correctness in speaking, speaking fluency, or affective questionnaire results. Students in general liked both approaches and elementary subjects preferred Suggestopedia. Motivation was stronger with students towards Suggestopedia to continue further language classes. Similarly, students taught suggestopedically had a higher regard for their learning abilities than before vs. students taught the Silent Way. The author concluded that it is the teacher who is basically responsible for the important variations in the outcomes of this study rather than the particular approach used.

Oller and Richard-Amato (1983) present a smorgasbord of ideas for language teachers, ideas that work. In addition to Suggestopedia, Silent Way and Total Physical Response, they introduce other proven methods of foreign language teaching, such as Rassias' Madness, Curran's Counseling-Learning, Moreno's Sociodrama, natural orientations, along with fun and games approaches. Refer to their interesting book for details.

In summary, we can say that there are other effective methods besides Suggestopedia for foreign language teaching. Some are quite similar to Suggestopedia; some are dissimilar. Many of them could be used in a complementary fashion to Suggestopedia, especially in the practice phase in Suggestopedia.

C. NON-LANGUAGE STUDIES

Next we are going to review the literature for the use of SALT (Suggestive-Accelerative Learning Techniques) in accelerating classroom learning. We will emphasize controlled studies, but range over all grade levels in the public schools, and include studies with college students occasionally.

Schuster and Miele (1978) reported the minutes and recommendations of the working group of international experts at a meeting on suggestology as a learning methodology held in Sophia, Bulgaria, December 11–17, 1978. UNESCO and the Bulgarian Ministry of Education jointly sponsored the conference. The invited participants presented their research findings and made recommendations to UNESCO concerning further large scale implementation of Suggestopedia in the areas of research and experimentation, teacher training and suggestopedic centers. Complete proceedings were published later by UNESCO (1980) in Paris.

After careful deliberation, the UNESCO panel of experts agreed that Suggestopedia is a generally superior teaching method for many subjects and for many types of students compared with traditional methods. This consensus was arrived at following a study of the research literature, listening to the testimony of international experts, observing films portraying suggestopedic instruction and visiting classes in which Suggestopedia was practiced. Many recommendations were made for suggestopedic research and experimentation, teacher training and research centers.

Schuster and Prichard (1978) utilized a quasi-experimental design with pretest and posttest measures to evaluate the SALT method for ten teachers utilizing SALT vs. another ten teachers teaching the same subject matter conventionally at the same socio- economic level in the same area in central Iowa. Teachers were trained in the first year and appropriate pre and posttests developed. Volunteer teachers were trained in the summer of 1976 in a 120 hour training workshop. A workshop covered the background and principles of Suggestopedia such as openness, communicativeness, creative dramatics, some testing development and some research design. The subject matter areas taught included elementary school spelling, reading, and health, junior high earth science, life science, art and agribusiness, plus first year German. Grade levels ranged from first grade through the tenth grade. Criteria were achievement tests specific to each of the experimental teachers and secondly the Brooks Student Questionnaire which measured three dimensions of student attitudes: student-teacher affective relationships, perceived school stress and school learning orientation.

In this Schuster and Prichard (1978) study, there was considerable research support in terms of raw data for the SALT method for accelerating achievement, but essentially no support for improving student attitude. The SALT method appeared to be appropriate for both elementary as well as junior high students. There was no difference with low or middle socio-economic status students. Creativity was enhanced significantly. Specifically seven out of the ten teachers using SALT had their students achieve significantly more on the specific criterion tests for their subject than controls. An eighth teacher produced marginally significant (p = .08) achievement results. A ninth teacher had been apprehended for drunk driving for the fourth and hopefully for the last time and was not back in the classroom teaching with SALT until February. His students were pretested at that time and post-tested as usual in late spring. His students showed the same gains as the students taught conventionally over the previous eight months. Thus in only one case out of ten was the SALT method class merely comparable to the results for students taught conventionally. In summary for nine out of the ten classes, SALT produced better results than in the classes taught conventionally.

Leontiev (1976) reviewed intensive teaching methods in the Soviet Union, including the Lozanov method. He concluded that intensive studying methods were effective, but that they must be supported in addition by intensive material preparation by the teacher.

Applegate (1983) reported on a federally funded project administered to a school district in Paradise, CA. Utilizing the Super-Learning experience, the project dramatically increased student learning rates in reading, math, spelling and writing. Students were in regular and special education classrooms grades 2–6 and ranged in ability from learning disabled to gifted and talented. The study involved 20 experimental and 12 control teachers. Also involved were 538 experimental students and 517 control students. On standardized testing with the California Achievement Test, experimental students averaged a significantly higher gain (46.9) than did control students (33.4). There was a significant reduction in problem behavior referrals for the experimental teachers as compared with controls. At the end of the second school year, the California Achievement Tests again showed that the experimentally taught students were significantly higher in reading and math with higher average gain scores for the experimental group vs. students taught conventionally. Behavioral problems were again significantly reduced with students showing significantly more time on task in the classroom. The evaluation was done by a separate independent firm specializing in evaluation. The evaluation firm commented at the end of two years, given the alternative of standard classroom teaching, the accelerative learning techniques have the potential for dramatically improving the quality of education of regular students in our classrooms.

Schuster, Prichard and McCullough (1981) assessed the effectiveness of SALT in teaching spelling to elementary pupils (n = 275). Four of the six elementary teachers who applied SALT in their spelling classes achieved statistically significant gains (p < .05) vs. their controls and one approached usual significance standards (p < .08). The remaining teacher's students showed no difference than the control class. Attitudinal measures were insignificant for experimental vs. controls.

Prichard, Schuster, and Gensch (1980) evaluated the teaching of reading in a rural central Iowa fifth grade class with SALT. The achievement test was alternate forms of the California Achievement Test (14C and 14D). Pretests were given in the fall and posttests were given in late spring. SALT taught students (n = 19) gained significantly more in reading comprehension and vocabulary than did the control class (n = 12). There were no differences on three measures of affective change.

Johnson (1982) evaluated the effective use of group relaxation exercises on second and sixth grade children's spelling scores. She utilized a pretest-posttest experimental design with separate experimental and control groups. There was a pair of experimental and control groups at both the second grade and the sixth grade levels. Experimental groups were given relaxation training along with spelling instruction whereas the control groups had their spelling instruction without relaxation training. Second grade students, whether previously identified as good or bad spellers, benefited from relaxation training from pretest to posttest. Sixth grade students initially identified as poor spellers benefited more from relaxation training than did the initially identified good spellers. Relaxation training for good sixth grade students did not appreciably help the recall of written word lists. Overall short term relaxation training appeared to have had a beneficial effect on children's spelling performance.

Beer (1978) evaluated Suggestopedia in a Vienna public school in two first grade classes in reading, writing and arithmetic. There were no significant pretest differences between the two classes in intelligence, vocabulary, picture-test, or educational professional background of parents. The suggestopedic class received its instruction with a trained teacher and specially prepared materials. The comparison teacher taught conventionally. At the end of the school year the experimental pupils had achieved the goal for arithmetic, reading and writing, whereas the comparison group only achieved its first grade goals partially. Specifically in the experimental class some additional second and third grade materials were taught successfully. In reading, the experimental pupils were reading more material than the other first grade students by the end of the first semester. In writing, many of the goals for the 2nd grade were achieved as well.

Palmer (1985) systematically reviewed all the books and articles for the years 1976–1984 that utilized experimental/control group paradigms utilizing SALT or suggestopedic techniques. He reviewed 45 such data sources dealing with special students in the category of learning disabled, educable mentally retarded, remedial reading, behavioral/emotional disturbance, low socioeconomic status, remedial mathematics, low or poor or under achievers, normal and gifted or talented. The metanalysis indicated strong statistically significant findings showing that SALT is a promising procedure for special needs populations.

Nelson (1979) used a true experimental design in evaluating the Lozanov method in teaching word retention to children with learning disabilites. The children were 6 to 8 years in age with learning problems and had been referred to a special education diagnostic clinic at Kansas University Medical Center. Three students were randomly assigned to the experimental treatment and the remaining two students to the control treatment. All students had initial baseline criterion scores of 0. All experimental students had daily quiz and end of learning test scores of 75% or more. The control students taught traditionally had some daily quiz scores meeting this criterion, but no end of learning test scores doing so. In addition, the average acquisition and retention test scores of the experimental group were significantly (p. > .05) higher than those of the control group. Thus the Lozanov approach with learning disabled students provided higher achievement than the traditional approach.

Hales (1983) investigated the use of Suggestopedia in improving the word identification skills of mildly and moderately retarded children. He used a three way Anova study with one group of retarded students taught word identification skills with Suggestopedia and the others with traditional teaching. A second factor in the Anova design was I.Q., high or low. The number of words identified was not affected significantly by the suggestopedic teaching method. However, the retarded students with a higher than average I.Q. for this group identified more words. The author concluded that Suggestopedia did not significantly affect the number of words identified compared with using the traditional teaching approach.

In a quasi-experimental study Schuster and Ginn (1978) utilized the SALT method to teach earth science at the ninth grade level. A teacher using her own method of teaching earth science to low socioeconomic ninth graders was utilized for comparison. Students were pretested and posttested both with achievement and attitudinal measures. While the students were initially comparable on pretest measures, at year end the experimentally taught students were significantly better in earth science achievement scores and had better student-teacher affective relations, less stress at school, better attitudes toward school orientation and learning than the comparison group.

Prichard, Schuster and Walters (1979) evaluated the use of SALT in teaching ninth grade agribusiness. Two of four sections taught by the same teacher were randomly assigned to the SALT treatment and the remaining two served as comparison or controls. Before the SALT treatment started, the four groups were comparable on the first midterm test. After the experimental treatment had been employed, the final exam showed that the two sections taught with SALT had achieved significantly more than the control groups.

Edwards (1980) evaluated the effects of SALT on the creativity of low and middle socio-economic status fifth and eighth-ninth graders in central Iowa. A $2 \times 2 \times 2 \times 2$ nonequivalent control group design was used with univariate analysis of covariance to determine the effects and interaction of treatment, grade level, socio- economic status and sex on 11 verbal and figural creativity variables derived from raw scores on the Torrance Test of Creative Thinking (TTCT). The experimental group consisted of 175 pupils exposed to SALT by trained teachers. Results indicated that the uncontrolled effects of pretesting, history and maturation on posttest scores were small. SALT significantly increased creativity on five variables: verbal flexibility, figural fluency, flexibility and elaboration and a number of creative strengths. At the fifth grade level, verbal originality, figural fluency, and flexibility was significantly higher for SALT taught students than conventionally taught students. In conclusion, SALT significantly improved the creativity of SALT taught children with respect to conventionally taught students in Iowa public schools.

Gamble, Gamble, Parr and Caskey (1982) evaluated the effects of relaxation training and music on creativity. Undergraduate beginning art students were randomly assigned to one of three treatments, music only, music plus relaxation training or a no treatment control group. Seven measures from the Torrance Test of Creative Thinking and three writings from a panel of judges were used for evaluation. Analysis of covariance revealed that three of the Torrance test scores were significant at posttesting: the sum of scores, fluency and originality. Multicomparisons revealed that the relaxation plus music group was significantly more creative than the control group. Panel ratings of student drawings at posttesting failed to indicate any significant difference. The authors concluded that music and relaxation might prove more potent over a longer period of time as part of a regular class procedure.

Boyle and Render (1982) investigated the relationship between fantasy journeys in the classroom and students' scores on a measure of creative thinking. Three seventh grade classes were randomly assigned to one of three groups: group one received no treatment prior to testing; group two experienced one fantasy journey prior to testing; and the third group experienced five fantasy journeys, one per day prior to the administration of the criterion test, the Torrance Test of Creative Thinking (TTCT). The groups experiencing one or more fantasy journeys prior to testing received significantly higher scores on the creativity test than the control group, but there was no difference as to whether the groups had had one or five fantasy journeys.

Peterson (1977) utilized college students in two sections of a Navy ROTC class to test the effectiveness of the Lozanov Suggestopedic method. He utilized a Dr. Jekyll-Mr. Hyde procedure wherein he taught two sections of the same class in one quarter with different approaches. The control section was taught the instructor's usual way. The experimental section was taught with SALT in one-half the usual time each week. Before the instructor started teaching differently, he utilized the first mid-term exam scores to show that the two sections were comparable and that they had indeed almost identical scores. After the first mid-term the instructor started teaching the two sections differently. The final exam scores for the two groups again were almost identical but showed that the experimental group had learned as much as the control group but in one-half the usual time.

Seki (1981) applied SALT with a computer engineering class of approximately 200 students at Tokai University in Tokyo. Students during one semester served as their own controls, that is, they learned certain materials with SALT and certain other material without SALT. Items learned with SALT were learned appreciably better than comparable items without SALT.

Vannan (1981) used a non-equivalent research design over two years to evaluate the effects of SALT in a university science course. The control group was comprised of teachers and their scores in all sessions in 1975 and the experimental group was teachers in 1976 taking the same course for the whole year. Students when taught suggestopedically received 78% A grades vs. 11% A grades for those

Fig. 3-1.   Learning Is Easy

taught traditionally. The high achievement trend has continued through 1980 with a 76% A grade for the experimental years of 1976–80 inclusively.

We can summarize this section by saying that SALT appears to work quite well in accelerating the learning of many school subjects, and also has a favorable influence on increasing the creativity of students in the process. See Fig. 3-1.

D. LEARNING RESEARCH STUDIES

In this section we are going to review briefly more nearly conventional studies that have dealt with accelerating learning.

Jason et al (1976) instituted an academic support program at Southern Illinois University in Edwardsville, IL. The purpose of this was to prepare students for survival in the academic system by providing a conceptual and skill base for further academic studies and to motivate students to pursue careers in science, engineering and medicine. The remedial math program combined features of counseling, tutorial facilities, and conventional lectures with workshop sessions. Petschauer (1983) described the implementation of a student-to-student advising program sponsored by the Exxon Corporation. Advanced students were hired to teach beginning students basic college survival skills. Emphasis was placed on managing time, improving memory, taking lecture notes, textbooks, taking exams, writing themes and reports, making oral presentations, improving scholastic motivation, improving interpersonal relationships and improving concentration.

Thompson (1973) reported on project success of a three year project in Atlanta, GA directed toward academic underachievement in innercity schools. The program concentrated on the construction of a positive learning environment, a restructuring of the classroom that replaced the failure environment with a success environment that in turn promoted future successful experiences. The approach involved a classroom management system consisting of three components: behavior modification for positive contingency and mangement, classroom arrangement design to foster small-group and individualized teaching, and some revision of the standard curriculum. In terms of results, project pupils achieved at least one month gain in reading and arithmetic for each month of project participation in contrast to conventional schools where students show a loss, that is, they regress. The project was recognized as one of the top three exemplary programs during 1973.

Walken (1968) evaluated the use of behavior modification in getting disruptive fourth grade boys to attend class and to learn. Compared to the control group, token reinforcement in combination with program learning was more effective than either treatment alone or the Hawthorne effect treatment.

Mayer and Butterworth (1983) trained selected teachers in behavior mod techniques intended to make school more pleasant principally by praising and otherwise rewarding students for appropriate behavior. Hitting, throwing things, and not doing assignments decreased as the teachers acquired the knack of using positive reinforcement. The improvement carried over into the classrooms taught by teachers who had not had the training: in the overall school environment vandalism became less a problem. Vandalism went down an average of 75% without taking into effect cost inflation.

Masters (1975) reported on two studies designed to clarify the role of different performance standards for contingent reinforcement with preschool children. On a discrimination task, the children's performance had to meet low, medium, or high standards to be rewarded. In the accelerative standard condition, their performance had to surpass their performance on the previous trial. Learning was significantly more rapid with the high and accelerative standards than low. The self-dispensation of evaluative reinforcement produced such rapid learning that by the end of the experiment, the effects due to different standards had vanished.

Mayer (1979) reviewed studies on advance organizers (Ausubel, 1960) and their possible influence on facilitating learning. Mayer reviewed previous reports and discounted studies that inadequately represented theory, those that inadequately analyzed learning outcomes and those that lacked experimental control. He introduced 9 separate tests of the theories based on experiments which overcame the mentioned problems. These reports clearly favored an assimilation encoding theory, and provided consistent evidence that advance organizers can influence the outcome of learning if used in appropriate situations and measured properly.

McMurray (1975) developed an instructional design based on task analysis procedures and developed experimental lessons to accelerate subject matter concept by 4th grade students. Subjects were randomly assigned to treatment according to the Solomon Four Group Design. The experimental groups performed significantly better at both levels than control groups, both on immediate acquisition and retention tests two months later.

McMurray et al (1977) showed that 3rd and 4th graders who had received task analysis instructions performed significantly better than groups receiving placebo lessons at two levels of advanced mastery in the 3rd and 4th grades.

Pavio et al (1979) investigated the affect of an imagery mnemonic on second language recall and comprehension. He used the ''hook' technique which involves associating new items to be learned with an overlearned series of French stimulus words and images which could be retrieved during recall using a number code. The control group used a technique without imagery. The recall items varied in familiarity and concreteness. Recall following one study trial was approximately three times higher for words learned by imagery than by rote. There were very slight effects for familiarity and concreteness which also affected recall. Translation tests given before and one day after the recall experiment showed that the correct translations of unfamiliar items increased about twice as much after imagery than after rote study. Thus imagery simultaneously facilitated both recall and comprehension.

Galyean (1982) investigated the use of guided imagery in elementary and secondary schools. Working with teachers specially trained in wholistic education on several research projects, she concluded that imagery activities are used primarily for cognitive gains, affective development, and transpersonal awareness. Teachers also are using imagery activities to sharpen the focusing and attending skills of students.

Caskey and Oxford (1981) examined the use of mental imagery activities from SALT in early concept learning with kindergarten children. Children were randomly selected from three public school kindergarten classes and were assigned randomly either to one of two experimental groups or to the control group. The cognitive abilities test was the evaluative instrument; children who experienced the mental imagery exercises achieved higher levels of concept formation than children who did not have such mental imagery experiences. These differences became even more marked when age and intelligence were held constant.

Stein, Hardy, and Totten (1982) investigated the influence of music and imagery to accelerate information retention. Their research utilized three conditions: music plus imagery, music only, and a non-treatment control condition. All subjects received a pretest of vocabulary words identical to the posttest and a list of defined words to study. Subjects in the music plus imagery group heard Handel's water music as the experimenter read the words aloud. Subjects in the music only group heard the same music but control groups subjects did not hear the words read aloud nor hear the music. Analysis of covariance revealed a significant difference on the immediate criterion test for the musical condition. That is, the students who had heard only music while they studied the list had significantly higher scores than the other two conditions. The music and imagery group had intermediate vocabulary scores. On the delayed posttest analysis one week later, both the music only and music plus imagery groups had retention test scores significantly higher than the control group scores but there was no difference between the two treatment groups. The authors concluded that the baroque music used in their study was a contributing factor to increasing both immediate and delayed information retention and that baroque music plus imagery appears to have increased retention as measured later.

Render, Hall, and Moon (1984) evaluated the effects of guided relaxation and baroque music on college students' test performance. Students (n = 62) in four different sections of an undergraduate course in the foundations of learning were given unit tests under each of the four conditions: (1) guided relaxation administered prior to testing, (2) baroque music played during testing, (3) both relaxation and baroque music and (4) control (no relaxation and no music). A within-subjects experimental design was used where each class got each of the four treatments sequentially. Treatments were counterbalanced over the four classes. There were no significant differences among the four treatment conditions. The authors concluded that relaxation prior to testing and baroque music played during testing had no effect on students' test performance.

Borgen and Breitbach (1984) investigated the effects of different types of music on learning vocabulary and physiological measures. They used three types of music, hard-rock, soft-rock, and baroque music and a control group using no music while studying vocabulary. Subjects were checked on their arousal level during testing periods by using the galvanic skin response (GSR) and heart rate (HR). The baroque music condition produced the best acquisition scores for both sexes, but females scored better with hard-rock and easy-rock and males vice versa. Music appeared to affect arousal level and learning.

The baroque music enhanced acquisition non-significantly versus the control group, but the order of enhancement was baroque music, hard-rock, no music, and easy-rock. Learning appeared to be independent of galvanic skin response. Acquisition score, however, was related to heart rate with a Pearson Product Moment Correlation of 0.61. A higher heart rate was associated with greater acquisition.

Groff and Render (1983) investigated the effectiveness of three classroom teaching methods: programmed instruction, simulation and guided fantasy vs. a control group in terms of improvement and achievement in a unit of social studies at the fourth grade level. Results indicate that significant gains and achievement were made by all groups including the control group, but there were a number of significant differences among the groups as well. Specifically the students taught with programmed instruction and fantasy scored significantly higher than the control group while the simulation group had intermediate results. On the delayed posttest retention test, the fantasy group and simulation group mean gains were significantly higher than the programmed instruction and control group mean gains. The authors concluded that each method has something to offer specifically for teaching content and the differences among methods were not great. Teachers can choose from these methods without reservations regarding their effectiveness and this study suggests that these methods can assist teachers to help them reach their educational goals.

Schallert (1976) investigated two aspects of memory for prose: the amount of information remembered and the semantic interpretation of sign to ambiguous paragraphs. Task instructions and exposure duration of the passages were manipulated to induce different levels of processing to affect amount of information retained. The dependent variables of recall and recognition indicated that subjects remembered more information and more context-consonant information when given instructions which require processing the paragraphs at a deep semantic level. Thus, context was a powerful determiner of which meaning was remembered when incoming information was processed at a deeper more meaningful level.

Siegel and Siegel (1976) reported an experiment in remembering color with coding color verbally. Subjects with normal color vision who were taught a verbal code were more accurate and more consistent in their memory of colors than another group which was not taught that same code.

Bellezza (1983) taught students a word arrangement technique to help them learn words. Students were able to recall the simple patterns and then the definitions later as compared to students not taught this sequential arrangement.

Fuller (1982) in a series of provocative articles thoughtfully considered why Lashley's engram has never been located. She argues rather persuasively that the story may represent Chomsky's deep structure because of its universality and that its component parts may represent universal grammar. Further, the central nervous system may overcome the limits of chunk size by processing information in story form. The theory also suggests how memory is stored and retrieved.

Mantyla and Nilsson (1982) reported on the phenomenon of perfect recall. They performed two experiments to demonstrate a striking empirical phenomenon not previously reported, that of perfect recall performance after incidental learning instruction with only one trial for learning. The method used to establish this effect was to have subjects establish effects of each item presented to study and then at test time to ask subjects to recall the to-be-remembered items and the self-generated aspects again. Tentatively, the concepts of uniqueness and reconstruction account for this phenomenon.

Roth (1984) used a toy manipulation task to investigate language learning in children $3\frac{1}{2}$ to $4\frac{1}{2}$ years of age. They were taught linguistic structures beyond their developmental grasp and solid improvement was found in experimental conditions, but none was reported in the control condition.

Swanson (1975) used the theatre as a vehicle of increasing flexibility in students. He used an experimental design involving the testing of students before and after involvement in directing theatre productions. The Schaie Test of Behavioral Rigidity revealed increased personal flexibility after theatre experiences.

Berendt and Schuster (1984) evaluated the influence of suggestions to speed up mental processes to see if this would increase the number of vocabulary words learned consequently. College student subjects were randomly assigned to one of the four experimental treatment groups; control: no preliminary relaxation, no suggestion of mental speeding. Another group received mental speeding only, a third group received preliminary relaxation only and the fourth and last group received both preliminary relaxation and suggested mental speeding. The sophisticated speeding condition produced a 33% increment in speed of mental processes and this was accompanied by a 25% increase in the number of words recalled correctly immediately after practice. A corresponding but insignificant increase in retention was shown 7 days after the initial practice. Mental speeding thus may have some value in the classroom for increasing learning.

From these recent experimental studies in summary, we can conclude that behavior modification and advance organizers have been shown many times to be effective. Also effective are rearranging the environment academically, task analysis instructions, goal setting and imagery.

SUMMARY

In this chapter we approached the review of literature relevant to SALT/Suggestopedia from several viewpoints. First we approached the review from the theoretical consideration of demonstratedly effective psychotherapies, then from educational philosophies similar to Suggestopedia. Next came critical reviews of the SALT/ Suggestopedic literature first for foreign languages and then for regular classroom subjects. We concluded by reviewing studies dealing with accelerating learning from the educational and psychological literature.

We reviewed the theory for SALT/Suggestopedia by comparing its theoretical elements first with other effective therapies for helping people change and then with other methods for accelerating learning. We compared Lozanov's Suggestopedia with Satir's Conjoint Therapy, Erickson's Indirect Suggestion, Erhard's est Training, and Perls' Gestalt Therapy. Almost all of the 6 means in Suggestopedia have their counterparts in the other 4 effective therapies. Then we compared Suggestopedia with Caycedo's Sophrology, the Tomatis approach, Soviet hypnopedia, Suzuki's Talent Education Method and Machado's Emotopedia.

Most of these accelerative learning methods have the common elements of sympathetic teacher attitude, authority of the teacher, student confidence in the teacher, belief in tapping student mental reserves, and stress voice intonation and rhythm in presenting material. These methods promote indirect attention to the didactic material in a relaxed, pleasant environment with alternating active/passive phases.

We looked critically at studies using Suggestopedia or SALT in teaching foreign languages in the United States. To be able to state that a supposedly superior educational treatment like SALT caused superior achievement, random assignment of students to treatment and doing the study again are essential. Only a few studies survived the stiff requirements of such controlled research. Almost all of these carefully controlled studies that followed the philosophy and intent of Suggestopedia showed that a foreign language can be taught two to three times faster with SALT than conventionally.

SALT and/or Suggestopedia has also been used in many non-language classes, from elementary school through college classes, from the 3 R's to such subjects as naval science, art, agricultural education, among many others. While these studies haven't been as well controlled as laboratory studies, those studies using a control group have generally reported a significant benefit in achievement coming from SALT/Suggestopedia. While the results of improving student attitudes toward learning are unclear, several studies investigating creativity have consistently shown that it is increased significantly in classes taught suggestopedically.

Finally we summarized recent experimental learning studies. There is no doubt but that behavior modification and advance organizers are quite effective in facilitating learning. Goal setting, imagery, task instructions are also effective along with restructuring the learning environment.

QUESTIONS

1. What elements does Suggestopedia have in common with effective therapies that help people change and grow?
2. What does Suggestopedia have in common with Sophrology, the Tomatis method, the Suzuki approach, Soviet hypnopedia and Emotopedia?
3. What are the requirements for determining cause and effect in controlled experimental studies?
4. From how many, and from which studies listed in this chapter would you conclude that Suggestopedia is a generally superior teaching method? Consider only well-controlled studies.
5. List all the subjects you can to which Suggestopedia has been applied.
6. What specific educational techniques facilitate learning?

IV.

PRODUCTIVE PRINCIPLES (THEORY INTO PRACTICE)

In the previous chapter we discussed the basic theory behind SALT or accelerated learning. In this chapter we are going to discuss why the theory works and a first step on how to put the theory into practice. Putting theory into practice will take us several steps and several chapters. Specifically we are going to consider the twin bridging concepts of suggestion-expectancy and whole brain learning in this chapter.

One suggestopedic principle is "Joy and the absence of tension in learning." This sounds nice, but how do you implement it in class? Another principle is the "Unity of the conscious and paraconscious." Great, but how do you cut this down to classroom size? The final principle is "Suggestion is the link to the reserves of the mind." This sounds good, but how you do use it?

The first bridging concept is using suggestion to lead students to expect their learning will be accelerated above normal. This is the suggestive link to get students to expect that learning will be easy, fun, fast and efficient. Suggestion comes in a variety of forms: verbal — non-verbal, direct — indirect. We will consider these different forms of suggestion in detail and give lots of examples. Using suggestion in class is complex, but has always been part of the art of good teaching.

The second bridging concept is whole brain learning, or getting more of the brain than usual involved in the learning process. We consider right brain — left brain specialization, rational — emotional integration and learning in different levels of consciousness. We will review quickly several brain theories relevant to the theme of the unity of the conscious and unconscious. Each theory can be tied in with suggestopedic activities to improve learning.

Finally we will consider the part relaxation plays in learning as an application of the principle of joy and the absence of tension in learning. We will briefly review relevant research results.

A. SUGGESTION — EXPECTANCY

The basic factor on which accelerated learning depends according to Lozanov (1978) is the expectancy that students will learn according to what the teacher expects of them. The phenomenon that people perform according to what important people around them expect is well-known by the name of the *Self-Fulfilling Prophecy* or the *Pygmalion Effect*, and well documented by Rosenthal (1968) and many others. Suggestion by the teacher is the key to this enhanced learning expectancy. Therefore we need to discuss in detail various types of suggestion and ways of using suggestion in the classroom. But first we need a definition of what suggestion is.

Let's repeat how Lozanov (1978) defines suggestion, "Suggestion is a constant communication factor which chiefly through para-conscious mental activity can create conditions for tapping the functional reserve capacities of personality." By "constant" Lozanov means that it cannot be turned on or off; it is present always between teacher and students. By "functional reserve capacities" Lozanov means that we all have talents or abilities that are not normally used, developed, or brought into our normal personality. One such reserve capacity of the human mind is accelerated learning. By "para-conscious" he means beyond our normal consciousness, what we might call subconscious or unconscious.

The term "suggestion" ordinarily has two meanings; one casts light on hypnotic communication. This technical definition is the transmission of influence of ideas, and their uncritical acceptance by the recipient. Since this could be compared to molding plastic in a machine it may be called the mechanistic meaning of suggestion. It implies a passive recipient, a suspension of reason and the implantation of an idea in the recipient's mind. However, Young (1931) long ago pointed out a second definition, that suggestion is indirection, hinting, or intimating. The teacher presents ideas to communicate indirectly, in images, such communication as in the arts and humanities. A playwright does not say a person is bad; he shows his actions and lets the audience respond appropriately. An artist does not need to explain or argue; s/he communicates by presenting concrete images. This indirect communication may be called the humanistic aspect of suggestion. Instead of asking a person directly to do something, the teacher may ask him/her to let it happen involuntarily, or to imagine that it is happening and then to find that it does happen.

The reader may be questioning at this point whether suggestion as used in SALT or Suggestopedia is the same as hypnosis. Some people believe they are identical, but we believe there is a difference. First, hypnosis applied in the classroom does not generally work, whereas Suggestopedia in the classroom has been shown in many studies to accelerate learning. Second, Suggestopedia lacks the formal trance induction and the reported unusual subjective experiences of hypnotic subjects, such as being unable to take their clasped hands apart. Hypnosis and Suggestopedia emphasize suggestion to produce their effects, but even here, there is a difference. We feel that suggestion used in SALT is closer to suggestion as used in commercial advertising than it is to suggestion in hypnosis. The difference is that suggestion in advertising attempts to persuade you to do some thing that you might ordinarily do anyhow; suggestion in hypnosis attempts to compel you to do something that you ordinarily couldn't do. Carrying this to an extreme, if Suggestopedia is "hypnosis", then so is commercial advertising.

Lozanov (1978) printed out that students taught suggestopedically are *less* suggestible at the end of class than at the start.

One last comment here: recall just previously that Lozanov calls suggestion a "constant communications factor". This means that it is always present, even in the classroom. Since it is used negatively in most classrooms, why not use it positively for a change?

Let's tackle the analysis of suggestion. First, suggestion may be verbal or non-verbal. Suggestions may be given in words, "As you relax today, you will find learning is easy." Suggestion may come from the environment, as in having lively Spanish music playing when students enter for their Spanish lesson, the non-verbal suggestion is that learning Spanish will also be fun and exciting. Second, suggestion may be direct or indirect. A direct suggestion in words is, "Today you will find learning here is fun, easy and efficient." A direct behavioral suggestion is the teacher's manner and behavior in presenting the lesson; if the teacher is enthusiastic and relaxed in teaching, then the students absorb this attitude and feel the same way themselves. In summary, suggestion can be categorized as verbal vs. non- verbal and as direct vs. indirect, for a total of four types. Next we will discuss each type in detail.

1. Direct verbal suggestion

Direct verbal suggestion is illustrated a second time by the teacher's telling the class, "Learning will be easy for you today." Since this constitutes a direct frontal attack on students' barriers to accelerated learning, we recommend using it sparingly and judiciously. This type of suggestion is most effective when given after students have been relaxed physically and mentally. Refer to the section on classroom procedures for typical preliminary relaxation techniques.

2. Indirect verbal suggestion

Indirect verbal suggestion draws heavily on the work of Erickson (1980), who gives our second example, "Are you willing to find that out (with respect to today's lesson)?" Note that the implied answer is "yes", as most of the students are in class to learn today's lesson. There many types of indirect verbal suggestion; we present a few of them that have appealed to us for use in the classroom.

Truism

A simple form of indirect suggestion is the truism, a simple statement of fact about behavior that the student has experienced so often that it cannot be denied:

1. "You already know how to experience pleasant sensations like the warmth of the sun on your skin." (Helpful in relaxation.)

2. "Everyone has had the experience of nodding your head 'yes' without quite realizing it."

3. "On some days you learn better than on other days."

4. "Learning easily will probably happen just as soon as you are ready."

5. "Sooner or later you are going to do extremely well in class."

Note that the last 3 examples included time in some aspect. When Erickson made a request for a definite behavioral response, he usually tempered it with time — it could be a few seconds, minutes, hours, or even days. In a similar vein, these suggestions all become truisms because the time factor allows the students to use their own associations and experience to make them come true.

Not doing, not knowing

A basic aspect of Erickson's approach is to allow mental processes to proceed by themselves. We ask the student to "relax and let things happen." Not doing is thus a basic form of indirect suggestion of value in the classroom. Most people do not know that most of their mental processes are autonomous or primary; they believe that they learn by driving, working hard, and directing their own associative processes. So it comes as a pleasant surprise when they relax and find that associations, sensations, perceptions, movement and mental mechanisms can proceed quite on their own. This autonomous flow of undirected experience is influenced considerably by suggestion. When relaxed, the parasympathetic nervous system is dominant, and one is physiologically predisposed not to make an effort. Thus the following suggestions are easy to accept:

1. "You don't have to make any effort or even keep your eyes open here to learn."

2. "You don't have to bother trying to listen to me because your subconscious can do that and learn all by itself."

3. "People can sleep and not know they are asleep. Similarly people can learn and not know they are learning."

Simple binds

Characteristic of all simple binds is free choice among alternatives — but all alternatives lead in the direction desired by the teacher. Here is a simple example, "Would you like to learn to spell 20 or 40 words today?" The simple bind is a simple paradox that some people cannot easily resolve, and so they go along with the suggestion and let their behavior be determined by it. Thus the simple bind can be recognized as a determinant of behavior along with reflexes, conditioning and learning. Here are some further examples:

1. Would you like to relax quickly or slowly?

2. Are you going to be ready to learn faster this week or next?

3. Would you rather imagine yourself to be Aristotle or Einstein in learning math today?

Focusing questions

Questions are of particular value as indirect forms of suggestion when they cannot be answered by the conscious mind. Some examples:

1. Can you imagine yourself being Napoleon Bonaparte or the Empress Josephine at the height of the French Empire for today's history lesson?

2. Would you find your favorite place again for a few moments to relax and get yourself centered before we start? This is the room that you have made, decorated, and put all of your favorite things in.

Yes sets

This type of suggestion creates a cooperative frame of mind through taking the student through a series of statements, for which the obvious answer is "yes", ending with a suggestion as a final question. Hopefully, the student will continue answering "yes" implicitly to the terminal suggestion. Several examples are:

1. Today is Monday, right? And it's afternoon (or morning, as the case may be)? Is it a beautiful day outside? Are you ready to learn more?

2. If you can relax, your mind can help you in unsuspected ways.

3. Before you start to learn easily and faster than before, you ought to be comfortable sitting there.

Double binds

The student cannot answer these questions or decide among alternatives with the conscious mind. These double binds are a little more complicated than the simple bind. The student must first relax and let other parts of his/her mind work to get the answer. Examples are:

1. As you start to relax today, what part of your body starts to feel most comfortable?

2. There are little used parts of your mind that can help you learn

faster and easier than before. Will your mind help you learn quickly today or tomorrow? Will it happen quickly or slowly?

3. You can learn while your body relaxes. When it does, which do you like better, the feeling of a sharp, clear mind or a relaxed body?

Compound suggestion

The compound suggestion is made up of two independent statements connected by the conjunction "and". The first statement is a truism that elicits an implicit "yes" while the second part is the suggestion. some examples are:

1. Get yourself relaxed now, and I will help you learn easily.

2. Learning is going to happen, and you won't have to worry about it because it will be so easy.

3. Each of us has abilities we only know a little about yet. Learning faster and easier in this class is one of those abilities we all will experience more fully in this class.

Complex contingent suggestion

This has the form: Negative statement + suggestion + ongoing behavior. Some examples are:

1. Don't use your mind in a more helpful way until you are relaxed.

2. Don't get any higher test grades in here until some time passes.

3. Don't take part in today's lesson and have fun learning until you have your book open and pencil ready.

The teacher's voice intonation helps to make this more effective as follows: "Don't" might be spoken in a normal tone of voice, while the suggestion "get any higher grades in here" would be emphasized in a louder, firm tone of voice, and the trailer clause "until you are relaxed" again would be spoken in a normal tone of voice.

The general pattern in indirect verbal suggestion is to occupy the mind with processing one statement and then make the next statement the suggestion. The first statement may be complex and require some extra thought to be understood; during this time period the student's logical barriers are reduced and suggestions are accepted readily. Or, the first statement may be puzzling, confusing or ambiguous, with the same result.

For a fuller discussion of these and other types of indirect verbal suggestion, refer to Erickson et al (1976). The introductory discussion and presentation by Prichard (1979) also will be helpful.

3. Direct nonverbal suggestion

Gestures and mime (acting without words) to get students to imitate the teacher form the basis of direct nonverbal suggestion. An interesting incident that actually happened illustrates this. As part of training teachers some years ago, the teachers invited me (DHS) to come to their classes individually, and demonstrate to their students in the teachers' own classes how SALT/Suggestopedia works. Of course, this challenge couldn't be turned down. So I found myself in a fourth grade classroom in a public school in central Iowa giving a one hour spelling lesson with SALT. Initially I did brief physical stretching exercises with the 30 boys and girls, and then prepared to do mind calming. Located just before me for some unknown reason was an ordinary chair; I was standing facing the class with the regular teacher's desk behind me. As I started the guided imagery for the mind calming, a little boy left his desk, came up to the front of the room by me, and plopped himself down in the chair on his stomach. He said nothing and I ignored him.

The guided imagery started with my saying, "Boys and girls, in a minute we are going to take a walk in our imagination outdoors in the snow. (It was mid-January and about six inches of fresh powdery snow had fallen the night before.) But first, in your minds feel yourself putting on your warm coats, overshoes or galoshes, and mittens. You want to be warm for our walk in God's beautiful outdoors in the snow." The little boy lying crossways on the chair raised himself up and exclaimed, "Oh boy, I like to go outdoors to play in the snow!"

Continuing with my spiel, I ignored him, "All right boys and girls, we're warmly dressed now in our imagination; let's go outside." (Most of the boys and girls had their eyes closed and their heads down on the desks.) "Walk in the snow and feel the snow crunch as you walk along." My little friend came up off the chair with, "This is great fun walking in the snow!" I put my hand on his shoulder and gently pushed him down while I kept talking. "Now look boys and girls, there's a red bird singing over there in the top of that oak tree. Listen carefully and you can hear him singing," I intoned. The fourth grade boy tried to get up off the chair, "Hey, he's singing real pretty; I like that!" However, my 190 pound weight and arm held him solidly on the chair firmly but not hurting him.

The guided imagery continued similarly with my attention split. At the verbal level I went right on with the walk in the snow, focusing on the fun, the sights, the sounds and the feel of a winter walk in the snow. The students were doing exactly what I wanted them to do and experience. At the nonverbal level I was doing something completely different, coping with the little boy on the chair, keeping him from disturbing the rest of the class and calming him down. I continued my verbal guided imagery in a completely normal way and simultaneously used nonverbal suggestion on the boy. Every time he tried to get up off the chair, I kept him there forcibly but firmly, and patted his shoulder when he quieted down again. By the end of the four minute walk in the snow, he was lying calmly and quietly on his stomach on the chair. Just after I finished the guided imagery, the boy got up off the chair. With my hand on his shoulder I reinforced my suggestion verbally, "Son, you can keep quiet when you want to, can't you?"

Rather than return to his seat, the boy walked over to the window and lay there pensively while I went through my spelling lesson for the next 45 minutes. Since he just sat there without disturbing the rest of the class, I merely watched him from my position at the front of the room.

A SALT lesson concludes with an informal quiz. On the spelling test, my little friend spelled all of the words correctly to my surprise. The teacher, who had been watching all of this for an hour, was surprised also, but for a different reason. She was not surprised that he got all of the spelling words correct, for he was the smartest kid in class. What surprised her was that he was also the class cut-up and a continuing discipline problem for her, that he had quieted down in response to my nonverbal suggestion of physical restraint and reassurance, and that he had stayed quiet afterwards. This I learned afterwards.

There's one more note to this anecdote. When I saw the teacher for the last time late that spring, she told me that he continued a different boy for the rest of the school term, no more discipline problems with him. Both his parents were working, so the boy at home spent most of the time with his four older brothers without parental supervision. The boy simply had no model of disciplined behavior in school and no one had been able to show him. But four minutes of nonverbal suggestion (physical restraint? reassurance?) changed his behavior for months thereafter.

4. Indirect nonverbal suggestion

There are several aspects to this: teacher nonverbals, student nonverbals and classroom environmental suggestion. The teacher's behavior and attitude are critical indirect behavioral suggestions. The teacher's manner of speaking, eye contact, use of gestures and stance are important suggestions. If the teacher talks in a modulated, excited way, this carries across to the students. If the teacher talks in a dull monotone, this also carries across to the students that the subject, as well as the teacher, is dull and boring. Lozanov (1978) orginally recommended that a teacher deliberately say one sentence in a normal tone of voice, the next in a loud declarative tone of voice, and the third in a soft subdued voice. Then the cycle repeated. Now Lozanov recommends that possibly with theatrical training that the teacher modulate his/her voice dramatically and naturally in keeping with the subject matter. The purpose of course is to suggest to the students that this is an interesting course because the teacher talks excitedly.

Another important nonverbal is eye contact. The teacher who is really interested in his/her students continually looks one student in the eye, then another, another, and so on around the room. The roving eye contact seems to suggest, "Are you awake? Are you getting this? I want you to understand this." Without this eye contact many students feel that the instructor is not really interested in them personally, that they are merely blobs on the wall.

Yet another instructor nonverbal is his/her gestures, or lack thereof. Personally we find it difficult or impossible to lecture with hands in pockets and without using arm gestures. Motions made with the hands can be used to emphasize points made verbally. This also is part of the art of good teaching, and again, theatrical training or experience can help, as does any public speaking.

A final point here is physical posture and location while talking in class. Suppose we take a negative example first. Suppose you were to teach with your eyes downcast, facing the blackboard and stood behind your desk or podium. This suggests to your students that you are unsure of yourself and your subject matter and are defensive. Suppose instead that you stand in front of your desk, stand erect, smile and look the students in their faces. This suggests to the students that you are psychologically naked, but sure enough about yourself and subject matter to do so! Your confidence impresses them.

Here's an interesting incident of how we have used this nonverbal indirect suggestion in class. This happened in a psychology class of 200+ college students. One day two young men near the back of the class persisted in talking rather loudly while I (DHS) was lecturing. Rather than ask them verbally to shut up and be quiet, I walked slowly toward them at the back of the room, lecturing all the while. As I got to within 15–20 feet of them, I started asking questions of students near the two talkative young men. I occasionally looked at the two talkers, while I lectured and engaged nearby students in question and answer. Surprisingly and gratifyingly, the two talkers stopped their conversation rather quickly when I asked their neighbors questions; they probably thought I was going to call on them next! (I was prepared to do that, but didn't have to.) After seeing that the men were staying quiet while I continued lecturing, I slowly walked back to the front of the auditorium and finished my lecture there.

What happened? My physical presence as a college professor near them alerted them; further they became a little anxious when I started interacting with their neighboring students. My temporary physical nearness was enough of a nonverbal indirect suggestion that they quickly became quiet, and stayed quiet for the rest of the period. This type of suggestion works!

Another type of nonverbal suggestion is peer success and peer pressure. One student on one day sees other students do quite well on the ungraded quiz given at the end of SALT lessons. This student thinks to him/herself, "If my friends can do well in here, so can I." This is suggestion by the contagion of success. Peer pressure can add verbally, as has actually happened. Many students do very well with a SALT class, so well in fact that many do get perfect scores on the weekly quizzes near the end of the school term. In one class one spring, everyone was getting perfect scores on these quizzes, all except one teenager who was keeping the class from scoring an average of 100%. Another class member was observed to approach the holdout (who incidentally was doing much better than he had ever done before in school) with the suggestion, "Come on now, Bill, get 'em all right on the quiz today and I'll buy you a beer after class!"

The classroom itself is a final source of nonverbal indirect suggestion. The physical aspects of the room can make it more inviting than normally. Use light paint for walls and ceiling. Arrange the chairs if possible in a semicircular arrangement with teacher and desk at the gap. Use the dimmer light control on occasion to quiet the students down, or to help them relax psychologically. Put posters on the wall that are inspiring, such as "Super students work here." Put interesting travel posters on the wall for a history or foreign language class — ask the students for help and ideas. Put potted plants and flowers in various spots around the room. All of these features add up to the suggestion, "This room is a pleasant place to be in to learn." So use as many of these as you can.

Fig. 4-1. Orchestration of Suggestions

The teacher can control certain classroom features to help control her/his students' behavior. Controlling room lighting and playing appropriate music are 2 examples. For instance, if your students are hyperactive, and you want them to slow down and relax: play slow, relaxing music, and/or turn down (off) the lights. If you want to arouse your students, play lively music and turn up the the lights. You can also do this at a party when you're tired and you want your lingering guests to leave.... Try it!

This concludes our listing and discussion of different types of suggestions. The teacher's goal is to integrate all types of classroom suggestions with conscious and paraconscious elements skillfully combined to lead the students to expect that learning will be easy, fun, efficient and long-lasting. See Fig. 4-1. The teacher learns to orchestrate these aspects of suggestion in the same manner that a director leads an orchestra of musicians. This takes training and practice, of course. Studying this chapter with its many examples will certainly help you get started. We also suggest that you turn to the *SALT Teacher's Check List* further on in this book, and use it slowly bit by bit to help you implement systematically these different aspects of suggestion. Try one or two more each day; then after class, how did you do? Keep on using the suggestive elements you find working for you and that you can do readily; ignore the others temporarily. Later on, try them again. Soon you will find that you indeed are the orchestra leader of suggestions in your class of eager, efficiently learning students. Have fun!

B. WHOLE BRAIN LEARNING

Lozanov (1978) claims that the second major reason that students learn faster with Suggestopedia than students taught conventionally (whatever that is), is that their brains and minds are operating in an integrated manner, left-right, cortical-subcortical. Recent neuro-scientific findings tend to support his claims. Linguistic symbols such as language are generally associated with slightly increased cortical activity in the left cerebral hemisphere, while listening to music and visualizing a picture are associated with increased right hemisphere activity. Public schools in general tend to emphasize verbal or left brain activities in the classroom to the relative neglect of activities to stimulate the right brain. Research on teaching wherein more than one area of the brain is involved shows that both learning rates and retention can increase dramatically (Claycomb, 1978).

Lozanov structures classroom activities so that more than one area of the brain is stimulated during teaching by the use of music, relaxation, imagery, psychodrama and suggestion. Lozanov (1978) reported that foreign language words could be learned in a suggestopedic class at the rate of 0.6 words per minute in the first presentation, while the rate went to 1.2 words per minute in the second presentation. Part of the secret for the increase is attributed to the use of baroque music in the second presentation which in turn is effective due to its placebo effect, its psychological relaxing effect, and the effect of its rhythm, about 60 beats per minute.

We want to review the literature briefly for several current theories of brain functioning, and how they affect learning. Neuroscientists have advanced four general theories of brain functioning: interaction of the right and left cerebral hemispheres of the neocortex, interaction of the triune brain, locale and taxon memory, and holographic memory. These will be defined and explained below. Each theory suggests that the simultaneous and complementary interaction of more than one brain area in the learning process results in enhanced learning. Let's take these theories in turn.

1. Right brain — left brain specialization

The neocortex, or outer "bark" of the brain lies just under the skull and is deeply wrinkled or convoluted, folded in and tucked under itself. There is a major split straight down the middle, front to back, producing the left hemisphere and the right hemisphere of the brain. These two hemispheres are connected near the bottom of the brain by a large bundle of fibers, the corpus callosum. The earliest research on hemipheric specialization came from patients with brain damage, lesions or strokes (Milner, 1968 & 1971). An important advance occurred when Sperry (1964) cut these interhemispheric connecting fibers in an operation called a commissurotomy designed or intended to reduce epileptic seizures. As a result, the research formerly done only on animals was extended to humans to verify hemispheric specialization with these split brain patients. Data also were collected with special techniques from normal persons with intact brains. Electroencephalography (EEG) is one such technique used extensively to monitor brain electrical activity in certain bands or portions of the brain's electrical spectrum. Usually during alert states such as classroom learning, the high frequency beta waves (13–30 Hertz) are associated with increased activity in the left hemisphere compared to the right. Simultaneously, the left hemisphere shows a corresponding reduction in low frequency waves in the alpha band (8–12 Hz) and theta band (4–7 Hz); see for example Galin and Ornstein (1972). Another technique is to monitor hemispheric electrical activity while presenting visual stimuli separately to each hemisphere (McGlone, 1973). Yet another technique is to present separate sounds in dichotic listening studies while monitoring the brain's electrical activity (Kimura, 1967). There are other techniques currently being developed which may let investigators pinpoint brain activity even more precisely while the subject is learning (Gadian, 1982).

A bit of neuroanatomy is needed here. Below the level of the neck, the right side of the body reports sensations to, and is controlled by, the left cerebral hemisphere. The converse holds true for the left side of the body. Above the level of the neck, there is no general left-right crossover. Hearing is different. While auditory stimuli are sent primarily to the auditory cortex on the opposite side of the head, some aren't. For right-handed persons the brain area just above and slightly in front of the left ear is involved in speech. For left-handed people, this may be the case also, or located in the corresponding place on the right. A strange case is vision. Visual stimuli presented to the left half visual field of each eye are sent to the right visual cortex at the back of the head. Correspondingly within each eye, stimuli presented to the right half of the visual field are relayed to the left visual cortex. For further details see Milner (1970).

The left cerebral hemisphere controls most of the right side of the body in right-handers in Western culture. The processing of language also occurs in the left cerebral hemisphere near the left ear in the auditory cortex. Thus the left hemisphere is dominant for most Westerners. The left hemisphere processes information in a linear, sequential fashion similar to computers in their approach to solving problems. Words are processed primarily in the left hemisphere whether presented visually or orally. Words are processed for understanding and comprehension in Wernicke's area, while words are articulated or spoken under control of Broca's area, both in the left hemisphere for right-handers.

The right hemisphere processes information holistically, or the visual gestalt (overall pattern) for an idea. The right hemisphere also handles the non-verbal, emotional components of speech, gestures, music and imaging pictures. Ross (1982) summarized this division of processing language functions thus, "The left is responsible for what we say, and the right for how we say it."

Lozanov uses the label "double plane" to refer to what the teacher says and how it is said: tone of voice, gestures, posture and eye contact primarily. We listen to the "how" to assess the reliability of the spoken information. *Double entendre* for example, lets us say one thing and mean just the opposite by how we say it. Lozanov (1978) has suggested using the prosodic (emotional) functions of the right hemisphere along with the left hemisphere functions in the teacher's presenting material in a globally integrated fashion in the classroom. This facilitates learning in a whole brain fashion. Paivio (1975) for instance reported that simultaneously processing information to be learned through both hemispheres increased long term retention.

Music also is processed primarily in the right brain hemisphere (Gordon, 1970). Lozanov (1971) reported a significant 9% increase in subjects' alpha brain waves during the baroque music review phase and another 9% increase in the theta waves concurrently as compared with their previous levels of alpha (8–12 Hz) and theta (4–7 Hz). He also reported a significant slowing of pulse and blood pressure while listening to music, indicating a state of relaxed alertness. Lozanov also contends that bodily rhythms tend to synchronize themselves to the rhythm of the music; that is, breathing and pulse tend to follow the beat of the music. Further, he suggested that the slow, steady rhythm of certain composers in their music helps to induce a relaxed physiological state. Examples are Handel's Water Music or Vivaldi's Four Seasons. Bordon and Schuster (1976) reported that words presented rhythmically with such baroque music as background were learned and remembered significantly better than words merely given orally without such background. Schuster and Mouzon (1982) reported that different musical backgrounds while learning words affected this learning; baroque had the most effect, then classical as compared with no music as a control.

Imaging, especially picture imaging, is another primarily right brain function that affects learning. Although both hemispheres process pictorial information, the right hemisphere tends to be dominant here (Russell, 1979). Kimura's (1973) studies reported right brain dominance in stereoscopic depth perception. Paivio (1975) reported that visual imagery enhanced memory. Information can be processed either verbally (left brain) or imaginally (right brain). His studies reported an additional benefit when both are used simultaneously. For example, recall was significantly higher for subjects who imaged the words than for subjects who just pronounced the words. Lozanov (1978) recommends the use of imagery along with pronouncing words to be learned to increase learning. Based on this recommendation, Schuster and Wardell (1978) reported significantly better recall of words imaged than not during learning.

2. Triune Brain

This theory classifies the evolutionary development of the mammalian brain into three phases: the reptilian brain, paleomammalian brain, and the neomammalian brain (Maclean, 1973; Holden, 1979). The reptilian brain consists of the brain stem, the midbrain, the basal ganglia, most of the hypothalamus, and the reticular activating system. The old mammalian brain consists of the limbic system, with a concentric ring in each hemisphere. This limbic system in turn has the hippocampus which is important in long term memory, and also the pituitary gland which controls the endocrine system. The limbic system surrounds the older reptilian brain. Surrounding the limbic system in turn is the neocortex, split into the two hemispheres, and the largest of the three brains.

MacLean states that each of these three brains in our heads has its own functions. Each part is distinct from the others although they are interconnected neurally. The reticular activating system of the reptilian brain deals with such biological functions as hunger and the sex drive. The limbic system controls emotions and feelings. The neocortex deals basically with external, environmental events. MacLean's theory, according to Holden (1979) differs from the previous right brain/left brain theory in that creativity and emotional functions are localized in the limbic system rather than in the right hemisphere in hemispheric specialization. The neocortex can operate optimally only when the lower brains are satisfied. Memory is basically a function of the limbic system, but long term memory is a function of all three brain systems. In summary, all parts of the triune brain are involved in memory.

Lozanov (1978) recommends baroque music to help produce a relaxed state. In keeping with triune brain theory, the music and relaxation would affect the limbic system and reticular activating system. MacLean feels such an integration of portions of the brain would enhance learning.

3. Taxon and Locale Memory System

O'Keefe and Nadel (1978) have separated long term memory neurobiologically into two systems, the taxon system and the locale system. Hand (1982) classified the taxon system as rote memory rather than contextual or time referenced. An example using the taxon system would be memorizing the names of all the bones in the body in order from the tip of the toes to the top of the head. In contrast, Hand says that locale long term memory deals with context, using multiple channels and modalities to store anything and everything regarding a specific memory. In learning the names of bones in the body, the locale system is used when additional modalities are used, such as imagery, imagined sounds or fanciful exaggerations. Hand (1982) recommended adding verbal or graphic imagery to a text being studied, to construct a time-space context around the verbal information to help store it in the locale memory system. Lozanov (1978) has suggested using multiple modalities of sensory input to help students learn vocabulary words. Specifically, he recommended using music, relaxation, imagery, psychodrama and suggestion. These should help move the memory from the taxon system of short term memory to the relatively long term memory of the locale system.

4. Holographic Memory

Pribram and Goleman (1979) advanced a holographic theory of memory similar to the locale memory system. However they contended that all sensory inputs are interrelated and that a separate taxon memory system was not needed. They felt that the brain acts as a hologram according to the optical mathematical principles of physics. Brain cells act as frequency analyzers to process the input sensory stimuli; the resulting pattern is then stored over the entire nervous system. Anything about that holographic memory then may restimulate the entire memory hologram. The desire to remember the concept or incident, or some contextual cue may be the stimulus to recover the memory. Optically, when a small corner of a hologram is cut off, that small corner contains all the information in the original whole hologram plate, plus some noise depending inversely on the size of the cutoff fragment. Theoretically the number of waveforms associated with a given memory increase as the number of sensory modalities or channels used in learning increase. Thus more channels, more waveforms result in better memory.

Multiple modalities of sensory information input on a given subject lead to more information waveforms processed holographically and to storing the memory with many tags. All aspects of a given memory may be recovered by using any tag or memory location, as in the optical hologram mentioned above. This is quite similar to the concept of restimulation. Lozanov (1978) emphasized the use of multiple sensory inputs to accelerate memory. Such use is more than additive because of the distinctive interference pattern produced. Teaching vocabulary orally would produce primarily an auditory waveform. Adding visual input simultaneously (seeing and hearing the words) adds a second channel, while the brain in addition produces a third, the interference pattern produced by the interaction of the visual and auditory patterns. The addition of a third input modality such as writing the words produces further interference patterns between visual — motor, visual — hearing, hearing — motor, and all three, visual — hearing — motor. Thus Lozanov's deliberate use of several modalities probably increases long term memory through the increased number of multiple waveform patterns and increased memory accessibility. See Fig. 4-2.

This concludes the brief summary of current theories of whole brain functioning and its possible effects on learning. We don't pretend to be able to decide which is most appropriate, if any. Our purpose is to show the reader that whole brain theories need to be invoked to explain the enhanced learning found in SALT or Suggestopedia, a

Fig. 4-2.   Right Brain — Left Brain Integration

view shared by Lozanov (1978). The interested reader may want to study further these fascinating theories of brain functioning. A short summary of these theories is given in Stein et al (1982). A fairly recent book is *The Integrated Mind* by Gazzaniga and le Doux (1978). Parlenvi (1982) has some interesting things to say about writing, language and the brain. Ferguson (1973) has done a highly creditable job of bringing research in this whole area down to the layman's level.

O'Boyle (1984) surveyed the existing literature on hemispheric brain functioning and concluded that one should be rather cautious when generalizing the few proven experimental findings and transferring these to the classroom. Specifically it is inaccurate to say that in the normal human brain that one brain hemisphere can perform some specialized cognitive task while the other is completely void of such capacity. For example, it is not the case that only the right brain hemisphere can recognize faces while the left hemisphere can not; both possess the necessary capacity. One hemisphere may have a propensity to process information in a given style or dimension, but we should always keep in mind that in a complex task like learning to read or painting that both brain hemispheres make substantial unique contributions toward learning that skill.

O'Boyle feels that to rely upon hemisphere laterality as a cureall of our educational woes would be a serious mistake. As teachers we should acknowledge the vast potential this area has, but at the moment remain cautious with respect to specific classroom use.

In spite of the possible abuse, O'Boyle suggested that one possible application of hemispheric laterality pertains to the teaching of reading skills. Instead of relying only on the phonetic method or the spatially oriented method, teachers should combine the two into a wholistic word technique. Such a multi-dimensional approach would seem to benefit the student. The important point is that the teachers should emphasize the interactive contributions of the right and left hemispheres to the mastery of any given skill. The utilization of various instructional designs or modes of presentation would seem to be the most effective style of teaching. The reason is that the multiple modes of instruction typically result in better learning than reliance on a single method. Pedagogical techniques which use the contributions of both hemispheres to learn a given task may prove to be the most beneficial application of brain laterality studies in the educational setting.

We tend to be more forward here in this book in promoting the use of whole brain research applications in the classroom than is O'Boyle above. Lozanov's claim that whole brain learning is the second major factor that makes Suggestopedia effective seems to us to be supported by research. Thus we favor classroom activities derived from whole brain learning theory. The extent to which our optimistic applications here are appropriate remains to be seen.

C. RELAXATION

The subject of relaxation needs to be discussed briefly before we go on. The opposite of relaxation might be considered to be anxiety, which does not have a simple relation to learning. Crawford (1978) reported that college students with high achievement needs and low fear of failure did increasingly better on criterion posttests as the difficulty of the instructional material increased. However, students with low need for achievement and high fear of failure decreased their performance as difficulty increased. Hanson and O'Neil (1970) found that highly anxious students responded with significantly greater amounts of state anxiety than low trait anxiety students throughout learning. Students working on difficult learning materials increased their state anxiety significantly but decreased it reliably when they worked on easy materials. Caracciolo et al (1973) studied forgetting in an induced emotional situation, whether the teacher would promote the student or not. Students who were told that the teacher would give them a negative judgment because they probably would do badly on the test did indeed do significantly less well than others.

Vorkel and Urban (1977) found a significant relationship between the results of psychological tests and the memorization performance of people via their EEG records. Better memorization performance was more frequently associated with lower EEG activation indices. In other words, people learned better when relaxed.

Carter (1981) investigated the use of biofeedback relaxation procedures with handicapped children to help them learn. Independent variables were treatments and all possible combinations of EMG biofeedback, relaxation tapes, handwriting practice and home practice. The effects of these treatments were determined by improvement scores on the Slosson Intelligence Test, all subtests of the Peabody Achievement Test, the Gray Oral Reading Test, and the Gestalt Auditory Memory and Handwriting. Results indicated that the

EMG biofeedback was the most potent treatment and listening to relaxation tapes second. The biofeedback treatment resulted in significant gains in 9 of the 11 independent measures. The relaxation tapes had a significant link to biofeedback on 3 measures and was the most potent on reading comprehension. Handwriting practice contributed only significantly to penmanship, while home practice yielded a low order negative relationship to 6 of the 11 measures.

Since anxiety/relaxation interacts with so many variables to influence learning, Schuster and Martin (1980) performed a complex study to try to untangle the relationships. Their study investigated the effects of biofeedback induced tension or relaxation of the forehead muscle during learning and testing, subject chronic anxiety level, vocabulary test easiness, facilitating suggestions and sex of subject on the learning and retention of rare English words. From 108 introductory psychology university students tested with the Spielberger et al (1968) Self-Evaluation Questionnaire, 16 subjects were selected with the highest chronic anxiety level, 16 from mid-range and 16 from the lowest level with half male and half female at each level. These 48 subjects were trained in one hour to approximately double or halve their forehead muscle tension with the aid of electromyographic biofeedback monitors. In a later experiment, psychological anxiety went up and down with these requested physiological changes in forehead muscle tension. The learning task consisted of 25 paired associates of rare English words and their common meanings. Subjects spent 10 minutes attempting to learn the 25 words on a given list, with the acquisition test given immediately afterwards.

They reported many significant effects on acquisition which could be summarized in two major conclusions. First, state-trait or state-state matching occurred for simple or low-level interactions. That is, highly anxious subjects typically did significantly better when tensed in the learning situation than when relaxed. The converse was true for chronically low anxiety subjects. Subjects with medium anxiety performed the worst regardless of induced tension or relaxation. Second, for higher order interactions, the results significantly favored overall relaxation in keeping with suggestopedic concepts. Even the chronically anxious did better when given suggestions with an easy test and when relaxed with biofeedback prior to learning, during learning and during testing.

For our purposes here, the general conclusion seems to be that students learn better generally when they are relaxed thoroughly and consistently in the classroom than when they are anxious and nervous.

Accordingly we recommend that teachers strive to get their students relaxed as much as possible in the learning situation. The teacher's manner itself can promote this in many cases, but in others, we recommend using the preliminary physical and mental relaxation exercises described later on in this book.

SUMMARY

In this chapter we took the first step in putting SALT theory into SALT practice. Considering that suggestion is the link to the unconscious reserves led us to the use of suggestion to set up the students psychologically to expect accelerated learning. We introduced the Pygmalion Effect or the Self-Fulfilling Prophecy in which students achieve according to their teacher's expectations. Then we analyzed suggestion into 4 types based on the dual split, verbal vs. non-verbal, and direct vs. indirect suggestions. We further split this into finer detail and presented many examples of suggestion that are directly useable in class.

Next we considered what 4 current brain function theories have to say relevant to the unity of the conscious and unconscious. These theories of brain functioning were, right vs. left brain hemispheric specialization, taxon — locale theory, theory of the triune brain, and the holographic theory of the brain. These have direct implications for teacher activities in the classroom.

Finally we covered the research on relaxation in the learning process as a corollary of the principle of joy and the absence of tension in learning. There are considerable differences in how people learn, or learning styles in this area. However, a general conclusion seems to be that people learn best regardless of different learning styles when they are relaxed consistently in class and expect learning to be easy.

QUESTIONS

1. What are the theoretical principles of SALT and Suggestopedia?
2. How do you go from the "suggestive link to the mind's reserves" to classroom activities?

3. How do you go from the "unity of the conscious and paraconscious" to classroom activities?

4. How do you go from "joy and the absence of tension in learning" to classroom activities?

5. Describe in your own words what is meant by the Self-Fulfilling Prophecy.

6. What are the major points of the right brain — left brain specialization theory? How can you apply these to class?

7. What are the major points and applications of the taxon — locale theory of brain functioning?

8. Ditto for the triune brain theory.

9. Ditto for holographic brain theory.

10. Why is relaxation in learning important?

11. Make up and write down a direct, verbal suggestion that you can use in class or for your own study.

12. Make up two different indirect, verbal suggestions that you can use for your own class or study.

13. List two direct, nonverbal suggestions that you feel you can use in class.

14. List two indirect, nonverbal suggestions that you can see yourself using in class.

V.

PHILOSOPHICAL CONSIDERATIONS (TEACHER ATTITUDES)

Lozanov (1978) presents six additional minor principles or means that guide the teacher's behavior to start and maintain accelerated learning. We will consider them and discuss their applications in this chapter.

Authority of the teacher is the first such means: authority of knowing the subject matter as an expert, and also authority in knowing how to teach.

Infantilization on the part of the students is the second means: learning with a childlike, open attitude.

Double planeness is a third means; the teacher communicates the classroom message at conscious and paraconscious levels simultaneously.

Intonation in which the teacher speaks is a fourth means; the teacher should present the material originally in a lively, dynamic fashion to encourage student imagery.

Rhythm is a fifth means; repeating the material in the lesson in a soft and calm manner with baroque music rhythmically helps learning.

Passive concert is the last means to implement suggestopedia.

The six techniques or means that must be used to develop rapid and easily learned and long remembered material are each only a part of the total picture. Each of these could help but the "snowball effect" will only happen if all six are worked into the teaching. "Snowball effect" is a term for the common reaction that as the students slowly begin to change, the teacher adds more techniques. The students will change even faster, allowing the teacher to change even further and faster. The order that we list these techniques is not to imply that any one is first or last in importance.

The chapter ends with desirable teacher characteristics and behaviors. The concept of the teacher as a totally positive person summarizes these points. We list desireable teacher attitudes and characteristics in several summary tables organized around the six basic suggestopedic means.

A. MEANS FOR IMPLEMENTATION

1. Authority

The authority of the teacher is not to be confused with authoritarianism. We are talking of the fact that you would learn more mathematics from Albert Einstein than anyone less respected. The classroom teacher must have a command of the subject that is observable from the students' position.

The student does not know or care what grade point the teacher had in college so many years ago (maybe only two or three in fact, but so long ago in the life of a child). Students will ask questions, not for the answer, but to test the teacher to see if there is an answer.

Subject mastery is just the first part of authority. Does the teacher show prestige or self-confidence? One easy way to observe self-image is the manner of dress. There are only a few students who need a dress code but the teacher needs to display self-confidence every way he can, and dressing the part can be a big help. Physical appearance can vary, but physical fitness is the obvious way.

The second part of authority is that the teacher is an authority on how to teach. Mastery of this book and lots of practice will make you an authority in this sense. Then you can say as Lozanov (1978) recommends, "You students don't have to worry about learning in this classroom. You show up everyday and let me help you learn easily and well. That's my job."

The teacher must display the belief that "knowledge is important", that being in school is also very important for both himself and the students. Having a lesson prepared for every day that fits into the expectations of the child for that subject is essential. This belief can be shown by the physical aspect of the classroom. The presence of flowers, art objects or pictures show the pleasantness of the place. They are not used to show off but to make a pleasant place for both the teacher and student. School is a special place and this classroom is the most special of this special place.

Lozanov uses a phrase that means a closeness, but yet remoteness. Teachers should understand the student's position because once upon a time they were also students themselves. Do we show that understanding so the students feel it? But a separation must be maintained because of the mastery of material and authority role. Teachers are not in competition with the students for attention or approval and should not let themselves be trapped into it.

There is a great deal written about subliminal communication within any society. The students are not aware of the culture's habits, but the teacher must understand them. They may be very different from the teacher's, but the teacher should not try to mimic theirs at the subliminal level.

"A totally positive person" is a very large statement, but it needs to be a part of every teacher's personality. Satir (1972) states that "people who are around someone who says 'You do it because I say so,' or, 'It is so because I say so,' suffer personal insult constantly. It is as though the other person were saying, 'You are a dummy. I know best,' all the time. Such statements have a long-range crippling effect on the victim's self respect. Effective learning cannot be done in an atmosphere of distrust, fear, or indifference."

Authority can be used to harm or belittle students. Negative input, sarcasm, and one-upmanship do not belong in the classroom. Hart (1983) uses the term "downshifting" in the triune brain to explain the effect of stress on learning that causes the automatic use of reflex reaction under stress or in stressful situations, not learning.

Authority properly used can be a very important positive influence in a learning situation as it is in the life of an infant. Why not in the classroom?

The commercial world is well aware of the effects of authority in advertisements: it helps sell products. Its commercial use has been researched. Sternthal and others (1978) investigated experimentally the effects of credibility of the speaker in promoting the persuasibility of ads. In this same sense, teachers need to "sell" their authority to their students.

2. Infantilization

Learning is the natural state of an infant and does not require an active mental process, but occurs in the random order of the real world. They learn their mother language this way. It is the best method to react to the world around them. Can we use this playful attitude in the classroom? Yes, by making the classroom a place to interact with the material to be learned in the relaxed, playful, spontaneous, creative way of a child at play. Playful, not childish, in games, physical movement, marches in rhythm and the other activities of children.

Nothing is impossible in the minds of children at play. We need to build a playful mentality in a non-threatening situation. The imagination of children does not need correction or criticism, just release to make an enjoyable reaction with the material. If learning is a normal mental activity of a human and does not require a conscious mental process, the teacher needs to reflect this joy of learning. This is a joy that we have all had when some new ability has been achieved. Let the students take this joy and pride in learning, and give them a chance to use their new skills in different ways.

Adults have rigid masks that are used to cover their personalities and protect them from the world. These masks, even the intellectual rational forms, stand in the way of learning and make the teaching of adults harder. The teacher must control the situation to allow students to take off these protective masks without harm. The younger the student, the fewer activities and direction will be needed.

3. Double Planeness

Lozanov (1978) uses this term "double planeness" to refer to our communication at the conscious and paraconscious levels simultaneously. But he really focuses on their *integration*. The unity of the conscious and paraconscious is a fundamental principle of suggestive teaching. Very little has been written about this unity in education. Each teacher needs to be aware of the messages that their paraconscious is sending out and how that meets the cultural requirements of the student population. The student can't be expected to realize that this is part of the classroom. If the teacher is not pleased with the room they are assigned, that displeasure will be constantly in his/her paraconscious interfering with the learning. Make your classroom a place that you can take pride in and enjoy being in, and that will be your paraconscious message.

If your classroom is expected to be a learning station, physical condition is secondary to your mental expectations. Knapp (1972) reports that the perceived attitudes of the students are 7% verbal, 38% vocal intonations, and 55% facial expression. Do you spend this same ratio of time in the preparation of a lesson as a lecture? You can work with your "George" to the extent that only you can control; the student doesn't have that skill yet. Only the teachers know that you can't be psychological opposites at the same time, simultaneously joyful and tense, mad and relaxed. The teacher can put on a happy face in just 5 minutes, just "as if" you were whatever character you want to be. Five minutes play-acting the role will cause you to start in fact to be as you want to be in school. If you take the time while you go to school each day to act "as if" you will have a good day, you will. James (1979) uses this method "as if" to cause something to become true as you believe it to be.

Your double-planeness is trainable if you are aware of the need. It is not easy and many teachers will have to change their basic personality to become effective in the classroom.

4. Intonation

To stop the boring monotones that are so popular in college lectures, it is important to practice voice dynamics for the classroom. The dramatic delivery of any material is possible for every one, but most teachers don't take the time or make the effort to try to spice up their classroom presentation.

You could act out scenes from history, use stand-up comic routines, or ham it up as only the artistic professional can. The children are not too sophisticated to enjoy even an amateur's attempts and usually will join right in.

Voice locus, change of pace, building suspense, getting excited yourself or charged with interest over your subject causes the students to change their mental sets. For the teacher, controlling the mind set is the key reason for voice dynamics.

McLuhan (1982) states that those who draw a distinction between education and entertainment don't know the first thing about either one. His point is well taken in teacher interest arousal techniques. Just standing there telling them won't do it. Be alive and dynamic!

A quote from James Thurber (1983) may be in order here to help make a point that the teacher can use. "After a little Einstein there ought to be a little Cole Porter; after talk about Kierkegaard and Kafka should come imitations of Ed Wynn and Fields. Humor is counterbalance. Laughter need not be cut out of anything since it improves everything. The power that created the poodle, the platypus, and people has an integrated sense of both comedy and tragedy."

5. Rhythm

We use rhythm separately from intonation because it as important and may be used in all phases of the presentation. Rhythm should be used in vocal presentation but we'll settle for the musical component.

Minsky (1983) treats music differently, but try his thought out: "Now, I have asked myself, what on earth could this thing (music) be for- why are so many people doing this? I've made up several theories . . . . One is a cynical theory and that is that music is indeed very much like a language but doesn't mean anything and so gives you a feeling of thinking. It uses up part of your brain that normally is understanding stuff, but without the unpleasant consequences of understanding. So music is relaxing in the sense that it exercises the part of the brain that has a drive to think of thinking about things that are meaningless. . . . The cynicism is saying that thinking is actually unpleasant and so people like this thing going on that relieves it."

The use of rhythm is musical in the context of this section. The music is baroque, that is the music from the 1700's, and largo (4/4 time), and a slow 60 beats per minute in measure. Any pre-classical music can be used, but the best is that music that has endured for 200 years and is still being played.

Make your presentation in time with the music rhythm, play lyrical games with the melody and the students will have little trouble remembering the material.

6. Passive Concert

The passive review concert is the one thing that most people see as so different from cornrow lecturing in the traditional classroom. It is not any more important than the other parts of the presentation. It may require some training that is not in the teacher's academic background but don't consider it more important. The review of material is a valid practice in a presentation. There are some new review sequences that add a great deal to the level of memory.

Lozanov (1978) refers to this means as "pseudopassive concert review". By this he means that when a person goes to a concert of his/her favorite music, that s/he goes to the concert hall with an expectant attitude of being entertained in a pleasant, relaxed, enjoyable way. The SALT teacher should strive to induce this same attitude in the students during the passive concert.

Passivity on the part of the student is not new, but the teacher trying to control the review in conjunction with music is. The passivity is to be of the same type you experience at a recital or movie, physically inactive, ignoring the setting and people around you, concentrating on the experience mentally. The teacher is to be in a very active mode if s/he is going get the students to concentrate together at one time.

B. PRACTICAL CONSIDERATIONS

Now our problem is to go from Lozanov's means to practical aspects of the classroom. First we will consider developing the proper teacher attitudes and then in the next chapters what the teacher does.

1. Philosophy and Beliefs

We tend to think of ourselves as rational people working for a solution to a common problem, but first here is a definition of "rational" that has a different broader meaning than usual:

> "A rational mind, based on the impression that it receives from its limited perspective forms structures which thereafter determine what it further will and will not accept freely. From that point on regardless of how the real world actually operates, this rational mind following its self-imposed rules, tries to superimpose on the real world its own version of what must be." (Zukaw, 1979)

Based on this definition, we will then look at schools from different vantage points, and come to different answers for the same problems. Here is a description of our view:

"I have come to a frightening conclusion. I am the decisive element in the classroom. It is my personal approach that creates the climate. It is my daily mood that makes the weather. As a teacher I possess tremendous power to make a child's life miserable or joyous. I can be a tool of torture or an instrument of inspiration. I can humiliate or humor, hurt or heal. In all situations it is my response that decides whether a crisis will be escalated or de-escalated, and a child humanized or dehumanized." (Ginott, 1972)

"On this basis, if I am paid to teach, not baby sit or socially promote, how do I teach? What is the best method or most effective way to teach? Did you know SALT has the best track record that we can find?" (Palmer, 1984)

Fast drivers can see no farther than slow drivers, but they must look farther down the road to time their reactions safely. Similarly, people with great projects afoot habitually look further and more clearly into the future than people who are mired in day-to-day concerns. These control the future because by necessity they project themselves into it. They do not easily grow sad or old; they are seldom intimidated by the alarms and confusions of the present because they have something greater of their own, some sense of their large and coherent motion in time. (Grudin, 1982)

It seems that every time I (CEG) talk to teachers someone asks, why you? I don't know; it is just a part of my basic belief system that drives me to continue to try. I have tried all of the other techniques that have come down the road in the last twenty years. Most of them didn't work after the original excitement wore off.

We can teach much more effectively now than is generally perceived. You will need a good support group that will be available whenever you feel the need of them. A good psychiatrist or psychologist, minister, an older experienced teacher, a friend, or a good spouse.

This may offer an idea of why I need to teach and to try to improve my techniques:

Those who want to leave an impression for one year
   should plant corn.
Those who want to leave an impression for 25 years should plant a
   tree.
But those who want to leave an impression for 100 years should
   train and educate a human being.
          —An Ancient Chinese Proverb

I wanted to change, I needed to change to satisfy my beliefs that teaching can help others and, I have, with the help of Dr. George Lozanov, M.D.

The questions are: "Do you want to change?" "Do the schools want to change?" "Are the 'threats' real enough to force us to change"? Only time will tell. But SALT will allow us to change to a more effective influence whenever the classroom teachers are ready.

2. Belief System

Your beliefs and mine are the product of our rational thought and training. The "state of the art" has changed in psychological theory as fast as it has in other areas. But what changes can we show for the basic differences in teaching techniques between the 1890's and now?

Can we change? YES, but slowly. It is harder to change the basic structure of society than some people think. But then it is reported that Shakespeare said, "Assume a virtue if you have it not." Now let's take this great truth and follow some of its implications. In assuming a virtue, you are assuming it via your imagination. To become the person you would like to be, you create a mental picture of your newly conceived self. And if you continue to hold it, the day will come when you are in reality that person. So it is with the accomplishment of desires. (Bristol, 1949)

If we follow the writings of William James, founding father of American psychology, he stated, "In this case (and it is one of an immense class) the part of wisdom clearly is to believe what one desires; for the belief is one of the indispensable preliminary conditions of the realization of its object. There are then cases where faith creates its own verification. Believe, and you shall again be right, for you shall save yourself; doubt, and you shall again be right, for you shall perish. The only difference is that to believe is greatly to your advantage." (James, 1979) So I will believe it can be done until I am shown a better psychologically based method of teaching.

What we need is an atmosphere that nurtures change. To change is required and to stay the same is to repeat the mistakes of the past. The risk of change is required if the district is to grow. Change, not on the surface for show, but in the basic level of learning theory. The risk is not to change, and thus have the public education system destroyed.

But change is in itself threatening and depressing to the individuals, so a strong support system must be a basic priority. The teacher needs a support system that encourages change. That support system must have "free" "experts", who will "come show me in this classroom with these kids". Support that the teachers know is not part of their evaluation process. It needs psychological, philosophical, physical components on top of the pedagogical help that is to be instantly available to face the immediate problems.

For example, learning and memory are processes of the unconscious mind. (Brown, 1979) I (CEG) was not trained in unconscious processes while I was in college and still have trouble rationalizing some of the things that the unconscious mind does and/or its limits. Who can I turn to for help with a feeling of safety and security now?

We know that schools are not doing a very good job now! But the generalizations of the various reports don't get down to the specifics of what a teacher must do or not do in the classroom. SALT does. We feel that SALT is a large improvement over the unorganized mixture of things that work for only a few teachers and a few students. Most of the time the students learn in spite of us rather than because of us. SALT reverses that so virtually all students learn the lesson faster and remember longer than with today's methods.

3. Teacher Attitudes

The classroom teacher is faced with the seemingly impossible task of educating another human being. Is there any help? We think so, with the newer ideas of psychology. We do not, in 1985 have a complete picture of how or even where learning takes place. The study of the human brain has reached some interesting new insights but they are not yet ready for classroom use.

We know the brain to be an electrochemical mechanism that has certain requirements for its continued successful operation. What its nutrient requirements are is still not clear. It does need certain building blocks to function and others to clean up the refuse of chemical activities of functioning. Okay, but there are no pills for learning, yet.

We know that the brain needs lots of stimulation to grow. To reach its potential is still a larger story. And we still need an explanation of intuition and creative insight. Then how to apply that in a classroom of students is just starting.

Of the four fields of psychology, Freudian, Behavioral,

Humanistic, or Transpersonal, which is best? We think the last comes close to covering all the various aspects of SALT.

Cognitive Theory needs to include more of the facts that are known. How does the cognitive theorist explain dreams, intuition and other psychic phenomena that are listed as normal human psychic functions?

4. The Totally Positive Person?

As one example of the depth of thought that has been used in forming the bases for SALT try a "Totally Positive Teacher". A Totally Positive Teacher (Lozanov's Speech, 1975) was a very upsetting phrase. Lozanov stated in all dealing with the student the teacher needs to be positive and that includes the double plane level, no sickness or death in any form in the classroom. Real life has enough of them. That was a large order for an ex-drill sergeant in the army and ex-wrestling coach. It at least makes an attempt at improving your outlook on life and your job as a teacher.

Psychologically you can't be opposites at the same time, tense and joyful, mad and relaxed. Know that a teacher can be positive only in a positive supported situation. Tell them that you can put on a happy face in just 5 minutes every day to prepare to face the happy faces of great learners.

Some do's and don'ts that have come up in various talks George Lozanov has given:

1. Do be a totally positive person (Put on a happy face, you can control your mood by acting for five minutes in the mood that you want: a happy, positive person).

2. Don't try to be an artist if you are not.

3. Don't try to be an musician if you are not.

4. Don't use you or your abilities as a standard for the children to compare themselves to. They are not adults with your background and training!

5. Do be yourself.

6. Don't, do not, never ever say "You're wrong" or any other put-downs — no irony — no sarcasm, no put-downs in any form.

7. Don't wait more than 15 seconds for a response to a question without giving it tactfully.

8. Do repeat or resay the mistakes correctly a couple of times later in the correct way without drawing any attention to it or cause any embarrassment to the student.

9. Do allow the students to call "Time-Out" or "King's X" to stop the class for questions or help.

10. Do give the student a pseudo-personality, something to protect themselves. Going to school can be a very threatening, dangerous place to expose oneself; it is dangerous to change. Protect the students' self-image some way in all situations. For example, you might hang a sign on a student's neck for one day, a sign for $+$, $-$, $\times$, $/$, $=$ or each of the digits to make the problems walk around. At least assign the character in a story to go through the actions. Here the student is the sign character temporarily, and not his/her usual self.

In various speeches, George Lozanov has listed the following items of what learning depends on:

1. Attitude, not aptitude.

2. Internal experience, not behavior.

3. Receptive mode, not an active mode for the student.

4. Intuitive level, not the rational thinking or logical level.

5. The limiting factor to the amount of learning is how fast the teacher can talk.

6. Psychological relaxation is similar to that which you would experience if you went to a concert or movie.

7. Psychological relaxation is different from physical relaxation.

8. To learn is the natural state and is normal activity for a human.

9. The teacher's unconscious opinion of the students and the student's abilities become the nucleus to build upon.

10. Maintain a proper distance and yet a closeness to the students.

11. Promote a positive expectation in the student, but without building it too high for the student's age and/or abilities.

5. Assumptions about Teaching

What assumptions do we make about learning that is done in school? Duhl (1983) has listed certain assumptions about learning that we like well enough to repeat here:

1. The exsisting structure needs changing, but that is not the purpose of this book.

2. Learning is an unconscious process. According to Brown (1975), all learning is subconscious.

3. Learning is an effortless process on the part of the learner.

4. Memory is an unconscious process.

5. Most students learn the most in a relaxed, non-threatening situation.

6. Unconscious communication between humans takes place constantly.

7. Limited repetition is useful in a classroom situation.

8. Act as though learning to read and write will help people to think better and differently. Assume that starting with centuries' worth of other people's knowledge is more efficient than starting from scratch and will provide a launch pad for new ideas. Expressing and shaping ideas through metaphor and other forms of rhetoric make the ideas more fully our own and amplifies our ability to learn from others in turn.

We do make assumptions about students, teachers and learning. As we present our paradigm for teaching, here are our assumptions that underpin our way of training. We assume that people learn best:

1. When taught in an atmosphere of respect, with a base of safety or equivalency from which one can take risk. This means that people are free to learn from each other as well as from life experience, books, tapes, teachers, other schooling, and with regard and respect for each one's areas of expertise and vulnerability. It means respecting, with tender nurturance, budding new ideas and images. It means the support and protection for "I wonder if . . ." and "What if . . .?", so that beginning ideas are not judged against complete and long-finished theories. It includes room for new ideas and recognition that all the answers about human beings and human systems are not yet in.

2. When learning takes place from the inside out, in gradual increments, when new learning is based on previous learnings, in a mastering of techniques that are embodied in the culture, and that are passed on in a contingent dialogue by agents of the culture. External reality is changed so that the organism may remain the same.

3. When learning takes place from the inside out in abrupt bursts: Gordon states that learning is connection-making between strange and familiar. Making the familiar strange is innovation. According to Piaget, making the familiar strange is the process of accommodation, when "the organism changes itself to adapt to the environment."

Successful interventions, and teaching processes, make the familiar strange and the strange familiar. (Some leave the familiar familiar, and the strange strange!)

Our assumption is that people learn when the new activity, new information is not too far removed from that which was last known, when it is "novel." Piaget, Bruner, Kagan and others have found that the mind tends not to take in, but reject and/or ignore information which is too discrepant from that which is already integrated into one's schema or assumptive world.

In learning both from the inside out and outside in, we assume that each person learns best when he/she can locate him/herself in connection to the information.

4. When each person's learning style, that optimum idiosyncratic mode of processing information is respected and honored. We believe that people do not learn, grow and change unless the information is available to them in their own mode of representation, their own input channels.

5. When the modes of teaching incorporate multiple ways of learning. We believe that people learn by immersion and reflection, by analogy and metaphor, by detailed analysis, by imagery, by doing, seeing, looking, hearing, feeling, writing, drawing, reading, describing, modeling, imitating, exploring, by challenge, by making the strange familiar, the familiar strange, using right and left brain functions, and probably other ways as well.

6. When there is invitation, room for and appreciation of the "having of wonderful ideas" that keep the spark in life and the sparkle in living.

7. When the body is involved in physical activity, in which the integration of meaning and concepts recapitulates each stage of cognitive development, from sensorimotor through formal operational functions. The body has memories and associations the verbal mind knows not of, which we uncover in sculpture and spatialization, as well as other action metaphors.

8. When any aspect of processes, person, or content is grist for the

learning mill of human systems. Thus aspects of trainees' or trainers' lives, institutions, families, cultures, as well as the thinking behind any exercise, intervention or idea is open for discussion, questioning, experimentation, challenge, and change.

9. When all can be safe enough to take risks of new integrated methods, then is time for laughter. Humor is a needed item in every teaching/learning setting, if not in all settings. Not only is humor a great teacher in and of itself, but we assume it is an absolute necessity in the classroom.

Oliver Wendell Holmes said, "The mind, once expanded to the dimensions of larger ideas, never returns to its original size." We hold all of this to be important even though reading and writing seem to be quite hard and take years to master. Our society declares that this kind of literacy is not a privilege but a right, not an option but a duty. (Kay, 1984)

These philosophical considerations and assumptions are detailed in Tables 5-1 through 5-4. There are many practical applications here that the thoughtful teacher can use in the classroom.

Table 5-1.   Suggestive linkage in learning

Suggestopedia	*Indirect Suggestion*
AUTHORITY: (Positive personality required)	Prestige, Truism: Most Important, Pause with expectation, Acceptance Set, Bind and Double Bind
DOUBLE PLANE: (Physical Exercises) (Mind calming)	Two-level communication, Multiple levels of communication, Interspersal technique, Implied Directive, Dissociation, Distraction
INFANTILIZATION: (Fun and easy to learn)	Analogy, Allusion, Metaphors, Puns, Jokes, Pantomime, Depotentiating the learned limitations, Confusion, Paradox, Non Sequiturs
RHYTHM: (Metronome)	Rhythm
INTONATION: (Dynamic Delivery)	Vocal intonations, Voice dynamics, Voice locus, Folk language
PASSIVE CONCERT: (Sound reproducing equipment)	Not doing, Not knowing: Second Most Important, Parasympathetic activation of the unconscious

Outward sign of the inner search include pupil dilation, flattened cheeks, increased skin pallor, lack of movement, slowed blink and swallow reflexes, and lowered and slowed respiration. Essentially, these are the signs of light trance — concentrated inner attention and decreased motor output. (Lankton, 1983, p. 66.)

Table 5-2. Unity of the conscious/unconscious in learning

Teacher's *Conscious/Unconscious*		Student's *Unconscious/Conscious*
AUTHORITY		
Accept responsibility to teach, Rules are appropriate, Constructive, Overt, truism, No criticism, No resistance to criticism. Personalized room, Pictures, Plants.	Learned limitations, Automatic patterns of living.	Agreement to respect others, Accept role as a student.
INFANTILIZE		
Games, Marches, Jokes, Role playing, Metaphors, Puns, Analogy, Patience & response to new learning with joy & support.	Release to spontaneity, Transform into something we are not.	Ham it up.
DOUBLE PLANENESS		
Relaxed, Centered, Dissociate, Leveling, Distraction, Imagery (fantasy), Allusion, Confusion.	Aware of one's inner self.	Imagery, To center one's self, Awareness.
PASSIVE CONCERT		
Timing, Pause with expectations, Folk language, Physical posture and movement.		Relaxed, Not Doing, Not Know, (Sit, Do Nothing)!
RHYTHM		
Baroque and classical music, Timing.		
INTONATION		
Vocal intonation, Voice dynamics, Voice locus, Folk language, Roller coaster, Silences, Nuances, Posture image.		Listen to the sounds not the words.

Table 5-3.   Joy and absence of tension in learning

Teacher's Conscious/Unconscious	and	Student's Unconscious/Conscious
Relaxed,		Go with the flow,
Centered on one's self,		
Awareness of inner self,		Accept the role
Patience,		of the student,
Room setting,		
Music in background,		
Imagery,		Centered on one's
Positive personality,		inner feelings,
Reality Therapy,		
Globalized materials,		
Encouraging risk taking,		Respect the rights
No sarcasm of students,		of others.
No criticism of students,		Relaxed,
No ridicule of students,		
No correction of errors,		Awareness of inner
Reflection of content and affect,		self,
Pace of speech, Summarizing,		
"I" messages,		Self correction,
Posture, eye contact, facial expression,		
and other nonverbal behaviors,		Self-verification.
How to take notes,		
Clarifying, Confrontation,		
Positive reinforcement,		
Methods of identifying reinforcers,		
Extinction, Time-out,		
Reinforcing alternative responses,		
Modeling, Response cost,		
Contracts (If, Then, By when),		
Using certificates and awards (behavioral and achievements),		
Teaching students to get positive recognition,		
Teaching students to reinforce teachers,		
Positive reinforcement bombardment,		
Secret Pal Game,		
I Spy Game, Token systems,		
Good Behavior Game,		
Daily report cards (accomplishments),		
Bonus points,		

BAD INFLUENCES ON STUDENTS:

Negative reinforcement,
Punishment and its side effects,
Readability assessment procedures,
Adapting material to students' reading level,
Overcorrection, Quiet warnings.

Table 5-4. Reserves of the mind

Here is a list of mental reserves that are generally recognized and the first is most important for this book:

Accelerated learning,
Accessible memory,
Creativity,
Valid self-image,
Self-actualization,
Doing things according to one's will,
Accelerated healing, (Cf. Muñoz, 1984; Schuster, 1975)

(With a combination of repetitive sensory deconditioning and sensory imaging of being healed again, it has proven possible in controlled experiments to speed up the healing process by a factor of 3:1 or more in some cases.)

Here is another short list of abilities that have been written about and instructions given to develop each: Replications are inconsistent. There are probably many more that we do not know of at this time in human history.

Faith healing,
Telepathy,
Clairvoyance,
Clairaudience,
Effulgence,
Out of body experiences,
Remote viewing,
Precognition,
Psychokinesis.

If your belief system includes other abilities, they are a part of your reality. Supernatural powers are not occult, mysterious or miraculous interferences with the laws of nature, but are part of that nature which is still beyond the senses of the unenlightened person. (Mishra, 1974)

The classroom teacher should not be disturbed or distracted by students who report development of any of these abilities. They will not interfere with learning if we do not react negatively.

SUMMARY

In this chapter we have considered six minor principles or means that Lozanov uses as a bridge between his three fundamental principles of Suggestopedia, and what the trained teacher does in the classroom.

Authority is the first such means: the teacher should be an authority in two ways, knowing his/her subject matter and how to teach. This does not mean the teacher should be dictatorial in the classroom, far from it.

Infantilization is the second means: the teacher should induce a childlike, open attitude in the students to let them be receptive to the didactic material and soak up the lessons like a sponge. This does not mean they should be encouraged to act in a childish way like brats.

Double planeness is the third means: the teacher should give the same classroom message didactically at both the conscious and paraconscious (subconscious) levels simultaneously. In other words, the teacher should communicate the material verbally in such a manner that it is reinforced by his/her behavior and manner.

Intonation is the fourth means: the teacher varies his/her intonation in an active, dramatic way to present the material in a lesson. While this can be done in a repetitive normal/loud/soft cycle, we feel this is done better if the teacher reads the material against a background of classical music. The music will change in volume and tempo, and so the teacher in reading against this background will automatically vary his/her intonation accordingly. This artistic intonation is preferred to cyclical loud/soft/normal mechanical variation of intonation. This then helps students generate accompanying imagery to facilitate their learning the lesson material.

Rhythm is the fifth means: reviewing the material previously presented with baroque music in a rhythmic, cyclical manner helps memory. The rhythm, at times almost chanting, of the presentation provides another association for memory.

Passive concert is Lozanov's sixth means. The teacher reviews the material with the students in a frame of mind similar to when a person goes to a concert expecting to relax and enjoy his/her favorite music.

Next we discussed the teacher as a totally positive person, and what it takes to approach this ideal in terms of the teacher's personality characteristics and classroom behaviors. A number of specific do's and don't's were given.

In this chapter we also talked about psychological support for the teacher just beginning to use SALT in classes. It's not necessarily fun sticking your neck out, being first in your school to use SALT.

QUESTIONS

1. Describe how the six means help implement Lozanov's main principles (joy of learning, unity of conscious/paraconscious, and the suggestive link).

2. What is meant by "authority" as a means? How can you use it in your classroom?

3. How do you interpret "infantilization" as a means? What would you do in your classroom to bring it about?

4. What is meant by "double planeness" as a means? How can you use it in your classroom?

5. How do you interpret "intonation" as a means? What can you do in your classroom to implement it?

6. How can "rhythm" be a means to produce accelerated learning? How can you see yourself using it in the classroom?

7. What is meant by "passive concert" as a means to speed up learning? Can you use it in your classroom? If so, how?

8. List the characteristics and behavior of the teacher as a totally positive person.

9. Referring to #8, in which areas could you as a teacher improve? Be specific. Make notes to yourself and try out your self-improvement ideas in class.

10. Compare your own attitudes and beliefs about how to teach with those presented here. Would you like to try any of ours? How would you go about doing so?

11. Name some of the important characteristics of a suggestopedic classroom. Are they different than yours? If so, which ones do you feel you could change?

VI.

CLASSROOM ACTIVITIES (HOW IT WORKS)

In this chapter we are going to discuss in depth the 3 major phases in sequence in a SALT lesson: preliminaries, presentation and practice. We recommend that you use them in this sequence until you are quite familiar with the basic concepts. Then later you can have more fun by being creative and putting them in a different order. There are only two aspects to this sequence that are best left in this initially recommended sequence: putting the relaxation and suggestive set-up first, and the ungraded check quiz at the end. It doesn't make much sense to put them elsewhere in a lesson. See Fig. 6-1.

The preliminary preparation phase is an important one for accelerated learning. Stop and think, can you concentrate well if physically you are restless, or hot or cold? Can you focus on what someone is talking about if you are preoccupied with personal problems? In order the recommended sub-phases are: physical relaxation, mental relaxation, and goal setting imagery.

In the presentation phase there are also 3 sub-phases in sequence: being alerted to the big picture of the lesson, a dramatic, imagery-provocative first presentation, and a quiet review with music. This is a recommended order; try it first before you play around with putting them in a different order. Ask yourself these questions: Do your learn better if you know what class you're in? If you brought the right notebook and you know you're in the math class, then you're set to learn math, and not geography in the geography class you might have walked into. Do you learn better if you're involved in the lecture and not asleep? If you have never gone to sleep in a boring class, you can't answer this question. Do you learn better if you reflect on a lecture you've just heard? Think about the times you wished you could have

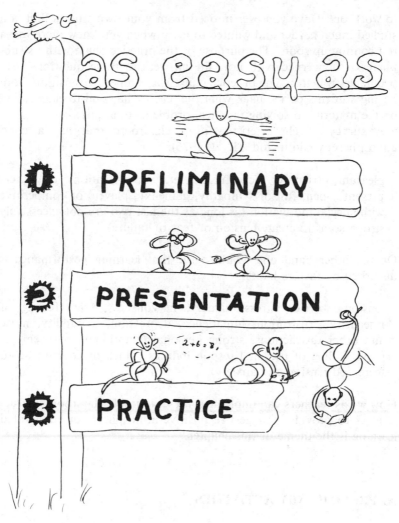

Fig. 6-1. As Easy As . . .

asked the teacher some questions after an interesting class rather than having immediately to go elsewhere. These points are all covered in the presentation phase in this chapter.

Here are some questions to get you thinking about the practice phase. Does it help you to learn something if you can apply it? Have you ever wished the teacher would give you some real world problems to work on? Have you ever noticed from your own studies that you studied much harder and wanted to learn when you knew there was a test coming up soon? The purpose of the practice phase with its sub-phases is concerned with how the answers to these questions help people learn better. The practice phase starts an easy transition from having students parrot back what the teacher has said to elaborating on the material to solving practical problems to a quiz.

A survey of characteristics of a classroom that has a good atmosphere would include (Ryzl, 1976):

pleasant, friendly, peaceful, quiet, warm-relations to others present, open, full of sympathy, gamelike, playful or competitive with special motivation (as long as the last two are not excessively strong so as to create tension or fear of failure).

On the other hand one would agree that learning performance is disturbed by factors like:

tension, worries, stress, anxiety, nervousness, fear, feeling of insecurity, frustration, impatience, depression, irritability, noise and other distractions, strong personal (emotional) involvement, grave feeling of personal responsibilities (which of course lead to increased tension and anxiety).

How we as teachers can implement these desirable classroom characteristics to provide a suggestive positive atmosphere for accelerated learning is the theme of this chapter.

A. PRELIMINARY ACTIVITIES

The purpose of these preliminary activities or exercises is to relax the student physically so that the student can be quiet physically and be ready to learn. The student should be relaxed, concentrating and interested in learning what comes next. There is a major difference here in what Lozanov recommended in his book *Sugestologia* (1971) and his subsequent book in English *Suggestology and Outlines of Suggestopedy* (1978). We will discuss these differences at the end of the chapter; first the reader needs to get the feel of these preliminary activities.

1. Physical relaxation

In general these simple physical activities are similar to gentle warm-up exercises or simple yoga stretching exercises. Refer to Devi (1959) for related exercises discussed in detail.

Stretching

What does a cat or dog do immediately upon awakening? It stretches.... Ask your students to stand up, and some of them immediately will start stretching. Encourage them and do something similar, such as rolling your shoulders around, putting one hand up over your head with the other down straight, etc. Add some encouraging comment, such as, "Doesn't that feel good?" You can add to this natural movement by saying, "Let's pick some apples. Pick an apple high up on the tree with one hand. Now put it down into the other hand, and pick an apple high up in the tree with the other hand. Put it down in the other hand. One day in class a SALT teacher asked the students what they wanted to pick. One ingenious student replied, 'Carrots'. So the class that day picked carrots off the tree. Okay, pick a carrot off the tree, put it down. Now pick a carrot with the other hand higher up in the tree; now put it down. (Teacher pantomimes all these actions.) Students like money as do the rest of us; another day the students wanted to pick money. So now it's a money tree. Reach high up to get that twenty dollar bill; put it down. Now reach for that $100 bill on top of the tree, and put it down." (Teacher as always demonstrates these actions.)

Bendovers

These are a favorite with teachers and students alike. Start with demonstrating the actions by bending down toward your toes. Then spread your feet apart somewhat, and use just one hand to try to touch the other foot. Then repeat with the other hand toward the other foot. Stress the gentleness: try to go just a little farther each time, possibly touching the foot, or if limber enough, touch the floor or put the palm flat on the floor. Avoid pushing hard to try to keep up with the athletes in class; stress trying to go a little farther than you did before. Compete with yourself, not the others. Several bendovers (2—3) are enough.

Sidebends

These are similar to bendovers, but sideways instead of down towards one's feet. Teacher should illustrate by bending sideways, with the down hand sliding down the leg toward the knee; the other hand can be relaxed or put over the head for more bending. Then the complementary motion is illustrated. Again stress the gentleness in trying to go a little farther this time than the previous time. Several bends (2–4) per side are enough.

Wave of tension/relaxation

This is a cumulative, wavelike exercise. Start by tensing the left foot, then the right foot. Keep this tension in both feet, then tense the left calf muscle (lower leg), next the right, then left hip, right hip. Keep all leg muscles tense. Next tense the abdomen, then stomach muscles, left chest, right chest in sequence. Keep all these lower muscles tense. Move on to tensing the left hand, right hand, left lower arm, right lower arm, left upper arm, right upper arm, left shoulder and right shoulder in sequence slowly one at a time. Now all the muscles in the body below the neck should be tense. Finally tense the muscles in a circle around the neck, jaw, face and head. All the muscles in the body should be tense.

Now slowly start relaxing these muscles in reverse order, starting with the head and neck. Next relax the left shoulder, right shoulder, left arm, right arm, left hand, right hand. Continue downward in reverse, left chest, right chest, stomach, abdomen. Then left hip, right hip, left thigh, right thigh, left calf, righ calf, left foot, right foot, completely relaxed.

This process takes more time to describe than it does to do, but it should be done slowly, about as fast as it takes to say the words. The second time through (2 or 3 waves are recommended), the teacher need say only the name of the muscle to tense or relax. When finished, this exercise when properly done leaves one with a feeling of overall relaxation coupled with energy.

Head flops

These are good for students who spend much time reading with their head in one position, or anyone else for that matter who has as to keep their head relatively fixed, such as looking at a TV or computer screen. Start this exercise by relaxing the head and neck muscles, and letting the head drop (or flop) to the chest without any tension in the neck muscles. Then slowly raise the head with a moderate amount of tension in the neck muscles. Repeat, letting the head drop to the chest without any tension. Then raise the head again under tension. Two or 3 repetitions is enough. This exercise is also called the "turtle" exercise, as children enjoy pretending they are a turtle, trying to pull their head into their shell and then putting it out again.

Throat tension/relaxation

First tense both throat muscles, then the right part of the throat, then left, and pause. Repeat, both, right, left, pause. Do this cycle 2 or 3 times. When the students are in the middle of one of the tension phases, ask them to "freeze", hold that muscle tension, and look around to see who has the worst expression. This is good for a laugh, and explains the origin of students' name for this exercise, "the ugly man contest."

Twists

These are another good relaxing-in-place exercise. Ask your standing students to bend their arms at the elbows to avoid hitting their neighbors, then turn slowly to the left, then to the right, with most of the twisting action in the legs and torso. (If there is room enough, the students can extend their arms.) Repeat this twisting action slowly 2–3 times, trying gently to go a little further each time. This is good for the back and leg muscles.

Shoulder flexing

This is done as follows. Bend the arm and place the tips of the fingers lightly on each shoulder. Now rotate the arms slowly in one direction 3 times, then 3 times slowly in the other direction. Children call this the "chicken wing" exercise.

Walking-in-place

This is just what it sounds like: walking in place. Make an effort to lift the foot up high, possibly to the point of kicking oneself with the back of the heel. This is a good to relax the feet. Walking some 30–50 steps is enough. A more energetic variation of this exercise is to run in place some 30–50 steps.

Choked breathing

This is a good exercise to massage the abdominal organs internally. This is done by exhaling all the air from the lungs, holding one's breath, then attempting to breathe by expanding the lungs. Don't let yourself breathe in any air. The effect is to suck in and up one's abdomen; the chest will expand without taking in any air while the abdomen is pulled sharply in and somewhat upward. Do this 2–3 times while holding your breath. Repeat 1–2 times. Do NOT do this exercise within an hour after eating!

Eye rotation

This is good for the eyes after spending some time reading. First look upward to the maximum extent comfortable. Then rotate the eyes so as to look to the upper right as high as possible, then to the right horizontally as far as possible. Continue down to the lower right, then straight down, lower left, extreme left, upper left. Rotate the eyes slowly 2–3 times to the right in a clockwise direction, then do the reverse 2–3 times. Next imagine holding something a foot or so in front of the eyes and focusing on it. Then imagine looking at something off on the horizon. Focus your eyes back and forth several times in this fashion. This exercises your eyes in 3 dimensions. Finally, rub your palms together briskly several times and place your palms over your open eyes, imagining energy flowing into your eyes to relax and energize them. Hold this position for 1–2 minutes.

This is a good place to point out that these physical exercises to promote physical relaxation are optional. We recommend that the beginning teacher do them regularly when starting to use SALT. If your students have just come in from some physical activity as walking to class or recess at school, feel free to skip any preliminary physical exercises. Your students are probably ready to sit quietly for your lesson. But if you find your students are restless, edgy and squirming in their seats, consider having them stand up and doing some of these simple relaxation exercises.

Another consideration here is the difference in Suggestopedia from 1971 to 1978 according to Lozanov. The early version had a separate preliminary physical relaxation section recommended, but the later version doesn't. Instead, the teacher relaxes the students appropriately with physical exercises integrated with the teaching itself. Examples are dance, mime, plays, psychodrama, games.

Most of us have a sense of "push and work hard" which promotes physical tension. SALT when properly done replaces that concept with a sense of relaxation and "Learning is easy." We recommend that the teacher experiment with the use of preliminary physical relaxation exercises until the teacher is able to relax the students with didactic exercises that help teach, such as the mime, games, plays mentioned above.

2. Mental relaxation

Mentally relaxing exercises are done to get students' minds off their present problems and attending to what the teacher is saying. An example that demonstrates the need for training in mind calming and focusing your mind on or off of a given subject is the Monkey's Tail problem. Ask your students NOT to think of a monkey's tail during the next 60 seconds. Look at your watch and time your students for exactly 60 seconds. Ask them how many were successful in not thinking of a monkey's tail. Most people will admit to failure sheepishly and be ready to do your concentration exercises.

A number of such psychologically relaxing exercises are presented next. All should be read or spoken slowly, and with frequent pauses. If the teacher reads them fast, this suggests to the students that teacher is uptight or anxious, and the students tend to imitate teacher's behavior and attitudes. The pauses give the student time to carry out the desired action and also reinforce the idea of relaxation.

These mind calming or psychological relaxation exercises come in two types: self-directed after teacher-given instruction, and teacher-directed or guided imagery. We present several self-directed exercises first.

Watching-your-breathing

This exercise is also called Zen breathing, and is a very good mind-calming or mentally relaxing exercise. Its 3 simple rules are: 1. Watch your breathing, saying "in" silently to yourself as you inhale, and "out" as you exhale. 2. Simply watch your breathing; don't control it. if your breathing wants to go fast, let it. Similarly with slow breathing. 3. When your mind wanders (and it will...) gently bring your attention back to watching your breathing. Do not get irritated that you were distracted, merely come back to watching your breathing again. Time your students for 3–5 minutes, then get on with your lesson.

Watching a picture

Select a beautiful picture or flower to look at. Instruct the students to observe a part of the picture or flower, then close their eyes and try to see the image in their minds. An attitude of "relax and let the image form" is best here; do not work hard at this. Observe for 5–10 seconds, then close the eyes and try to see the image for another 5–10 seconds, and repeat for 3–5 minutes. This develops mental imagery along with a relaxed attitude if properly done.

Biofeedback training

Biofeedback machines can be used to train oneself to calm the mind and control one's thoughts. Suitable and typical machines are Galvanic Skin Resistance (GSR) and Brain Wave or Electro-encephalographic (EEG) machines. These devices have to be used individually and so are not appropriate for classroom use unless every student has a machine. But they do help most people who use them for several hours learn to quiet their minds and relax psychologically.

Candle staring

Staring at a lighted candle for 5–10 minutes a day is an excellent way for individuals or small groups to learn to control their thoughts absolutely. For instance, it is one way to solve the Monkey's Tail Problem mentioned above. Candle staring is done with these directions: Get a timer that will ding or make a noise at the end of the specified 5 or 10 minutes. Get a blank piece of paper and a pencil. The thought control direction is, keep your mind only on the candle flame. If your mind wanders off of thinking about the candle flame, keep your attention on the flame while making a tick mark on the paper to indicate that you were distracted once. Move your hand very slightly to a new position. Thinking about thinking about the candle flame is legal, but otherwise your mind should be preoccupied with aspects of the candle flame itself, the colors, the action, the flickering, its height, width, etc. Every time you are distracted, make a tick mark and keep your attention on the flame. If you get irritated with yourself for being distracted, then give yourself an additional mark for another distraction. At the end of the time period, add up the number of tick marks and plot them daily on a graph for your progress. You will find your progress uneven, and at times, discouraging. But with 5–10 minutes of daily practice of this candle staring, you will find you can control your thoughts, even to the extent of becoming aware that you are about to think a distracting thought and keep your mind on the flame without ever being distracted in the process. You may have to work at this for months or even a year. This ultimately is the answer to the Monkey's Tail Problem.

We're going to start a series of guided imagery exercises that are useful both for their mental relaxation effect and for providing training in developing mental imagery. As you as a teacher read this to your students, be sure to pause a fair amount of time (4–5 seconds) as indicated by the dots ... between phrases. They are best done with a teacher reading or speaking the words, or listening to a previously made tape of the words with appropriate pauses. As a teacher, you will emote and do guided imagery better for experiences you personally have had. So do your own thing here.

White cloud

"Imagine that you are lying on your back on the grass in a meadow or lawn on a clear, summer day. . . . Facing west, you notice the beautiful clear blue sky. . . . You feel very relaxed just watching the clear blue sky. . . . The sky is almost completely empty of clouds. . . . But over on the west horizon you notice a tiny white cloud. . . . That very slowly starts to drift towards you. . . . You are impressed by the purity of the tiny white cloud against the beautiful clear blue sky. . . . Completely relaxed, you simply enjoy the beauty of the little white cloud. . . . You watch in fascination as it drifts closer to you. . . . It's very beautiful against the clear blue sky. . . . You feel at peace, at home with yourself. . . . The cloud drifts closer and closer to you. . . . Now the little white cloud stops over your head and starts descending. . . . Yet completely relaxed, you watch it come down. . . . Now it surrounds you and you become the little white cloud. . . . Completely relaxed and peaceful. . . . Completely without tension just like the little white cloud. . . . Keep that feeling of complete relaxation, and get ready to learn today.''

Mountain sunrise

Imagine that we are walking up a gentle mountain slope just before sunrise. . . . The air is fresh and crisp; everything is so quiet. . . . You feel relaxed, just walking along comfortably up the easy slope toward the top of the hill or mountain. . . . The air is so clear you can see a long way in the valley. . . . Yet before sunrise, but now you can almost see the sun. . . . Now walking along very easily, we reach the top. . . . The sun peeks up on the horizon. . . . Creating a very beautiful sight. . . . Casting long shadows into the valley and peaks far away. . . . Feeling very peaceful, you enjoy this simple beauty. . . . Now the sun is farther up, and you can see things more clearly in the valley. . . . A new beautiful day is starting. . . . Enjoy it and let yourself be open to learning in this same relaxed way today.

Flower opening

Pick your favorite flower and imagine we have a bud or flower that hasn't opened yet. . . . Time is speeding up so that we can watch the blossom unfold. . . . It's going to be a pretty flower, of your favorite kind. . . . Watch the green covering slowly fall back. . . . The flower now shows its color. . . . You feel very relaxed and are enjoying watching the flower. . . . Now the petals of the flower start to unfold. . . . It's a beautiful sight. . . . The petals slowly unfold further into a very beautiful flower. . . . You simply enjoy watching it. . . . It's completely open now, your favorite flower is now fully open. . . .

You're completely relaxed.... Ready to learn in an open way like your favorite flower.

Walk along the beach

Note: if you have access to the Waves tape or record from the Environment series, (Refer to Music Section.) you can heighten the effect of this guided imagery. All right, let's imagine we're going to take a walk along the beach.... You can hear the waves crashing and see them come rolling in to shore.... The air feels and smells fresh.... There is a slight breeze you can feel on your face.... A peaceful and relaxing scene.... The waves crashing down and rolling to shore make a very pretty sight.... There are a few birds wheeling around over your head.... Occasionally the birds cry out.... You walk along very peacefully, enjoying the scene and relaxation.... You walk along comfortably and easily, relaxed.... Take a last look at the waves rolling in ... smell that fresh, salty air.... Feel your relaxed walking along ... and get ready to learn in this same easy way.

Flying a plane

Today we are going to fly a big jet airplane.... We have been through flying school ... and we know how to fly very well.... We walk up to the airplane easily.... Look over our "big bird" with pleasure.... Enter the cockpit and sit down in the pilot's chair.... We check things out with our copilot.... Everything is ok.... We start the jet engines ... listen to them whine.... We pull away from the dock ... feel the engines whining and just waiting to push us along.... We have clearance from the control tower to take off.... We push the throttles ahead.... Just feel the engines pushing us down the runway ... faster and faster ... until we start to feel very light ... and the airplane takes off.... We're in the air now and climbing rapidly.... Up to 5000 feet and climbing fast ... 10,000 feet and yet climbing.... It's really easy and fun with those big engines pushing us faster and faster.... Climbing higher and higher.... Now up to 20,000 feet.... Just see how far we can see ... 30,000 feet is where we level off ... feel the airplane straighten out.... Now we put the airplane on autopilot and the airplane flies by itself.... We can relax now....

We are getting close to where we're we want to go.... Yet relaxed, we start down.... Feel the plane tip forward and the air noises get a little quieter.... Now we're down to 20,000 feet already.... Going down smoothly and quietly.... Down to 10,000 feet.... Coming down easily.... Down to 5000 feet.... Now we're lined up with the end of the runway.... Everything is ok and all set to land.... Feel the landing flaps and wheels going into position with a thump.... Going more slowly now.... Just about ready to touch down.... There, feel the wheels screech and the slight bump as we touch down.... We reverse the thrust of the engines and rev them up.... We slow down quickly now.... We brake to taxi speed.... pull off the runway.... Taxi along the strip to the landing dock.... Very calmly and easily we pull our airplane up to the landing position.... Everything checks ok.... We shut off the engines.... We're home after a beautiful trip.

There is a very useful series of guided imagery tapes available, written by Mimi Lupin. An example is watching an eagle feed its young while on a trip to the mountains. One teacher and school used a tape from this series in this way: The teacher had a discipline problem with a boy and sent him to the principal's office. After some 15 minutes the boy returned to class, quite calmed down from his previous state, and behaved normally. The teacher later asked him what had happened in the principal's office. The unexpected answer was, "I listened to a tape." The tape however, was from Ms. Lupin's series of guided imagery and relaxation. See the later section on music for details.

Romen relaxation

A. S. Romen (1982) has combined Jacobsen's progressive relaxation (1938) and Schultz-Luthe's autogenic therapy (1959) into a very effective integrated physical and mental relaxation procedure. At the conclusion of this guided exercise, the students will be both mentally and physically relaxed. Tell your students,

"I want to help you get physically and mentally relaxed. I'm going to ask you to take my words, and put them into your own words if you like them better. The point is to talk to yourself, 'My left leg is relaxed ... relaxing ... relaxing.' ... As you tell yourself these words, check your left leg to see that indeed it is relaxing.... 'It is motionless.' ... Check that it is quiet and motionless.... 'It feels heavy.' . . . Feel your weight there in several spots. . . . 'It feels warm.' . . . Find several warm areas in your left leg. . . . Then tell yourself, 'I am calm . . . completely clam . . . I am resting.' . . . Next we will do the same with your right leg. . . . Tell yourself, 'My right leg is relaxed . . . relaxing . . . relaxing . . . relaxing.' Check that it is. . . . Then, 'It is motionless.' . . . Check that it is. . . . 'It feels heavy.' . . . Find some heavy spots there. 'Feels warm.' . . . Find some warm spots in your right leg. . . . 'I am calm . . . completely calm . . . I am relaxing.' Consider your hips, abdomen and lower back. . . . Tell yourself, 'They are relaxed . . . relaxing . . . relaxing.' . . . Next tell yourself, 'I am calm . . . completely calm . . . I am relaxing.'

The Romen relaxation continues with. chest and back, left arm, right arm, shoulders and neck, face and head. The person should slowly scan the part of the body under consideration during the pauses (. . .) to check the desired suggestion. At the end, the person will be quite relaxed if sitting, and possibly asleep if lying down. The complete procedure takes 3–4 minutes for a teacher to direct. After talked through this once or twice, most students can do this relaxation by themselves. It's worth learning and practicing as it's a very effective technique.

There are many other variations of guided imagery possible. Once the teacher has tried a number of the versions listed here, the teacher will be able to come up with a variation that works better for him or her. The result of all these mind-calming or psychological relaxation exercises however is the same: to leave the students with their minds relaxed and off of their previous problems, and ready to concentrate on what the teacher is going to say for today's lesson. We can also say that these exercises teach the student to learn to concentrate, a necessary prerequisite to learning. So mind-calming is also learning to concentrate.

3. Suggestive set-up

The purpose of the suggestive set-up is to convince the students that learning will be fun, easy, efficient and long-lasting. The suggestions here circumvent the barriers of the students to such easy learning, rather than tackling them head-on. Many suggestions for this purpose can be tacked on to the end of the guided imagery, as a careful reading of several of the previous examples will show; this is a generally recommended procedure.

A generally useful set-up is what we call Barber's Escape Hatch; see Barber (1969) for more details. This is particularly useful near the start of the very first SALT lesson. Our version of the escape hatch runs as follows: "I have been teaching this course and using this method of teaching for some time now. It's been quite successful and the students usually learn quite well and easily, and like it in the process. But occasionally I encounter a student who doesn't go along with the fun and interesting things I ask students to do. Sometimes I meet such a student who is more interested in trying to figure out what I'm doing rather than in doing it. If you want to know what I'm doing and why, just ask me and I'll tell you later. But such a student doesn't do the interesting things I'm going to ask you to do, and this student usually doesn't do as well as the other students or even fails. However, I've done this many times now. When I work with such students a second time, they let themselves do the fun and interesting things in this class, and then they succeed the second time. So what I ask now is that you let yourself do the fun and interesting things I'm going to ask you to do. That way you'll succeed, I'll succeed and we both will have fun and learn in the process. Just leave it to me, and I'll help you learn."

The George Concept of course is readily adaptable to goal-setting as a holistic suggestive set-up. An example is this for a typing class: "Okay students, let's get ourselves psyched up for today's typing lesson. . . . See yourselves taking the ungraded practice quiz at the end of the hour today. . . . Feel yourself typing away easily and accurately . . . all of your attention and thoughts on typing . . . feeling your fingers going along fast and relaxedly almost by themselves . . . no problems, just typing along relaxed . . . feel yourself sitting there looking at the page . . . the material seems to come off the page almost by itself . . . the words flow to your fingers accurately . . . you feel pleased with yourself . . . hear the machine click. Now you see yourself finished. . . . Score the results and see yourself pleased with the results. . . . Exclaim to your neighbors. . . . Maintain this relaxed attitude and let me help you achieve your goal today."

A major difference between Lozanov's approaches from 1971 to 1978 is that now he recommends skipping these direct preliminary activities and starting immediately with the lesson. Of course the teachers are trained in the more subtle and sophisticated methods of relaxing students and in the suggestive set-up. Reliance thus has to be placed on indirect verbal suggestions and nonverbal suggestions. Refer to the earlier sections in this book for details. Indirect verbal suggestions can be used initially and throughout the SALT class, limited only by the ingenuity of the teacher. A simple example here is, "As you students take your seats, get ready to have another nice day learning in this class." And of course, all the teacher non-verbals, voice, eye contact, clothes, expressions, gestures, relaxed manner, need to be used deliberately to relax the students and get them set-up when the preliminary exercises are skipped.

As always, imagery can be used as suggestion. Here is an interesting example that happened one day in the classroom: The teacher started, "Think for a moment of all the trouble that you have had in other classes learning.... Some subjects simply are hard for your.... Sometimes you have flunked a test.... Think of all the bad days you have had in school.... Occasionally you have hated school and the teachers.... Feel how hard learning is for you.... Now we are taking a vacuum cleaner to your head.... All those bad things about learning are being sucked up and away.... All the reasons you can't learn now are gone.... Now you can replace them with good thoughts about learning after today." One student was seen to put his hands on top of his head protesting, "No, no, you can't take my problems away; I don't want to learn easily." He learned anyway.

Early pleasant learning restimulation

The idea is to develop a positive attitude and a positive feeling toward learning. Make sure the students know that at least once in their lives learning was fun and natural for them. By focusing first on the nonverbal components of this previous situation, the verbal and cognitive aspects of the same situation should come flooding back to them. A sequence of instruction should start as follows:

Pick some early pleasant learning situation, some time in your life when you were learning something that you liked and enjoyed. (Pause) This may be as early as several years ago when your mother was reading to you or it might be as recently as a T.V. show you liked best of all. Everybody got one? (Pause) (If not, suggest learning to ride a bicycle or ice skate, a birthday party, etc.) Be back there again and find yourself enjoying the experience. (Pause) Think about where you were. (Pause) Who was with you sharing the excitement? (Pause) What was the person's name that was helping you learn? (Pause) Recall now how your hands felt then. Everyone's hands feel different when they are excited. (Pause) Recall that feeling and let it spread up your arms (Pause) Let that feeling spread from the top of your head to the bottom of your feet. (Pause) Recall now how your stomach felt. Let your stomach feel that way again. (Pause) Now think about the thoughts you were thinking then. (Pause) Take a look at the eager feeling you had that day so long ago. (Pause) Maximize that feeling, hang on to it and bring it here today and use it to enjoy as much as you did that day so long ago. With those feelings and thoughts you will remember today as well as you did that day. You still have the ability to remember just as well today.

Note — the pauses must be long enough for the memories to return, so pick a day of your own and use yourself as a guide. When you have had enough time, the students will also. Emote all the feeling you can into the imagery.

Lifelong learning

This is a general purpose set-up. Learning is what life is all about, learning who and what we really are. This is our purpose in life. Learning how to get access to the reserves of the mind, getting around our self-imposed barriers, learning that limits are usually ones we have made ourselves. To know yourself is the goal of life. So in your mind, see yourself being a better knower, a better learner, a better person. Feel this with all your senses, and hold it in the back of your mind.

As a result of these 3 preliminary activities, the students in a SALT class should be relaxed, concentrating on today's material, interested, and expecting to learn easily.

B. PRESENTATION

The purpose of presenting material in a dramatic, dynamic way, and then reviewing it passively with quiet music is to provide as many "tags" or associations as possible to help the students learn and remember the material. In the first dramatic presentation, students are requested to make images in their minds to provide visual or kinesthetic associations to facilitate learning. Providing dramatic music as background and giving practice in imagery-making both help this process. When students are relaxed and enjoying the passive review focusing on the sounds of the didactic material, again this provides a different type of mental "tag" or association to help learning. A general principle is that the more tags, the more associations of different types, the better is the learning, the longer the memory. This follows from the taxon-locale theory discussed earlier (Hand, 1982).

Our recommended presentation phase, as usual, breaks down into several subphases: Review/preview, Dramatic presentation and Passive review with music. The first subphase may be shortened or lengthened as seems appropriate.

1. Review/Preview/Decode

The purpose here is to help students get the big picture: what is the gist or meat of today's lesson and how does it fit in with what we're doing in this course. For instance, a brief review of yesterday's material makes an excellent jumping-off place for starting today. Or the material as review could be worked into today's material as basic material to build on today.

Preview of what is coming today is what Ausubel (1960) called an "advance organizer" and is highly recommended. We're reminded of the story of a famous Southern preacher who was asked for the secret of his success in preaching. His laconic drawl and informative reply was, "First Ah tell 'em what Ah'm going to tell them; next Ah tells 'em, and then Ah tells 'em what Ah done told them." Obviously his success included an advance organizer. For those familiar with behavior modification terminology, this also is similar to behavioral objectives; the students are going to be able to learn and use, repeat, amplify today's material.

The preview can be very short and simple, such as in math class, "Today we're going to learn how to square algebraic expressions." Or the preview can be much longer, as in the Spanish lesson in the Appendix. Turn there now, and note that quite a few pages are devoted to going over the material to be learned before the dramatic first presentation with music ever starts. The purpose not only is to show the students precisely what Spanish they are going to learn today, but to show them that they already know many Spanish words from their English look-alikes or cognates. An extensive preview of this sort is called "decoding", because the Spanish is "decoded" into English words that the students already know.

2. Dramatic presentation (Concert #1)

The purpose of presenting the material to be learned in a dramatic, dynamic way with lively background music is to stimulate the production of visual associations in the students' imagination. The more mental pictures a student makes, the more associations are made and learning consequently is better than without these "pictures". Schuster and Wardell (1978) provided interesting experimental verification of this concept. Lively classical music helps imagery making.

There are at least two ways to approach this imagery-making, provide ready made images or ask students to make their own mental images. An example of ready made images is the use of prepared slides in teaching the Russian alphabet (Hall, 1982). A Russian letter is shown as the initial of a Russian cognate at the bottom of a slide illustrating that word; an example is the Russian word "MAMA" which is identical in spelling and meaning to its English cognate "mama". The slide shows a maternal-looking woman holding the hand of a small boy, and somewhat hidden in the design of the woman's dress is a large letter "M". The students are asked to look intently at the scene, then close their eyes and try to see the scene with their eyes closed. (The scene includes both the spelled word and its accompanying illustration.) Then students are to open their eyes, check the image, and to repeat this process.

A second way to facilitate mental-image making is simply to ask students to make mental images. But then show them how and give them practice! There are several ways to help make images. First is visual association, elaboration and distortion. For example the unfamiliar word "kerygma" means "preaching". Imagine a priest on the ridge of a house preaching and shouting; there's your image and association to help you learn. Another unfamiliar word is "dyspneic", meaning out of breath. Here you can analyze its roots "dys", meaning "dysfunctional", plus "pneic" as in "pneumonia" relates to breathing. "Dysfunctional breathing" would be a technical translation of "out of breath". With this same word, you can use a third approach to image making, focus on the kinesthetic aspects: feel yourself climbing a flight of stairs, and at the top, gasp, "I'm dyspneic, I'm out of breath." A fourth way is to make an associated ridiculous image. Frequently I give this permanent funny image to help people remember my name (DHS): I take off one shoe, hold it in my hand, ask the students to make an image of myself going into a shoe repair shop and asking the proprietor, "Mr. Schuster, fix my shoe!" in a loud voice while pounding my shoe on the table. People have told me years afterwards they have no trouble remembering my name after this simple demonstration. Yet another way to make images is Atkinson's (1975) keyword approach. This two step method first has students focus on some aspect of the unfamiliar word, some aspect that is outstanding. For instance in the Spanish word "caballo" the second syllable is emphasized in the pronunciation "kah-BYE-yoh". This second syllable "BYE" sounds like "eye"; so imagine a horse kicking you in the eye. Presto! there's our two step image: bye — eye, plus horse kicking in eye, and "caballo" is the Spanish word for "horse". Simple, but it does take practice.

Should the teacher give the students prepared images, prepared associated pictures, or teach the students how to generate their own images to help them learn? It depends, on whether you want students to get off to an excellent running start with your prepared images, or whether you want to help their own independent learning by teaching them the above imagery building techniques. We (Schuster and Wardell, 1978) did an experiment to answer this question. We asked students to learn 12 lists of 25 unfamiliar words each, as in the above examples. For one group of students we had prepared images we suggested the students use for each of the 300 words. The other group of students had the same amount of time to study each list, but without any of our prepared images. Instead, we taught the students to make their own images in keeping with the above techniques before the students started on the 12 lists. As you might guess by now, the best technique depended on the amount of practice or number of lists the students had already practiced on for learning. For the first four lists (100 words), giving the students prepared images helped them learn more words than the students who had the problem of making their own images to help learn the words. A cross-over occurred with lists 5–8, so that by the last four lists 9–12, the students who had had instructions from the beginning to make their own images surged ahead and had higher scores from then on in learning vocabulary words. Some of the people in the prepared-image group didn't like our images occasionally and this interfered with their learning. Probably the best long-term answer to this question is to teach the students to make their own images, but give them lots of practice after showing them how.

Here is an interesting example of using image making to wake a class up and get them to pay attention. See Buzan (1971) for details. I ask the class to write the name of a concrete (not abstract) noun, such as "car" on a scrap of paper, tear it off and pass it in to me. More than 20 students are required to make this work. Then I get two student volunteers to help me with the demonstration, without telling the class what I'm up to. The first student screens each concrete word that it is a legitimate word and also not repeated, and then reads it aloud to me. After I nod my head, the student reads the next word. The second student counts to 20 and then stops me. As each word is read, I make an image and build a story to associate the words in sequence. Here is an actual sequence: "car" standing by the curb on a "street", "tire" off the car and rolling down the street, running into a "tree", scaring a "cat" which ran yowling up the tree now standing by a "house", which fortunately contained inside it a "table", on which lay an "apple" which rolled off the table hitting a "dog" on the head causing it to yap furiously at an "airplane" flying by overhead in the sky through a "cloud" while a "man" in the plane is eating "soup" with his "knife" and a "bird" steals this to carve a "boat" on a lake with a "doll" doing the steering to avoid "rain" falling on a "computer" and a "radio" shooting off sparks in the rain. After hearing the student read this sequence slowly to my nodded approval (while making up the picture story), I can repeat back an average of 18 of the 20 words correctly in sequence, sometimes all 20. Of course I don't tell them my story. An obvious question students ask, is "How is it done?" I tell them and hold up a ten dollar bill saying, "Ok, after I tell you my picture story to remember these words in sequence, I bet that at least one of you can now do the same thing for $10. Anyone want to try? You now have heard the list of words three times and also my story." Usually a student volunteers at this point, and usually does at least as well as I did, thus getting the $10. I lose $10 this way, but the students learn much more in the process: how to use imagery in the learning process.

Intonation is an interesting thing to play with in keeping your class awake and learning. Of course, you could mumble as usual into your beard or bosom, and put your students to sleep as usual. Why not wake them up instead with a deliberate, dramatic, dynamic delivery? There are 2 ways of doing this, a mechanical variation cyclically in a normal-loud-soft pattern, and reading along with a lively musical background that encourages you to read with a naturally varying volume level so that you can be heard above the music. Here is an Spanish example of the first type, the mechanical normal-loud-soft cycle: (Normal) caballo — horse — caballo, ... (Loud) ojo — eye — ojo, (soft) hombre — man — hombre, ... (Normal) mujer — woman — mujer, ... (Loud) mesa — table — mesa, ... (Soft) silla — chair — silla. While this is effective for a short time in helping your students pay attention and make images mentally, it tends to wear out after awhile. Instead of repeating this cycle mechanically, try reading the words with an intuitively appealing volume level such as, (Loud) caballo — horse — caballo, ... (Soft) ojo — eye — ojo, ... (Loud) hombre — man — hombre, ... (Soft) mujer — woman — mujer, ... (Normal) mesa — table — mesa, ... (Normal) silla — chair — silla, or whatever volume level appeals to you as you think of reading the word. The pattern is unpredictable and the effect of helping your students make images due to your volume level changes will last longer.

But perhaps the best way is to read the material along with a lively classical musical background. To understand you, and to learn, the students must be able to hear you; so you must talk at or above the level of the background music playing at the moment. We did an experiment to test the effect of reading somewhat softer (Schuster and Pansegrau, 1977) than the accompanying music. The result was as stated above, you have to read at about the same level as the music or somewhat above it. Our data showed that learning suffered when the teacher-experimenter read the verbal material at a volume level somewhat softer (10 db.) than the music background. Reading along with music is new for most teachers, so we suggest you practice it alone before you try it in your classroom.

3. Passive review with music (Concert #2)

The purpose of this special review is to provide yet another set of tags or associations to help students learn. Here the students are asked to focus on the sound of the material in a relaxed fashion, and to appreciate (savor) any images that come along, but not to worry about generating any images this time — just let the ones that do appear flow along with the sounds and music, and enjoy the process. The relaxation, rhythm of the music, sound of the words, all tend to relax the students and produce appreciably more relaxed and dreamy brain waves (Lozanov, 1978) than in the previous dramatic first concert or dynamic presentation of the lesson.

Lozanov claims that this special mental condition is one of the special suggestopedic conditions that enable the accompanying accelerated learning. Our research (Schuster and Mouzon, 1982) tends to bear him out. When we had students learn our vocabulary lists with different types of background music in a simulated (lab) suggestopedic setting with a suggestive set-up, the students learned approximately 30% more words with a baroque music background than with no music. Classical music produced an intermediate effect of about 15% better than the no-music control group. These figures held both for studying the lists and while taking the quiz over the lists. However, a later report (Schuster, 1984) with a study done in an ordinary class setting without the suggestive set-up lead to a different conclusion: some music does facilitate learning, while other music actually hinders learning. General recommendations about types of music to use as background while studying are risky, and the teacher is advised to try suggested types of music and get students' reactions and test results before settling on certain music. The difference in these 2 recommendations is in the setting: a (simulated) suggestopedic class vs. studying in a non-class setting.

For details about different types of music to use in a SALT lesson, refer to the Types of Music section of this book.

C. PRACTICE

The purpose of this rather conventional practice phase is to get the students to activate what they have just learned in the previous presentation phase. In the terms of Bloom's Taxonomy (1956), the change is from knowledge and comprehension to application, analysis and synthesis, possibly evaluation. The purpose of the ungraded quiz is to confirm to the student that learning has occurred.

Approximately 50% of a SALT class lesson is spent here in the practice phase. The teacher's activities here constitute what has been acknowledged as "good teaching", however defined down through the years. The emphasis is on actively involving the student in the learning process, getting the student to use and apply material previously learned. We will give examples. Several subphases are also used here, with the idea of starting with simple, easy activities, and moving on to more complex, harder activities.

1. Activation

Here the students are required to do something actively with the material for the first time. In a foreign language class for instance, the instructor can lead the class in choral reading of previous material, so that students for the first time have to speak the material. This is rather easy, as the students merely have to follow along with the instructor's voice. That is, it's easy if the phonemes (word sounds) are familiar, as in learning Spanish for English-speaking people. It can be hard if the same English-speaking students are in a Russian or Japanese class and the sounds initially are quite different. If the phonemes are different, then considerable choral reading may be used. Of course the teacher should read the material in a loud voice so that the students can hear the instructor over their own voices.

Laboratory exercises of the "canned" or carefully prepared type can be used with good effect here. Lab problems in science and math come to mind at this point. An interesting example occurred when a junior high school teacher wanted to dramatize distances in the solar system. He had students successively represent the sun, Mercury, Venus, Earth, Mars, Jupiter, Saturn, Uranus, Neptune and Pluto. Most of the students as planets were close together at one end of the hall, but poor little Pluto was down off at the other end of the hall unable to talk to anybody!

Songs are very appropriate practice time exercises to help pronounce a foreign language correctly, get the feel of sentence construction and to enjoy the process of cultural learning and elaboration. But surprisingly enough, they can be used in other subject matter classes as well. Several years ago I taught a beginning statistics class with SALT; but at the end of the first two evening classes, things weren't yet going with the usual SALT vigor and enthusiasm. Before the next class, I (DHS) wrote new words to the old American folksong "Jimmy Crack Corn". The words poked fun at the concern and tension of the students in learning statistics, and posed a solution by applying SALT to statistics. The next class evening I took my banjo to class and sang the song for the students, encouraging them to join in. After they sang the songs several times with me, they were ready to learn stat. That evening after class, I heard them talking to themselves, that for the first time, they really understood the subject. Score one more for SALT! For those of you who are curious and also possibly perplexed about learning statistics, here are the words I made up:

STATISTICS AND I DON'T CARE

(pronounced "STEH-tis-tics")

Tune: Jimmy crack corn (The Blue Tail Fly)

Chorus:
  Statistics and I don't care,
  Statistics and I don't care,
  Statistics and I don't care,
  My misery's gone away.

1.
  When I was young I used to fear
  Statistics with a passion dear
  An' clutch up tight when I got nigh
  To problems mumbling with a sigh.

2.
  De problems blur'd, I could not see
  To solve them very easily.
  But lo by magic there appeared
  Lozanov with his method queer.

3.
  With calculator in my hand
  And sharpened pencil here I stand
  Awaiting for de promised land —
  Statistics now I understand.

An interesting way to perform drill exercises is to involve the students in a ball-tossing game. This livens up any normally dull routine exercise. The teacher takes a basketball, bean bag, etc. that can be thrown easily and accurately short distances in the class. In a third grade arithmetic class the teacher might ask, "What is 4 times 3?" and then immediately toss the ball to one of the students whom teacher thinks knows the answer. The student answers. If correct, the teacher confirms the correctness with some verbal praise; if not, the teacher softly corrects the student. Then the student gets to phrase the next question aloud, and then quickly throws the ball to another student. The question must be posed before the ball is tossed to a selected student, so as to get all the students to answer silently. Similarly the teacher must make sure that the question is answered correctly before the next question is posed. The teacher also needs to watch that everyone is involved eventually. Children and adults enjoy a few minutes of drill with this psychomotor activity, whether the subject be math, spelling or grammar drill.

The Total Physical Response (TPR) is an excellent example of verbal and/or physical activity for the practice phase. James Asher (1969) wants to keep all the students in small classes actively involved at all times. He advocates a rapid fire set of questions and answers from students such that involvement is 100% as well as fun. The tension level may be high, but so is learning.

Another fun and interesting activity for practicing foreign language vocabulary is an adaptation of confluent education by Beverly Galyean (1982). A piece of note paper is pinned to the back of each student. Other students take a felt pen and write an adjective that describes in a positive way that person. The teacher helps with vocabulary as necessary. After each person has three adjectives on his/her back, the guessing game starts. The student goes around the room, asking other students questions in an attempt to guess what the other students have written on his/her back. In a Spanish class for example, the student might ask, "Soy yo hermosa?" (Am I pretty?) If "hermosa" is one of the adjectives listed on the girl's back, the asked student answers, "Si, tú eres hermosa." (Yes, you are pretty.) If "hermosa" is not one of the adjectives listed on that student's back, the asked student is constrained to reply, "Si, tú eres hermosa y también inteligente." (Yes, you are pretty and also intelligent.) The purpose is to provide vocabulary drill (in this example) and provide practice in saying nice things about other students who might otherwise not hear them. Of course, we all like to hear nice things about ourselves.

Wenger (1974) has developed and elaborated several techniques that are appropriate here in the practice phase. Perhaps the best in our opinion is this: What you describe in as precise and as great detail as you can, will not only help you learn that material but will also expand your intellectual abilities in general. An application that I have used in a Pascal computer language course is this: Ask the students to work in pairs; one of the pair in turn describes in as precise terms as possible to the other person the major points in today's material. The emphasis is on preciseness and brevity, with the other person having the right to chime in to correct or add to what the first person is saying. Then after 5 minutes, the roles reverse: the second person now has the major responsibility for stating precisely and briefly the major points on the second topic.

2. Elaboration

Here the students are required to use the basics of the lesson in new and different ways. For instance in an eighth grade history class, the teacher asked the students to make up a skit on Lewis and Clark's expedition up the Missouri river and down the Columbia river to the West coast. The students had a lot of fun in writing the skit (which obviously had to stick fairly close to historical fact). The students relished the idea of using their ingenuity in improvising props, and then putting on their play for the benefit of the teacher and other students.

The Appendix gives several examples of elaboration in the Spanish lesson. Other variations possible in a foreign language class are having students pretend to go to a hotel or restaurant as a customer, and then with the connivance of a local business, have the students actually go to such a place, and conduct their business in the foreign language. Another example here is foreign language night at the instructor's home: food, games and conversation are from the given language. A night of fun and learning!

An interesting question is the place of competition vs. cooperation in the classroom. We recommend the use of group rather than individual competitive games in a SALT classroom. This way, a large percentage of the students will be winners, rather than just one person winning in an individually competitive game. The losers can console themselves with, "My team lost, but next time we may win." In an individual competition, the losing persons lost individually, with a possible increase in their learning barriers due to having lost. We want all the students to have a good self-concept that includes, "I am a good, capable learner." Refer to Johnson and Johnson (1975) for further details.

The use of different names and backgrounds than actual in a foreign language class serves this same purpose. When a student makes a mistake when he/she has a fictitious name, the result is different than usual: "The fictitious person made the mistake, but not the real me." This again preserves the self-concept of the student as a capable learner and avoids the establishment of barriers against learning. A longer example is given in the Spanish lesson in the Appendix.

Error correction is an interesting concept in a SALT lesson. How do you correct student errors and at the same time maintain the good self-concept of the student? Following Lozanov, we recommend three general approaches. First, if the error is not too serious, simply ignore it; there will be many opportunities to learn correctly in the next part of the lesson. Second, turn aside near the student who made the mistake, and whisper the correct answer without looking at the student. If appropriate, an arm placed on the student's shoulder non-verbally serves to give a message that the student is ok, supporting the student's self-concept as a capable learner and worthwhile person. Third is correction in passing. The teacher her/himself recognized the mistake, but apparently did nothing about it. However, the teacher in the next few seconds correctly uses the same material where the student goofed. The student had partially learned the material, but guessed wrong. When the teacher uses the same material correctly in the next few moments, the student notices this, and says to him/herself, "Aha, so that's how it is." We recommend that the teacher practice both the whispering and in-passing methods of correcting student errors.

3. Tests

Finally we come to the issue of quizzes and tests in the SALT classroom. Ungraded quizzes are given at the end of every lesson for the purpose of showing the students how much and how well they have learned the lesson. Grades however, are given on the basis of announced or scheduled exams, such as monthly or end of term.

Ungraded quizzes are questions of all types taken from today's lesson. The teacher needs to be careful that the students have been exposed to the material in one or more forms, and that the students have had practice with that type of question. In following Bloom's Taxonomy (1956) for example, if you ask questions that tap evaluation, be sure that your students have had practice with evaluation in your lesson. The students usually do quite well on these ungraded quizzes, so well that they may want to turn in their papers to count toward their course grade. This is particularly true with students who are or have been borderline when taught conventionally; when they see themselves learning well and getting good scores on tests, they want the test scores recorded. So perhaps the class will vote on whether to turn in the (previously) ungraded quiz for a grade.

Grades are given on the basis of announced tests, such as end of term exams. These are conventional tests, but also include psychodrama. Yes, psychodrama can be used for grades. In my SALT teacher training short courses, I (DHS) use psychodrama in this way: I ask the students to split the available time (usually 2–3 hours) up into four equal parts as follows. First, the students in groups of 8–10 students discuss what is important in SALT in the way of theory, principles, means, practices and applications. (Each group also needs to appoint a timekeeper who insists that the group move on when each successive fourth of time allotted has passed.) Second, the group creatively writes the script for one or two skits or plays that incorporate these ideas. Third, the group has to practice their skit(s) at least once. Fourth and last, the group has to perform their skit for the other students and the teacher. During this time the teacher can determine whether the students have learned their SALT lesson satisfactorily or not. Sometimes this can be determined by the volume level during the practice. Once in Brisbane, Australia, I thought an accident had happened or that someone had had a heart attack because of all the commotion, the whooping and hollering going on. But it was merely the students practicing their skit! Students won't believe that a final exam can be fun — wait until they get to the final exam psychodrama in a SALT class!

SALT principles also can help on regular tests. While I (DHS) was involved in teaching Spanish with SALT for the first time, some students challenged me about the importance of goal-setting with the George Concept after watching their breathing. So we did an experiment the next class, which was quiz-time. I made up two parallel forms of the quiz, originally making up a pair of questions to measure each concept that day. Then one question of each pair was assigned by the flip of a coin to Form A, and the other question in that pair to Form B, etc. Thus I had two parallel forms of the same quiz covering exactly the same material and each was administered in exactly 17 minutes each. In a completely counterbalanced design, half of the students took Form A and then Form B second; half had regular test taking instructions first followed by SALT instructions second, and the other half had the complement. Each student served as his/her own control, as each student took both forms of the quiz, one with regular instructions and the other with SALT instructions (stop and watch your breathing for 8 in/out cycles, then expect the answers to come floating into your mind.) There was a 14% improvment when the students had used these 2 SALT techniques before and during each form of the quiz. This improvement by itself isn't much, but it is enough to change your grade on most tests by one letter grade. I tried this experiment again in another class, but during a final examination. This time there was absolutely no difference! Comparing the two experiments, what was different? The amount of time that the students had had to practice these SALT techniques.... The Spanish class students were well practiced in using imagery for goal setting and in relaxation by breathing-watching. But the other students had had no practice with either, letting me conclude that a final exam is no place to teach students how to relax! They must know and be proficient in using these techniques before the stress of a test.

SUMMARY

In this chapter we have covered the three major phases in a SALT or suggestopedic lesson: preliminary preparations, presentations, and practice activities. We recommend that you as a teacher spend about 5–10% of the total class time in the preliminary activities, about 40% on the presentation phase, and about 50% in practice. Each phase has sub-phases in turn.

The preliminary phase has a set of activities at the start of a lesson with the purpose of relaxing the students physically and mentally, and then getting them set-up for the lesson psychologically. First come physical exercises to relax the students so that they can sit still and learn. Then come mind-calming exercises whose goal is to get the students to stop worrying about other things and to start concentrating on today's lesson. Finally goal-setting imagery is used to lead the students to expect that they can learn today's material well and easily.

The presentation phase has its sub-phases of review/preview, dramatic presentation of material, then passive review with music. The review/preview shows how today's lesson fits on to yesterday's, and can simply or elaborately give the big picture about what the students are going to learn today. The dramatic presentation uses an active, dynamic style of presentation to help students generate their own mental imagery about the lesson. The teacher can supply these images in a prepared form, or teach the students how to generate their own images about the lesson. Classical music (type A) may be used to stimulate the students' imagery in the first presentation or first music concert presentation. In the second music concert or passive review with music, the teacher reviews the material a second time, but in a monotonous tone rhythmically with baroque (type B) music in the background.

The practice phase with its subphases aims at getting the students to use and apply the material in different ways. First is an activation wherein the students may repeat with little or major variations what the lesson is. Next the students elaborate or do something with the material they have just learned. This is the fun and games part of the SALT lesson — songs, skits, mime for example. Finally at the end of each lesson is the ungraded quiz whose purpose is to show the students that they have learned the material. Grades are given on the basis of performance in announced or scheduled tests, including a final psychodrama if used.

QUESTIONS

1. List the 3 major phases in a SALT lesson with the sub-phases in each.

2. List the purpose in your own words for each phase.

3. Give an example you can use for each preliminary sub-phase.

4. Give an example of how you would do each presentation sub-phase.

5. Give an example of how you would do each sub-phase of practice.

6. Could you use a movie first in your class as a dramatic presentation? Why or why not?

7. Could you use a short-answer, open-ended quiz covering today's material right after doing mind-calming in the preliminary phase? Could you use these questions to focus attention, say on Spain in a history class? What would be the purpose? Would you use this or not?

8. In a high school class you are thinking about having a guest

lecturer on consumer credit in your class on consumer affairs. When would you work this into your course? Would you prepare the class in any way; if so, how?

9. Turn to the SALT Teacher's Check List, either form in the next chapter. Which of these activities did you do in your last class? Are you satisfied with what you did?

10. Keep your fingers on the SALT Teacher's Check List. What can you do from each section to improve your class tomorrow?

VII.

CLASSROOM APPLICATIONS (WHAT DO I DO IN CLASS?)

Ok, you've just finished the previous chapter on SALT Classroom Activities. Lots of possible ideas were presented. But, what do I do in my classroom tomorrow? How do I get started? This chapter answers these questions.

There are several ways to help you plan your daily classroom activities, an overall approach to a lesson at a glance, a short model, or a week of plans. Specifically, what you might do for imagery, music and its type, what to do for a support group. There are two different forms of a lesson check list.

Several types of music are discussed along with appropriate times to use them in the classroom. Lists of music we have used are given.

A framework for systematic review to enhance memory is considered.

CLASSROOM PROCEDURES OUTLINED

Your school day or period must have all of the suggested pieces every day, in the format that is outlined, at least in the beginning while you and the students become familiar with the "new way". This means the material you will cover at the beginning will be very short. Later you can spread your lesson over 2–3 days.

Here are the points or steps we feel you should include in your SALT lessons, even for single 50–60 minute periods:

1. Physical stretching
2. Mind-calming

3. Positive suggestions

4. Preview of materials (globalization)

5. Active presentation (Hands-on material.) This is a dynamic presentation. Hams and prima donnas do very well in SALT presentations.

6. Passive concert of material (psychological relaxation with music)

7. Practice with material, playlike situation, practice in small groups

8. Review of material

9. Self-corrected quiz, for students' reassurance that they have learned today only — non graded, non collected. If you need to know what progress has been made, walk around and peek while the students are correcting their papers.

10. A minute of quiet at the close of the class period. (Don't forget to rearm them for passage; some hallways are not for the relaxed person.)

The three main principles are (A) Joy and the absence of tension; (B) Unity of conscious & unconscious; (C) Suggestive linkage to the reserves of the mind. As you follow and practice this outline you'll have more time to follow more suggestive linkage with the unity of which we speak.

Your classroom should reflect your personality — big plants, fish tanks, nice pictures; whatever it is that makes you happy to be there. That makes the suggestive atmosphere much easier to build.

Now about that sound system — you can never have too much quality but you can get by with something less. Cassette recorders are easy to use and tapes to make. Marking the various sections you want to use will make set up time short. It does take two or three different recorders in the room to be able to change music when you want. Volume should not be louder than your normal voice level to allow you to vary above or below as the setting requires.

To get a fresh start with a new group of students, here is one series of daily plans: Here is a model to use when you have students for half a day at a time. We suggest four periods of 45 minutes with a few minutes between the first and second, and a fifteen minute break after the second.

1. Stage — explanation of the material and method of presentation.

2. "Counselor section" — the student is "active" by reading or following the teacher's presentation.

3. The teacher repeats the material while the student is "passive" in a darkened room.

4. Practices or activities using the material in creative ways, e.g. plays, art, music, dance.

1. A WEEK OF INTRODUCTORY PLANS

Next is a way spreading one lesson at 50–60 minutes per day over several days to a week:

Monday's Plan

Introduction of the relaxed mental state to get the cooperation of the students.

1. Go through the physical exercises
2. Mind calming (Early Pleasant Learning Restimulation)
3. Metronome and Music with breathing (Ex-hale-In-hale-1-2-3-4-Ex-hale-In-hale-1-2-3-4)

Tuesday's Plan

1. Physical Exercises (5 to 7 minutes)
2. Mind Calming (2 to 3 minutes)
3. Globalization of this lesson (3 to 5 minutes)
4. Presentation — Active (20 minutes), with Type A Music

Students are to interact with the materials, that is, hands and eyes on the material. Don't expect to cover very much material until they know what is expected of them.

5. Presentation — Passive; that is, the students are to be passive (eyes closed, physically and mentally relaxed). (8 to 10 minutes)

Type B Music, Baroque 4/4 time, slow rhythmic movements
Use a metronome at 60 hertz to synchronize the breathing of students.

6. Quiet closing (1 minute)

Wednesday's Plan

1. Practice Session (Joy, absence of tension)

Games, dances, marches, songs, stories, playettes which students organize.

Feedback of progress — self-corrected questions, not to be collected.

2. Globalize tomorrow's concepts

Films, teacher prepared playettes, TV presentations of the big picture. Always work from the big picture down to the little facts that are needed to perform any task.

Thursday's Plan

Back to the first day of the cycle.

Friday's Plan

Be creative and use your own variations for elaboration. Try student skits and psychodrama.

We recommend that you start each day's lesson with a few minutes of physical and mental relaxation. See the previous chapter for examples, such as stretches, side bends, and early pleasant learning restimulation. Here are a few additional mind calming examples, where you as teacher provide the necessary guiding phrases.

Imagery examples:

Mind-calming ideas that have been used:

1. Walk up a high hill and look back and see where we were when we started and how high we have come.

2. Walk through a grocery store with your cart. Don't you want to fill it with ideas?

3. When climbing a stairway, do you remember each step until you reach the top?

4. Go to your favorite place and enjoy it again.

5. Let's take a walk in the park.

6. Let's take a walk in a flower garden and enjoy the flowers.

7. Let's go for a walk in a rose garden. Pick out your favorite for size, color and shape. Don't pick it. Let it grow in your mind.

Music

Type A music — emotional in nature, Classical — if it is still played after 200 years it must have some good qualities.

Type B music — philosophical or intellectual in nature — Baroque 4/4 time.

"... In the first part, the students listen to classical music of an emotional nature; while, in the second part, they listen to classical music of a more philosophical nature.

The new material that is to be learned is read or recited by a well-trained teacher; once during the first part of the concert (solemnly, slowly, with clear diction) and once during the second part of the concert (closer to the normal way of speaking).

At the same time, the teacher must, while taking into account the peculiar features of the music when reading the material and dual-plane wise with intonation and behavior, get a feeling of conviction across to the pupils...."
(Lozanov, 1978, p. 270)

Refer to the music list for music selections of various types.

Table 7-1.   Teacher's check list for a SALT lesson

Physical Arrangement of the Classroom	*Used*
1. Circular arrangement with the teacher closing the circle.	____
2. Class size limited to 12, preferably.	____
3. Alternating seating by sexes.	____
4. Comfortable chairs.	____
5. Subdued lighting, controllable.	____
6. Quality music reproduction equipment.	____

Teacher preparation
  7. Authority role, self-confidence. ____
  8. Subject area mastery and preparation. ____
  9. Positive beliefs and expectations. ____
  10. Positive personal communication (body language, facial expression, rhythms and mental images). ____
  11. Acceptance and respect for all students. ____

Student preparation
  12. School is a place to learn. ____
  13. Learning is important. ____
  14. Teacher as a center of learning. ____
  15. Respect for other individuals; share the world and teacher. ____
  16. Physical relaxation exercises. ____
  17. Mind calming exercises. ____
  18. Early pleasant learning restimulation. ____

Presentation of materials
  19. Positive expectation of learning. ____
  20. Review of previously learned material. ____
  21. Preview of new material to be studied. ____

Active session
  22. Dynamic, dramatic delivery. ____
  23. Three level variation of intonation. ____
  24. Students have materials to watch and in their hands. ____
  25. Background music from the classics, type A. ____

Passive Session
  26. Students physically relaxed, mentally alert. ____
  27. Done in rhythm with Baroque music, Type B. ____
  28. Synchronized breathing and music rhythm. ____
  29. Synchronized breathing (2/4/2) and delivery. ____

Practice session
  30. Role playing, games or songs. ____
  31. Psychologically protective personalities (new identities). ____
  32. Frequent self-corrected quizzes, not collected. ____
  33. Non-graded, non-evaluative situation. ____
  34. Error correction done indirectly and immediately. ____
  35. Mind calming at close of class. ____

Table 7-2.   Format of a specific lesson

Day of Week:_____   Date:_____

I will achieve JOY, UNITY, and SUGGESTIVE LINKAGE by:

Physical Exercises   *Minutes*
  Bend overs
  Whole Body Tension
  Waves of Tension
  Diagonal Stretching
  Side Bends   _____

For Mind Calming I am going to use
  Early Pleasant Learning Restimulation
  Imagery Example
  Tape No.? from Lupin Set   _____

Suggestions I will use
  Enjoy Learning
  I Have Learned Much
  Relaxing is easiest   _____

Preview of Information Unit
  Where does this fit into the course?   _____

Active Presentation
  Background Music
  Baroque or Classical   _____

Practice Activity
  Work Sheet
  Game
  Work alone or in groups?   _____

Passive Concert
  Summary Outline
  Metronome 60 hz.
  Music Baroque Largo   _____

Self-assessment
  To collect or not to collect?   _____

Review of Information Unit
  Did it fit into the course?   _____

Review and repetition schedule

Guttmann (1979) reported that scheduled repetition can help memory if repetition is done with the following in mind:

Preparation Unit

Deactivation, this is lowering arousal level so all students are at the same level. This is the MOST IMPORTANT phase (2 to 4 minutes of exercises and gymnastics; muscular tension and relaxation followed by calm imagery) to develop the student's ability to use just music and imagery.

Information Unit

A change to a higher level of activation together. Another form of music to signal the change. It will not last for more than 5 to 7 minutes. Guided imagery is used with the information.

Consolidation Phase

This phase takes hours or even days. The brain needs time for the learning process, longer than the presentation of the information. No other operation influences during this processing. It would be best to sleep, but in the classroom we need to change to some other activity.

Guttmann thus recommends this teaching sequence:

BREAK — a short shift from the material.

First repetition of the information unit

BREAK — longer with another shift away

Second repetition of the information unit

BREAK — very long

Third repetition of information unit

BREAK — very, very long — wait until the next day

Fourth and final repetition of information unit.

Rest Principle

Projection of the teacher's mental processes is a double-planeness procedure and another part of "suggestive linkage". Review of materials is necessary because of the "rest principle". This is the reason for four repetitions of the material. There are several phases of memory consolidation:

1. During the first few minutes, as electrophysiological activity gives rise to protein synthesis.

2. Over the next night's dreaming.

3. Over the next week or two, as the synaptic changes are made more permanent.

Review

Repetition of the initial learning will always enhance memory, and it will be particularly valuable at these crucial stages of memory consolidation. It is therefore always a good plan to establish an organized system of review whenever you undertake any form of study or remembering of any new material.

A good system is to have your first review of the material start about five to ten minutes after the end of study. This not only reinforces the consolidation of protein synthesis, it also makes the best use of the reminiscence effect, since memory is at its peak at about this time. Research has shown that a five-minute review at this time considerably improves later recall.

The second period of review should be about twenty-four hours later and should take only two to three minutes. This makes maximum use of the consolidation occurring during sleep and will compensate for any initial decline in the memory trace.

The third review should be about one week later for two to three minutes. This will make use of the long-term reminiscence effect and stabilize the memory for a much longer period. There should be another review after about one month, again for two to three minutes, and a final review after six months. After this final review most material will be permanently recorded in memory. The consolidation can be further enhanced by appropriate study techniques and note-taking systems so that virtually all the required material can be recalled.

It may be thought that with continual study the reviews would accumulate and take over most of the study time. Actually, this is not the case. Supposing a person studied every day for one hour a day and set up a review program for this study. On any one day he would need to review the work from one day, one week, one month, and six months before.

Review of work done:	Time taken
1 day before	3–5 minutes
1 week before	2–3 minutes
1 month before	2–3 minutes
6 months before	2–3 minutes

Maximum review time on any one day: 14 minutes

If the extra 20 percent of time spent reviewing leads to an improvement in long-term memory from 10% to 90%, the overall gain in efficiency is about 750%. Thus a few minutes devoted to review makes the hours spent worthwhile (Russell, 1979).

There are a number of things that can help the teacher: darkening the room, using special music only at this time, physical posture of the students, synchronizing breathing of both students and teacher, practicing physical relaxation to be used during this concert, pleasant experiences only.

The student should not "fall asleep" during this concert. The evidence about sleep learning is conflicting and is of little help. But do you remember the movies you have slept through? The entire setup is aimed at a sleep-producing physical attitude so some method to stop sleep must be understood by all. A gentle touch can be used, counting the beats to music and breathing, anything that keeps the student awake.

This passive review is done with baroque music and a breathing sequence of 4 beats to breathe and 4 beats to talk. Both the teacher and students are to breathe, but only the teacher is to do the talking. The rate of the teacher's talking will control how long the review will take and the points that need to be reviewed.

The sequence should be: Ex-hale-In-hale-Hold, 2, 3, 4; Ex-hale-In-hale-Hold, 2, 3, 4; Ex-hale-In-hale. This can be practiced with a metronome set at 60 beats per minute. Students can count the four beats while you are talking without losing the review. It seems to keep them mentally active while physically inactive.

B. TYPES OF MUSIC

Music is used in a SALT lesson to help students learn better for several reasons. The use of music in a classroom is unusual, and when a teacher does use it, the students think something unusual is going on that is going to help them learn — an example of the Hawthorne placebo effect. (If the doctor gives you a sugar pill, it's going to help you get better.) Secondly, the use of baroque music especially helps the students to relax, and this in turn helps students learn better than otherwise. Finally the rhythm of the music provides an additional input to the right brain hemisphere that helps provide an additional tag to learn the material. The relaxation also helps produce lowered activation (mental relaxation) which in itself is another tag. The more tags, the better the learning as we have said before. Let's consider four different types of music useful in the SALT classroom.

1. Classical music

Classical or sometimes romantic music is recommended for use during the dramatic presentation or first music concert. This type of music is characterized as lively, relatively unpredictable (unless familiar), and variable in volume level and tempo. This music tends to excite students, and stimulates their imagination to assist in developing images with the didactic material. As examples, we have used these selections, listed with a source where possible:

Beethoven: 1. Symphony No. 5, Leonore Overture No. 3, CSRV-190. 2. Symphony No. 6 in F (Pastoral); Fidelio Overture, CSRV-193. Vanguard, New York, NY 10010.

Haydn: 1. Symphony No. 100 in G (Military); Symphony No. 101 in D (Clock), CSRV-187. 2. Symphony No. 103 in E flat (Drumroll); Symphony No. 104 in D (London), CSRV-166. Vanguard, New York, NY 10010.

Music for Imaging, LI-201. Lind Institute, San Francisco, CA 94114.

Rimsky-Korsakov: Symphonic Suite for the Thousand Nights and a Night, Opus 35, #3026, Everest.

Tchaikovsky: 1. Romeo and Juliet; March Slav; Mozartiana, 3463, Everest. 2. Sleeping Beauty; Swan Lake, SUM X45056, CMS, Mt. Vernon, NY 10553.

We list here without a source 10 pairs of classical/romantic (A) and baroque (B) music (discussion below) as recommended by Lozanov (1978):

1. (A) Joseph Haydn, Symphony No. 67 in F Major, and No. 69 in B Major. (B) Archangel Corelli, Concerti Grossi, op. 4, 10, 11, 12.

2. (A) Joseph Haydn, Concerto for Violin and String Orchestra, No. 1 in C Major and No. 2 in G Major. (B) J. S. Bach, Symphony in C Major and Symphony in D major; J. C. Bach, Symphony in G minor, op. 6; W. F. Bach, Symphony in D Minor; C. P. E. Bach, Symphony No. 2 for String Orchestra.

3. (A) W. A. Mozart, Haffner Symphony, Prague Smphony, German Dances; (B) G. Handel, Concerto for Organ and Orchestra; J. S. Bach, Choral Prelude in A Major, and Prelude and Fugue in G Minor.

4. (A) W. A. Mozart, Concerto for Violin and Orchestra, Concerto No. 7 in D Major. (B) J. S. Bach, Fantasy in G Major, Fantasy in C Minor and Trio in D Minor, Canonic Variations and Toccata.

5. (A) L. V. Beethoven, Concerto No. 5 in E Flat Major for Piano and Orchestra, op. 73. (B) Antonio Vivaldi, Five Concertos for Flute and Chamber Orchestra.

6. (A) L. V. Beethoven, Concerto for Violin and Orchestra in D Major. (B) A. Corelli, Concerto Grosso, op. 6, No. 3, 5, 8, 9.

7. (A) P. I. Tchaikovsky, Concerto No. 1 in B Flat Minor for Piano and Orchestra. (B) G. F. Handel, The Water Music.

8. (A) J. Brahms, Concerto for Violin and Orchestra in D Major op. 77; (B) F. Couperin, Le Parnesses et l'Astree, Sonata in G Minor; J. P. Rameau, Pieces de Clavecin No. 1, 5.

9. (A) F. Chopin, Waltzes; (B) G. F. Handel, Concerto Grosso, op. 3, No. 1, 2, 3, 5.

10. (A) W. A. Mozart, Concerto for Piano and Orchestra No. 18 in B Flat Major; (B) A. Vivaldi, The Four Seasons.

2. Baroque or preclassical music

This music is used primarily during the passive review with music, or the second music concert. This music is characterized as being generally relaxing, with a 4/4 rhythm and 60 beats per minute. The relaxation happens due to psychological entrainment or synchronization of body rhythms. The normal human heart rate of 70 to 85 beats tends to slow down when the listener hears 60 beats per minute, and the 4/4 measure tends to slow down the breathing to about 15 breaths per minute.

Examples of baroque music are the (B) selections in the list above for Lozanov's 10 pairs of music. The user should make a tape recording of "A" music on one side of a cassette and "B" music on the other. If a piece of music quits before the end of the cassette, simply start playing that piece of music all over again.

Here are examples of other music we have used of this type:

The Baroque Lute, N5-1229, Nonesuch, New York, NY 10022.

Baroque Music for Recorders, N5-1064. Nonesuch, New York, 10022.

Handel, G. F. 1. Water Music, Sum X45044. 2. Four Sonatas for Flute, Opus 1, Sum X45046. CMS Records, New York, NY 10007.

LIND: 1. Largos and Adagios, LI-301. 2. Encore, More Largos and Adagios, LI-302. Lind Institute, San Francisco, CA 94114.

The Top 15 of 1750, CT-4762. (Baroque music of 1750.)

Vivaldi, A. Concertos for Piccolo and Orchestra, N5-1022. Nonesuch Records, New York, NY 10022.

3. Meditative or mood music

This music is appropriate for use during mind-calming exercises and guided imagery trips. This music is characterized by a very slow or no rhythm, flighty or dreamy. Examples we have used are:

David and Amanda Hughes. 1. Dreams of Immortality. 2. Flowers from the Silence. Vedic Research Institute, Sunnyvale, CA 94086.

Environment Series. (A series of records and cassettes of different environment sounds, such as, waterfall, rain, wind in the trees, surf, waves, brook, etc.) Syntonic Research, 175 Fifth Ave., New York, NY 10010.

Georgia Kelly. 1. Birds of Paradise, Heru-103. 2. Seapeace, Heru-101. 3. Tarashanti, Heru-102. Heru Records, Topanga, CA 90290.

Japanese Flute for Meditation: Sohkabu Reibo, VCK-2039.

Japanese Flute: Yasuragi o kimi ni; Akira ito.

Kitaro: 1. Ki, MC-057. 2. Silk Road; Oasis. Canyon Records,

Kuckuck SchollPlatten.

Lupin, Mimi: Harmony and Awareness: A Relaxation Program for Children. Learning Concepts, 2501 N. Lamar, Austin, TX 78705.

Meditative Entspannungsmusik. Psychologische Lernsysteme, D2800 Bremen 1, W. Germany.

Music of Gotzen (Japanese lute), VCK-3210.

Steve Halpern: 1. Starborn Suite, SRI-780-C. 2. Spectrum Suite. 3. Eastern Peace, HS-782. Spectrum Research, Palo Alto, CA 94302.

When we were in Tokyo, Japan, at a hotel, the day started delight-fully when the alarm clock played birds chirping for 30 seconds alternating with waterfall sounds.

4. Subject-appropriate music

This music is appropriate to helping the teacher teach the day's didactic material itself. In a German class, German ompah-pah music can be used as background during the practice phase appropriately to set a pleasant atmosphere. Also, German folksongs can be used appropriately to teach German sentence construction and help correct pronunciation. The characteristics of this type of music of course vary widely, depending on what the teacher is trying to do and teach. Spanish songs and music of course are useful for teaching Spanish, but what about non-language courses? Is music inappropriate here? Not at all, but you do have to be a little more resourceful. For instance you might try Ferdi Grofe's Grand Canyon Suite for a geography lesson, or Holst's The Planets for an astronomy lesson. Moreover, you might try the students' favorite instrumental (non-vocal) music as background while practicing.

Here are some examples and sources for this type of music:

Andriopoulos, 1. Instrumentals with Bouzouki, YAP-19004. General Publishing, Athens, Greece.

Australia, Our Land, Our Music, TC-Aust-1-1 & Aust-1-2. EMI Music Group, Sydney, Australia.

Charijayac (Incan instrumental, S. America.) D-E107. Discobal, Barcelona, Spain.

Grofe, F. Grand Canyon Suite.
3044, Everest.
Century City, CA 90067.

Holst. The Planets. MKC 1827, WRCA 2049. Everest Record Group, Century City, CA 90067.

Isiphiwo, Soul Brothers, (South African songs), 70–700. Masterpiece CBS, New York, NY.

Lieder der Heimat, (German songs), 3158–256. Polydor, Hamburg, W. Germany.

Stunde der Blasmusik, (German om-pah-pah band), 818-252-4Q. Phillips, Hamburg, W. Germany.

Ustad, Ali Akbar Khan. Indian Ragas, 4TCS-02B-1154. EMI, Gramophone Co. of India.

Ustad, Vilayat Khan. Enchanting All the Way, 4TC-04B-1244. EMI, Gramophone Co. of India.

A natural question arises, how often should the teacher use music of various types in the classroom? There is no set answer here; it depends on the teacher. We recommend that the teacher as a minimum, use music appropriately during the second presentation of material, the passive review with baroque music. This takes about 10–12% of the total class time, and the rest of the time, the teacher can get by with no music. Some teachers on the other hand, have music of one type or another playing all the time in their classrooms: Mood music (type C) during the preliminary phase, classical (type A) during the first music concert or dramatic presentation, baroque music (type B) during the second presentation or passive review, and subject-relevant music (type D) going the rest of the time during the practice phase. Thus teachers have extreme latitude in the amount of time they have music in their classroom. But we recommend that they experiment with using different types of music and settle on what they and their students like and benefit by.

SUMMARY

In this chapter we have discussed a number of specific items to help you the teacher plan on how to start using SALT in your classes. Probably the easiest way is to wade in slowly, rather than jumping in headfirst. Scan this chapter and start thinking what you can do to start using SALT. Take the *Teacher's Check List for a SALT Lesson*, or the *Format of a Specific Lesson*. For the first day, pick some one element that appeals to you and do it in your classroom. How did it work? Did the students like it and learn a little better? If it did, fine; do it again. If not, try a different element. For the moment, use only the things that worked for you and your students. Then try other different elements or things from the check list. Keep adding to the list of things that you are using each day, keeping only the ones that you like and that work for you and your students. Eventually you will be using possibly half of the elements in the check list in each of your lessons. At that point you are using SALT in your class. You will be using significant items from each major category in the list. It's also time to take stock and look again at the things that you did that didn't work the first time. Try them again. Specifically we have found that using suggestions and music in the classroom doesn't come easily for some teachers. These elements are critical, so if they didn't work for you the first time, try them again. Your students will like them and they will learn faster.

Review of a lesson after progressively longer periods of time can be an important part of a memory framework. The teacher needs to schedule this appropriately.

Music is another means: the use of appropriate types of music in the classroom helps learning. Music is a placebo, a relaxant and another association to promote memory. Type A music is lively classical/romantic music recommended as background during the first major presentation of classroom material. Type B music is slow, rhythmic baroque music recommended for use during the second major presentation of a lesson for review. Type C music is slow, dreamy, possibly arhythmic music recommended for relaxing the class before the lesson proper. Type D music is subject-relevant, such as the use of Rimsky-Korsakov's *The Young Prince and the Young Princess* while studying Shakespeare's *Romeo and Juliet* in an English literature class. Several examples of each type of music were listed for reference.

QUESTIONS

1. Go through the Teacher's Check List for SALT Lessons. Pick one item per major category to try in your class. Do it. How did you do? Try it again. Do you want to modify it?
2. Study the Format of a Specific Lesson. What can you do in each

major section? Decide, do it, evaluate yourself.

3. Go through the Week of Introductory Plans. Make notes to yourself: what will I do Monday? Tuesday? Wednesday? Thursday? Friday? Then do it. How did you do?

4. Name the four different types of music recommended for classroom use. When and where would you use them?

5. List the name of a music piece or selection of each type of music on record or cassette.

6. What is a recommended schedule of lesson review? How can you use it in class? How about applying it to a topic your students have had trouble with in the past?

VIII.

USE IN YOUR OWN STUDYING

The purpose of this chapter is to help the student apply SALT principles to his/her own studying and learning. We feel that applications of SALT to your own study are quite straightforward, but some of them may not be obvious. As an example some years ago in teaching Spanish (DHS), one of the students in the middle of the term near Christmas came in one day with a long face. I asked him what was the trouble. His reply, "I just flunked a test in Economics." My question of course was, "Didn't you apply what you have learned here in this Spanish SALT course?" His unexpected answer was, "No, I didn't think of it." Another day about a month later he came in with smiles on his face, "I got a B on my Economics test this time." His drastic turnaround happened because he had applied SALT meanwhile to his own studying outside of class. So perhaps the biggest thing to do for your own studying is to apply SALT principles deliberately. For instance, get the SALT Teacher's Check List, and go down through it systematically, seeing what you can do for yourself. To help you in this effort, we're going to go through a typical lesson, and give you some explicit advice on things you can do to help you learn more efficiently in your own studying with SALT. Obviously, we give only a few examples; as we go along more SALT things to do will occur to you.

A. PRELIMINARIES

The purpose here is to take 3–5 minutes, get yourself relaxed physically and mentally, and set-up for an hour of efficient studying.

Repeat this preliminary break every hour. This is 5 minutes well spent, and certainly is not wasted; you simply will study better again.

Physical relaxation

Get up out of your chair, and walk or run around the block. Failing that, go to the bathroom, get a drink, talk to friends for 2 minutes. Always excellent of course, is to pick your favorite exercise from the Classroom Activities chapter, and do it!

Mental relaxation

We happen to like watching your breathing for 10 in/out cycles, but by now you probably have your own favorite from the list in a previous chapter. We also like the Romen Progressive Relaxation for combined physical and mental relaxation in one exercise.

Set-up

At the end of a mind calming exercise like progressive relaxation, be sure to include a little mental imagery for goal setting. See and feel yourself studying the material, understanding it, and then doing well on the test. Of course, be sure to do this with activity and imagery appropriate to you and your goal(s).

B. STUDYING

The purpose here is to make associations or conceptual tags that will increase your learning. As an example, several years ago I (DHS) taught myself the Japanese katakana alphabet or syllabary of some 50 characters in 2–3 hours with imagery and wild associations. A katakana character is a combination of our alphabet, with one character for instance representing the two sounds "ka" pronounced "kah". As a result, I was able to go into a Japanese restaurant, take the menu, and puzzle out laboriously such Americanized words in katakana as, "ham-bur-gay-sah". After saying it once or twice, aha! it sounds like "hamburger" and actually means that. But see what you can do with the following suggestions in the presentation phase of your own studying.

Review/preview

Get an overview of the chapter: what is it all about? Read the chapter introduction if there is one. If not, read the chapter summary if there is one. If not, make your own preview! Skim the chapter lightly, what are the important topics covered, or if you have to read sections, see if you can make headings to substitute for the non-existent ones. It helps tremendously to know what you're learning as you start.

Dramatic presentation

Imagine yourself involved in the learning process; the book author is talking directly to you. Or contort yourself in your imagination to follow the text. Or make weird, sexy, odd associations as a reaction to the text. Remember, your associations do have to be relevant in some odd way to the material you're working on, but the weirder, the better. Once you've made some mental imagery, elaborate on it: make it move, take on different colors, etc. Your imagination here can help you extremely well; use it! See Figure 8-1.

A variation on this theme is to ask yourself, "What are the major concepts or points here?" List these mentally. Then predict the effects or outcomes of using and applying them in practice.

Passive review

Get your favorite baroque music tape or record and start it playing as background music. Read the material over again, pausing frequently to let your mind play with the significance and meaning of the material being reread. If you're studying a foreign language, make a vocabulary tape with vocabulary words and sentences to learn, then play this tape for yourself.

A friend of mine, A. E. van Vogt is a language buff, due to his frequent travels in foreign countries. His Two Hundred Language

Fig. 8-1.   Make dramatic images

Club has available cassette tapes in the usual foreign languages French, German, Spanish, Russian and many more. You can play these prepared language tapes for a passive review with music by adding your own music, or you can simply listen to these tapes while preoccupied with a routine task as driving or housework. They cover the basic necessities of traveling in a foreign country, such as travelling itself, customs, hotels, taxis, sightseeing, etc. They're an easy, practical way to learn the spoken language. The club address is: 200 Language Club, Box 1727, Beverly Hills, CA 90213.

C. PRACTICE

The purpose of practicing the material is to make it yours. Not only do you know and understand it, but you can use and apply it in different ways. Here are some recommended examples to make this happen.

Skeleton outline

Now that you've gone over the material twice or more already, make your own skeleton outline of the chapter. Create this in your mind, and then promptly check yourself when done by skimming the chapter again. Are you satisfied with your outline? If not, change it until you are. When finished, you should have this skeleton outline as if it were actually section headings.

Complete outline

Fill in the flesh on your skeleton outline: what details are necessary to fill out the information actually given in the chapter? Check yourself when done. Modify your full outline as necessary until satisfied. Why were the changes necessary?

Problems

If there are problems given at the end of the chapter, work them. In particular, do those where you will get some feedback from answers given at the back of the book. If no problems are given, make up your own problems and answer them. For each major section, ask yourself, "What is the point of this section? What kind of problem or question can the teacher ask, based on this section?" Of course, answer your own question. And again, check your answer by skimming back over the chapter.

Work with friend

Find a friend or fellow student who is in the same class, and take turns asking each other questions and problems. You both will do better this way than alone, as your blind spots probably are different for the two of you. That is, what you only half-know, your friend probably knows correctly.

Quiz

Finally, see if you can get a complete quiz or test to try your knowledge out on before you have to take the actual test in class. An old exam from the previous time the class was taught is excellent in this regard. Teachers have even been know to repeat some questions from old exams on current tests. The old test will give you a feel for the type of questions covered previously, and you can even give yourself simulated "for real" practice by timing yourself. Make sure you set a goal image of yourself taking the test while relaxed and feel yourself doing well on the test.

Review

Remember that Russell (1979) recommends a cumulative review of your studying. Glance over your material at progressively longer intervals after studying: 5–10 minutes, 1 hour, 1 day, 1 week, 1 month, 6 months. This will fix the material permanently in your memory. Set up a review schedule with yourself on a daily basis. Scheduled review each day really takes very little time each day, but it provides a tremendous gain in memory.

In summary, we have given here in this short chapter a number of examples of how you can apply the SALT preliminary exercises, presentation techniques, and practice concepts to your own studying. Students report that they seem to be effective. However, controlled research on these applications to your own studying remains to be done. Perhaps you can help?

QUESTIONS

1. What are the main points for each of the 3 SALT phases in applying SALT to your own studying?

2. Make a mental holistic image of yourself applying these points to your own studying.

3. As you finish a study session, check yourself, what techniques did I use? Looking at the SALT Teacher's Check List, which things do I want to use in my next studying?

Bibliography

(Note: we have included a few general interest references that are not referred to in the text or author index. — DHS & CEG)

Alesandrini, K. L. (1981) Pictorial-verbal and analytic-holistic learning strategies in science learning. *Journal of Educational Psychology*, *73* (3), 358–368.

Applegate, R. (1983) Accelerating learning potential. Paradise, CA 95969: Paradise School District. An ESEA Title IV-C research project report.

Applegate, R. L. (1985) Accelerating learning potential. Paradise, CA: Paradise School District. Project report, 7 pp.

Asher, J.J. (1969) The total physical response technique of learning. *Journal of Special Education*, *3* (3), 253–262.

Assagioli, R. (1980). *Psychosynthesis*. N.Y.: Penguin Books.

Association for Research and Englightenment. (1970) Circulating file on Thought, Concentration and Memory. Virginia Beach, VA: ARE.

Atkinson, R. C. (1975) Mnemotechnics in second language learning. *American Psychologist*, *30* (8), 821–828.

Ausubel, D. P. (1960) The use of advance organizers in the learning of meaningful verbal material. *Journal of Educational Psychology*, *51*, 267–272.

Bancroft, W. J. (1975) The Lozanov method in Hungary. *Educational Courier*.

Bancroft, W. J. (1979) Sophrology and Suggestology/Suggestopedia: The same system with a different name? *Journal of Suggestive-Accelerative Learning and Teaching*, *4* (2), 78–86.

Bancroft, W. J. (1981). Language and music: Suggestopedia and the Suzuki method. *Journal of the Society for Accelerative Learning and Teaching*, *6* (4), 255–266.

Bancroft, W. J. (1981) Suggestopedia and Soviet sleep-learning. ERIC Documents of Foreign Language Teaching and Linguistics, 19 pp. ED 206161.

Bancroft, W. J. (1982) The Tomatis Method and Suggestopedia: A comparative study. *Journal of the Society for Accelerative Learning and Teaching*, 7 (1), 3–18.

Bancroft, W. J. (1983) Yoga factors in accelerative learning. *Journal of the Society for Accelerative Learning and Teaching*, 8 (3 & 4), 115–128.

Barber, T. X. (1969) *Hypnosis: A Scientific Approach*. New York: Van Nostrand.

Bartel, R. (1983). *Metaphors and Symbols*: Forages into Language. Urbana, IL: National Council of Teachers of English.

Beer, F. (1978) Report on the school experiment, "Suggestopedia in elementary school". *Journal of Suggestive-Accelerative Learning and Teaching*, 3 (1), 21–37. ERIC 181721.

Berendt, J. & Schuster, D. H. (1984) Mental speeded practice in learning words. *Journal of the Society for Accelerative Learning and Teaching*, 9 (2), 113–141.

Bettelheim, B. (1977). *The Uses of Enchantment, the Meaning and Importance of Fairy Tales*. N.Y.: Vintage Books.

Bettelheim, B. and Zelan, K. (1982). *On Learning to Read, The Child's Fascination with Meaning*. N.Y.: Alfred A. Knopf.

Bloom, B. et al. (1956) *Taxonomy of Educational Objectives, Handbook I: Cognitive Domain*. New York: David McKay.

Bordon, R. B., & Schuster, D. H. (1976). The effects of a suggestive learning climate, synchronized breathing and music on the learning and retention of Spanish words. *Journal of Suggestive-Accelerated Learning and Teaching*, 1 (1), 27–40. ERIC 180–234.

Borgen, S. & Breithbach, D. (1984) Music and vocabulary words: The effects on physiological measures. Unpublished report, Psychology Department, Iowa State University, 19 pp.

Bower, G. H. (1974) Selective facilitation and interference in the retention of prose. *Journal of Educational Psychology*, 66 (1), 1–8.

Bower, G. H. & Karlin. (1974) Depth of processing pictures of faces and recognition memory. *Journal of Experimental Psychology*, 103, 751–757.

Boyle, C. L. & Render, G. F. (1982) The relationship between the use of fantasy journeys and creativity. *Journal of the Society for Accelerative Learning and Teaching*, 7 (3), 269–281.

Bristol, C. M. (1949). *The Magic of Believing*. N.Y.: Pocket Books.

Brown, B. (1975, July) *Psychology Today*, p. 4.

Bruni, C. W. (1977) Body-mind work toward a holistic learning theory based on a psychotherapeutic model. *Dissertation Abstracts International*, 39–11/B, 5539.

Bry, A. (1976) *est, 60 Hours that Transform Your Life*. N.Y.: Avon Books.

Bushman, R. W. (1976a) Effects of a full and a modified suggestopedic treatment in foreign language learning. Unpublished master's thesis, Brigham Young University, 34 pp.

Bushman, R. W. (1976b) An intuitive vs. a rational presentation mode in foreign language instruction. Doctoral dissertation, Brigham Young University. University Microfilms 77–4818.

Buzan, T. (1971) *Speed Memory*. London: David & Charles.

Caracciolo, W., Colombo, A. & Perini, S. (1973) Relation between the oblivion rate and the action of an induced emotional situation. In Ganovski., L., *Problems of Suggestology*. Sofia: Izdatelsvo Nauka i Izkustvo, 488–489.

Carter, J. L. (1981) Application of biofeedback relaxation: Procedures to handicapped children. Annual report on Project No. 443CH00207, Grant No. G008001608, with Bureau of Education for the Handicapped, U.S. Department of Education. 16 pp.

Caskey, O. (1980). *Suggestive-Accelerative Learning and Teaching*. Englewood Cliffs, N.J.: Educational Technology Publ.

Caskey, O. & Oxford, P. A. (1981) Mental imagery in early cognitive development. *Journal of the Society for Accelerative Learning and Teaching*, 6 (3), 196–205.

Caycedo, A. (1973) *Diccionario Abreviado de Sofrología y Relajación Dinámica*. Aura.

Claycomb, M. (1978) *Brain Research and Learning*. Washington, D.C.: National Educational Association.

Crampton, M. (1969) The use of mental imagery in psychosynthesis. *Journal of Humanistic Psychology*, 9 (2), 139–153.

Crawford, J. (1978) Interactions of learner characteristics with the difficulty level of the instruction. *Journal of Educational Psychology*, 70 (4), 523–531.

Devi, I. (1959) *Yoga for Americans*. Englewood Cliffs, N.J.: Prentice Hall.

DeVore, S., DeVore, G. & Michaelson, M. (1981) *Sybervision, Muscle Memory Programing for Every Sport*. Chicago IL: Chicago Review Press.

Dhority, L. (1984) *Acquisition through Creative Teaching*: ACT. Sharon, MA 02067: Center for Continuing Development. 209 pp.

Duhl, B. S. (1983) *From the Inside Out*. N. Y.: Brunner/Mazel.

Edwards, J. D. (1980) The effects of suggestive-accelerative learning and teaching on creativity. *Journal of the Society for Accelerative*

Learning and Teaching, 5 (4), 235–253.

Erickson, M. H. (1980) *The Collected Papers of Milton H. Erickson on Hypnosis*, Vols. 1-IV. N.Y.: Irvington Publishing.

Erickson, M. H. & Rossi, E. L. (1981) *Experiencing Hypnosis, Therapeutic Approaches to Altered States*. N.Y.: Irvington Publ.

Erickson, M. H. & Rossi, E. L. & Rossi, S. I. (1976) *Hypnotic Realities: The Induction of Clinical Hypnosis*. N.Y.: Wiley.

Fassihiyan, A. (1981) The notional analysis of "Suggestology" and its application in the teaching of a foreign language. 165 pp. *Dissertation Abstracts International, 42/04-A*, p. 1615. Language, linguistics.

Fast, J. (1970) *Body Language*. N.Y.: Pocket Books.

Fast, J. (1977) *The Body Language of Sex, Power and Aggression*. N.Y.: Jove Publication.

Feldenkrais, M. (1972) *Awareness Through Movement*. N.Y.: Harper & Row.

Feldenkrais, M. (1981) *The Elusive Obvious*. Cupertino, C.A.: Meta Publ.

Ferguson, M. (1973) *The Brain Revolution*. N.Y.: Taplinger.

From, E. & Shor, R. (1979) *Hypnosis: Developments In Research and New Perspectives*. N.Y.: Alinde Publ.

Frydman, M., Dierkens, J. & Abels, R. (1978) De la suggestopedie a la prise de conscience du corps: Etude experimentale de deux variables. (From Suggestopedy to body awareness: An experimental study with two variables.) *Langage et l'Homme, 37* (May), 11–17.

Fuller, R. (1982) The story as the engram; Is it fundamental to thinking? *Journal of Mind and Behavior, 3* (2), 127–142.

Gadian, D. (1982) *Nuclear magnetic resonance and its applications to living systems*. Oxford: Clarendon Press.

Galin, D. & Ornstein. R. (1975) Lateral specialization of cognitive mode: An EEG study. *Psychophysiology, 9*, 412–418.

Galyean, B. C. (1982) The use of guided imagery in elementary and secondary schools. *Imagination, Cognition and Personality, 2* (2), 145–151.

Gamble, J. A. (1981) The effects of relaxation training and music upon creativity. 107 pp. *Dissertation Abstracts International, 42/08-B*, p. 3399.

Gamble, J., Gamble, D., Parr, G. & Caskey, O. (1982) The effects of relaxation training and music on creativity. *Journal of the Society for Accelerative Learning and Teaching, 7* (2), 111–123.

Gassner-Roberts, S. & Brislan, P. (1984) A controlled, comparative and evaluative study of a suggestopedic German course for first year university students. *Journal of the Society for Accelerative Learning and Teaching, 9* (3), 211-233.

Gazzaniga, M. S. & LeDoux, J. E. (1978) *The Integrated Mind.* New York: Plenum Press.

Ginott, H. (1972) *Between Teacher and Child.* N.Y.: MacMilliam.

Glasser, W. (1976) *Positive Addiction.* N.Y.: Harper & Row.

Gordon, H. W. (1970) Hemispheric asymmetry in the perception of musical chords. *Cortex, 6,* 387-398.

Groff, E. R. & Render, G. F. (1983) The effectiveness of three classroom teaching methods: programmed instruction, simulation and guided fantasy. *Journal of the Society for Accelerative Learning and Teaching, 8* (1 & 2), 5-14.

Grudin, R. (1982) *Time and the Art of Living.* N.Y.: Harper & Row.

Guerin, G. R. (1976) Accelerated learning: A strategy for the instruction of pupils with learning disabilities in the regular classroom. Paper at the International Scientific Conference of IFLD. ED135154.

Guttman, G. (1979) Optimizing the presentation of classroom information. *Journal of Suggestive-Accelerative Learning and Teaching, 4* (4), 207-215.

Haines, P. R. (1981) Modifying mathematics instruction for gifted students using "SALT". 208 pp. *Dissertation Abstracts International, 42/11-A,* p. 4790. Education, Special.

Hales, V. E. (1983) Suggestopedia: Its effects on word identification skills of mildly and moderately retarded children. 94 pp. *Dissertation Abstracts International, 44/04-A,* p. 1053. Education, Special.

Hall, L. (1982) Reading Russian: A strategy for rapid mastery of the Russian alphabet (Lozanov approach). *Russian Language Journal, 36* (125), 211-220.

Hand, J. (1982) Brain functions during learning. In, *The Technology of Text,* D. Jonassen (ed.) Englewood Cliffs, N.J.: Educational Technology Publications.

Hansen, D. N. & O'Neill, H. F. (1970) Empirical investigations versus anecdotal observations concerning anxiety in computer-assisted instruction. *Journal of School Psychology, 8* (4), 315-316.

Hart, L. A. (1983) *Human Brain and Human Learning.* Hauppauge, N.Y.: Longman.

Hendricks, G. and Carlson, J. (1982) *The Centered Athlete: A Conditioning Program for Your Mind.* Englewood Cliffs, N.J.: Prentice-Hall.

Hendricks, G. and Roberts, T. (1977) *The Second Centering Book*. Englewood Cliffs, N.J.: Prentice-Hall.

Hendricks, G. and Wills, R. (1975) *The Centering Book*. Englewood Cliffs, N.J.: Prentice-Hall.

Holden, C. (1979) Paul MacLean and the triune brain. *Science, 204*, 1066–1068.

Houston, J. (1982) *The Possible Human*. Los Angeles, C.A.: J.P. Tarcher, Inc.

Jacobsen, E. (1938) *Progressive Relaxation*. Chicago, IL: University of Chicago Press.

James, W. (1979) *The Works of William James, The Will to Believe*. Cambridge, M.A.: Harvard University Press.

Jason, E., Gaonkar, G., Douglas, B. & Krishnan, K. (1976) Accelerated program in mathematics for disadvantaged students. Paper given at the TRIO Programs Conference, Nov. 8, 1976, 36 pp.

Johnson, P. L. (1982) The effect of group relaxation exercises on second- and sixth- grade children's spelling scores. *Journal of the Society for Accelerative Learning and Teaching, 7* (3), 239–253.

Johnson, D. and Johnson, R. (1975). *Learning Together and Alone: Cooperation, Competition, and Individualization*. Englewood Cliffs, N.J.: Prentice-Hall.

Jones, R. A. (1977) *Self-fulfilling Prophecies*. Hillsdale, N.J.: Erlbaum Associates.

Kaplan, P. et al. (1974) *It's Positively Fun: Techniques for Managing Learning Environments*. Denver, CO: Love Publ.

Kay, A. (1984) Computer Software. *Scientific American, 251*, (3).

Kimura, D. (1967) Functional asymmetry of the brain in dichotic listening. *Cortex, 3*, 163–178.

Kimura, D. (1973) The asymmetry of the human brain. *Scientific American, 228*, 70–78.

Knapp, M. (1972) *Nonverbal Communication in Human Interaction*. N.Y.: Holt, Rinehart & Winston.

Knibbeler, W. (1982) A closer look at Suggestopedia and the Silent Way. *Journal of the Society for Accelerative Learning and Teaching, 7* (4), 330–340.

Krippner, S. (1975) *Song of the Siren, A Parapsychological Odyssey*. New York: Harper & Row.

Kurkov, M. (1977) Accelerated learning: An experiment in the application of suggestopedia. *Journal of Suggestive-Accelerative Learning and Teaching, 2* (1&2), 27–35. ERIC 181–723. Reprinted by permission from *Innovative Instruction*, 1973.

Lahey, L. A. (1974) An empirical test of suggestopedia and suggestion in language acquisition. 63 pp. *Masters Abstracts*, *12/03* Education, general. AAD13-05697.

Lankton, S. and Lankton C. (1983) *The Answer Within: A Clinical Framework of Ericksonian Hypnotherapy*. N.Y.: Brunner/Mazel.

Leathers, D. G. (1976) *Nonverbal Communication Systems*. Boston: Allyn and Bacon.

Lee, I. J. (1981) Listening comprehension: A combined strategy for accelerated learning. 202 pp. *Dissertation Abstracts International*, *43/06-A*, p. 1863.

Lemyze, J. C. (1978) Teaching French composition through Suggestopedia. *Journal of Suggestive-Accelerative Learning and Teaching*, *3* (2), 129–133. ERIC 181722.

Leontiev, A. A. (1976) Sotsialnaya psikhologiya v obuchenii inostrannym yazykam. (Social psychology in teaching foreign languages.) *Inostrannye Yazyki v Shkole*, *2*, 70–74.

Lozanov, G. (1971) *Sugestologiya*. (Suggestology) Sofia, Bulgaria: Izdatelysvo Nauka i Izkustvo.

Lozanov, G. (1978) *Suggestology and Outlines of Suggestopedy*. N.Y.: Gordon and Breach.

Machado, L. (1985) *Principles of Emotology and Emotopaedia*. Pilot edition, Rio de Janeiro, Brazil: L. Machado. 109 pp.

MacLean, P. (1973) *A triune concept of the brain and behavior*. Toronto: University of Toronto Press.

Maltz, M. (1960) *Psycho-Cybernetics*. N.Y.: Pocket Books.

Mantyla, T. & Nilsson, L. G. (1982) The phenomenon of perfect recall. Umea,Sweden: Umea Psychological Reports, 163, 15 pp.

Masters, J. C. et al. (1975) Achievement standards, externally dispensed tangible reinforcement, and self-dispensed cognitive reinforcement as determinants of children's learning. Paper at the Biennial Meeting of the Society for Research in Child Development, April, 1975. 21 pp.

Mayer, R. E. (1979) Can advance organizers influence meaningful learning? *Review of Educational Research*, *49* (2), 371–383.

Mayer, G. R., et al, (1983) Preventing School Vandalism And Improving Discipline: A Three-Year Study. *Journal of Applied Behavior Analysis*, *16* (4).

McLuhan, M. (1982) *Institute of Noetic Science Newsletter*, *10* (1), Spring.

McMurray, N. E. et al. (1975) An instructional design for accelerating children's concept learning. Madison, Wl: Research and

Development Center for Cognitive Learning, Technical Report No. 321. 25 pp.

McMurray, N. E. et al. (1977) Instructional design for accelerating children's concept learning. *Journal of Educational Psychology*, *69* (6), 660–667.

McGlone, J. & Davidson, W. (1973) The relation between cerebral laterality and spatial ability with special reference to sex and hand preference. *Neuropsychologia*, *11*, 105–113.

Milner, B. (1968) Visual recognition and recall after right temporal lobe excision in man. *Neuropsychologia*, *6*, 191–209.

Milner, B. (1970) *Physiological Psychology*. New York: Holt, Rinehart & Winston.

Milner, B. (1971) Interhemispheric differences and psychological processes. *British Medical Bulletin*, *27*, 272–277.

Minsky, M. (1983) *Psychology Today*, *4*, (3), page 10 from Computer Music Journal.

Mishra, R. S. (1974) *Fundamentals of Yoga*. Garden City, NY: Anchor Books.

Moreland, R. L. & Zajonc, R. B. (1979) Exposure effects may not depend on stimulus recognition. *Journal of Personality and Social Psychology*, *37*, 1085–1089.

Morris, D. (1977) *Manwatching, a Field Guide to Human Behavior*. NY: Abrams.

Muñoz, J. (1984) *Trabajos para la Paz*. (Studies towards the Peace.) Sabadell, Spain: Graficas Perfil.

Nelson, W. (1979) Experimentation with the Lozanov Method in teaching word retention to children with learning disabilities. *Journal of Suggestive-Accelerative Learning and Teaching*, *4* (4), 228–271.

O'Boyle, M. W. (1986) Hemispheric laterality as a basis of learning: What we know and don't know. To appear in *Cognitive Instructional Psychology: Components of Classroom Learning*. G. D. Phye & T. Andre, Eds. (In preparation.)

O'Keefe, J. & Nadel, L. (1978) *The hippocampus as a cognitive map*. New York: Oxford University Press.

Oller, J. W. & Richard-Amato, P. A. (1983) *Methods That Work*. London: Newbury House.

Ornstein, R. (1968) *The Nature of Human Consciousness, a Book of Readings*. San Francisco: W.H. Freeman and Company.

Ostrander, S. and Schroeder, L. (1974) *Handbook of Psi Discoveries*. NY: G.P. Putman's Sons.

Ostrander, S., & Schroeder, L. (1979) *SuperLearning*. New York: Delacorte.

Paivio, A. (1975) Imagery and long-term memory. In, *Studies in long-term memory*, A. Kennedy and A. Wilkes (eds.) New York: Wiley.

Paivio, A. & Desrochers, A. (1979) Effects of an imagery mnemonic on second language recall and comprehension. *Canadian Journal of Psychology*, *33* (1), 17–27.

Palmer, L. (1985) Suggestive-Accelerative Learning and Teaching (SALT) with learning disabled and other special needs students: A literature review and meta-analysis. *Journal of the Society for Accelerative Learning and Teaching*, *10* (2) (in press.)

Parlenvi, P. (1982) Language and the brain. *Journal of the Society for Accelerative Learning and Teaching*, *7* (3), 219–232.

Patterson, K. E. & Baddeley, A. D. (1977) When face recognition fails. *Journal of Experimental Psychology*: *Human Learning and Memory*, *3*, 406–417.

Pearson, D. and Shaw, S. (1982) *Life Extension*: *A Practical Scientific Approach. Adding Years to Your Life and Life to Your Years*. N.Y.: Warner Books.

Peale, N. V. (1952) *The Power of Positive Thinking*. Greenwich, Conn.: Fawcett Publ.

Perls, F. S. (1969) *Gestalt Therapy Verbatim*. Moab, UT: Real People Press.

Peterson, E. E. (1977) A study of the use of the Lozanov method of accelerated learning in a naval science classroom. *Journal of Suggestive-Accelerative Learning and Teaching*, *2* (1&2), 3–10. ERIC 181723.

Petschauer, P. (1983) Exxon and higher education: Reflections on one student-to-student advising program. *College Student Journal*, *17* (2), 145–150.

Philipov, E. R. (1978) Suggestopedia: The use of music and suggestion in learning and hypermnesia. Doctoral dissertation, U.S. International University, 1975. Condensation in *Journal of Suggestive-Accelerative Learning and Teaching*, *3* (2), 65–107. ERIC 181–722.

Pribram, K. & Goleman, D. (1979) Holographic memory. *Psychology Today*, *12*, 71–84.

Prichard, A. and Taylor, J. (1980) *Accelerative Learning*: *The Use of Suggestion in the Classroom*. Novato, CA: Academic Therapy Publications.

Prichard, R. A., Schuster, D. H. & Gensch, J. (1980) Applying SALT to fifth grade reading instruction. *Journal of the Society for Accelerative Learning and Teaching*, 5 (1), 52–58.

Prichard, R. A., Schuster, D. H., & Pullen, C. (1978) Adopting suggestopedia to secondary German instruction. *ADFL Bulletin, 12* (2), 31–34.

Prichard, R. A., Schuster, D. H. & Walters, R. (1979) Suggestive-Accelerative Learning and Teaching (SALT) and student achievement in ninth grade agribusiness. *Journal of Vocational Educational Research, 4* (3), 57–67.

Ramirez, S. Z. (1982) The effects of suggestopedia in teaching English vocabulary to Spanish-dominant chicano third graders. Master's thesis, University of Wisconsin, Madison, 66 pp.

Reedy, J. B. (1981) An investigation of the effects of a whole-brain learning/teaching model, bi-modal development and synthesis on tenth grade student writers. *Dissertation Abstracts International, 42–06/A*, p. 1615.

Render, G. F., Hull, C. R. & Moon, C. E. (1984) The effects of guided relaxation and baroque music on college students' test performance. *Journal of the Society for Accelerative Learning and Teaching, 9* (1), 33–39.

Roberts, T. (1978) *Four Psychologies Applied to Education*. Cambridge, Mass.: Schenkman.

Robinett, E. A. (1975) The effect of suggestopedia in increasing foreign language. Doctoral dissertation, Texas Tech University. *Dissertation Abstracts International*, 1976, (*11-A*), 7217.

Romen, A.S. (1982) *Self-suggestion and its Influence on the Human Organism*. M. E. Sharpe.

Rosenthal, R. & Jacobson, L. (1968) *Pygmalion in the Classroom*. New York: Holt, Rinehart & Winston.

Ross, E. D. (1982) The divided self. *The Sciences, 22*, 8–12.

Roth, F. P. (1984) Accelerating language learning in young children. *Journal of Child Language, 11* (1), 89–107.

Russell, P. (1979) *The Brian Book*. N.Y.: Hawthorn Books, Inc.

Ryzl, M. (1976) *ESP Experiments Which Succeed*. San Jose, CA: M. Ryzl.

Sadella, E. K. & Loftness, S. (1972) Emotional mazes as mediators in one-trial paired associates learning. *Journal of Experimental Psychology, 95*, 295–298.

Samuels, M. and Samuels, N. (1975) *Seeing with the Mind's Eye*: *The History, Techniques and Uses of Visualizations*. NY: Random House.

Satir, V. (1972) *Peoplemaking*. Palo Alto, CA: Science and Behavior Books, Inc.

Satir, V. (1983) *Conjoint Family Therapy*, 3rd ed. Palo Alto, CA: Science and Behavior Books, Inc.

Schallert, D. L. (1976) Improving memory for prose: The relationship between depth of processing and context. *Journal of Verbal Learning and Verbal Behavior*, *15* (6), 621–632.

Schank, R. (1983) *Psychology Today*, April, page 32.

Schultz, J. H. & Luthe, W. (1959) *Autogenic Training*. New York: Grune & Stratton.

Schuster, D. H. (1975) Preliminary evaluation of PAMFA: Psychological Assist to Medical First Aid. *Journal of Clinical Psychology*, *31* (1), 97–100.

Schuster, D. H. (1976) A preliminary evaluation of the suggestive-accelerative Lozanov method of teaching beginning Spanish. *Journal of Suggestive-Accelerative Learning and Teaching*, *1*(1), 32–51.

Schuster, D. H. (1984) The effect of background music on learning words. Paper given at the Annual SALT Conference, May, 1984.

Schuster, D. H. (1984) A critical review of American foreign language studies using Suggestopedia. In Wil Knibbeler & M. Bernards (eds.), *New Approaches in Foreign Language Methodology*, 119–127. Nijmegen, Netherlands: University of Nijmegen, Proceedings of the 15th AIMAV Conference.

Schuster, D. H., Bordon, R. B., Gritton, C. E. (1976) *Suggestive-Accelerative Learning and Teaching*: *A Manual of Classroom Procedures Based on the Lozanov Method*. Ames, Iowa: Box 1216 Welch Station. ED-136566.

Schuster, D. H. & Ginn, S. (1978) Evaluation of the suggestive-accelerative Lozanov teaching (SALT) method in teaching earth science to low socioeconomic ninth grade students. *Journal of Suggestive-Accelerative Learning and Teaching*, *3* (1), 16–20. ERIC 181721.

Schuster, D. H. & Martin, D. J. (1980) The effects of biofeedback-induced tension or relaxation, chronic anxiety, vocabulary easiness, suggestion and sex of subject on learning rare vocabulary words. *Journal of Suggestive-Accelerative Learning and Teaching*, *5* (4), 275–288.

Schuster, D. H. & Miele, P. (1978) Minutes of the Conference for Suggestology, Dec. 11–16, 1978, Sofia, Bulgaria, *Journal of Suggestive-Accelerative Learning and Teaching*, *3* (3), 211–222.

Schuster, D. H. & Miller, T. M. (1979) The effects of active dramatic presentation, passive review with music, practice sentence making, word list difficulty, and sex of subject on learning rare English words. *Journal of Suggestive-Accelerative Learning and Teaching*, *4* (1), 32–51.

Schuster, D. H. & Mouzon, D. (1982) Music and vocabulary learning. *Journal of the Society for Accelerative Learning and Teaching*, *7* (1), 82–108.

Schuster, D. H. & Pansegrau, R. (1977) The effect of background music volume relative to speaking volume, previous list exposure and sex of subject on learning rare English words. *Journal of Suggestive-Accelerative Learning and Teaching*, *2* (1&2), 20–26. ED-181723.

Schuster, D. H. & Prichard, R. A. (1978) A two year evaluation of the Suggestive- Accclerative Learning and Teaching (SALT) method in central Iowa public schools. *Journal of Suggestive-Accelerative Learning and Teaching*, *3* (2), 108–122. ERIC 181722.

Schuster, D. H., Prichard, R. A. & McCullough, J. (1981) Applying SALT to elementary school spelling instruction. *Journal of the Society for Accelerative Learning and Teaching*, *6* (3), 189–195.

Schuster, D. H. & Vincent, L. (1980) Teaching math and reading with suggestion and music. *Academic Therapy*, (*Sept*) *16* (1), 69–72.

Schuster, D. H. & Wardell, P. J. (1978) A study of suggestopedic features that can be omitted once students learn how to learn. *Journal of Suggestive-Accelerative Learning and Teaching*, *3* (1), 9–15. ED-181721.

Seki, H. (1981) Experimental application of the SALT method to a large number of students. *Journal of the Society for Accelerative Learning and Teaching*, *6* (2), 109–115.

Sexton, T. G. & Poling, D. R. (1973) *Can intelligence be taught?* Fastback 29. Bloomington, IN 47401: Phi Delta Kappa, Box 789.

Showers, B. (1983) *Transfer of Training: The Contribution of Coaching*. Eugene, OR 97403: Center for Educational Policy & Management, University of Oregon. 106 pp.

Siegel, M. H. & Siegel, D. E. (1976) Improving memory for color. *Bulletin of the Psychonomic Society*, *7* (5), 461–464.

Simon, R. (1985) Life reaching out to life: A conversation with Virginia Satir. *The Common Boundary*, *3*, (1), 1–4.

Sperry, R. W. (1968) Hemisphere disconnection and unity in consciousness. *American Psychologist*, *23* (10), 344–346.

Spielberger, C. D., Gorsuch, R. L. & Lushene, R. (1968) Self-

Evaluation Questionnaire. Palo Alto, CA: Consulting Psychologist Press.

Stein, B. L. (1982) The effect of an adaptation of the Lozanov method on vocabulary definition retention. 73 pp. *Dissertation Abstracts International*, *43/11-A*, p. 3573. Education, Teacher training.

Stein, B. L., Hardy, C. A. & Toten, H. (1982) The effect of baroque music and imagery on vocabulary retention. *Journal of the Society for Accelerative Learning and Teaching*, 7 (4), 341-356.

Sternthal, B., Dholakia, R. & Leavitt, C. (1978) Persuasive effects of source credibility. *Public Opinion Quarterly*, *42*, 285-314.

Stevens, J. O. (1971) *Awareness*. Moab, UT: Real People Press.

Sommer, R. (1969) *Personal Space*. Englewood Cliffs, NJ: Prentice-Hall.

Suzuki, S. (1973) *The Suzuki concept: An introduction to a successful method for early music education*. Mills, E. & Murphy, T.C., Eds. Berkeley, CA: Diablo Press.

Svyadosch, A. M. (1965) K istorii gipnopedii. (On the history of hypnopedia.) *Voprosii Psikhologii*, *3*, 147-149. (Available in American translation also.)

Swanson, C. H. (1975) A paradigm for a future of change in organizations; A new potential for educational theatre. Paper at the Annual Meeting of the American Theatre Association, Aug., 1975. 20 pp.

Szalontai, E. (1980) Suggestive teaching methods in the Soviet Union. *Journal of the Society for Accelerative Learning and Teaching*, 5 (2), 67-73.

Tart, C. (1975) *Transpersonal Psychologies*. NY: Harper and Row.

Taylor, G. R. (1981) *The Natural History of the Mind*. NY: Penguin.

Taylor, G. R. (1983) *The Great Evolution Mastery*. NY: Harper & Row.

Thompson, M. (1973) Project Success Environment. Paper presented at the American Vocational Association Annual Conference Dec. 5, 1973, Atlanta, GA. ED-089134.

Thurber, J. (1983) *Psychology Today*, March, page 12.

Tomatis, A. (1977) *L'Oreille et la Vie*. Paris: Edition Robert Laffont.

Tomatis, A. (1978) *Education et Dyslexie*, 3rd ed. Paris: Editions ESF.

Tung, T. (1981) *WU SHU! The Chinese Way to Family Health and Fitness*. NY: Simon and Schuster.

UNESCO. (1980) Reunion du groupe de travail sur la suggestologie et la suggestopedie, Sofia, 11-16 decembre 1978, rapport final.

UNESCO, 7 place de Fontenoy, Paris, France.

van Vogt, A. E. (1980) Foreign language tapes. Beverly Hills, CA: 200 Language Club, Box 1727.

Vannan, D. A. (1981) Adapted Suggestology and student achievement. *Journal of the Society for Accelerative Learning and Teaching*, 6 (2), 129–134.

Vorkel, W. & Urban, A. (1977) Psychophysiologische Untersuchungen bei Gedachtnisleistungen. (Psychophysiological investigations of thought processes.) *Medizin und Sport*, 17 (6), 213–214.

Wagner, M. J. & Tilney, G. (1983). The effect of "SuperLearning Techniques" on the vocabulary acquisition and alpha brainwave production of language learners. *TESOL Quarterly*, 17 (1), 5–17.

Walken, C. L. (1968) Accelerating classroom attending behaviors and learning rate. *Dissertation Abstracts International*, 30-03/A, p. 1032.

Walken, C. L. (1968) Accelerating classroom attending behaviors and learning rate. Eugene, OR: Interim report on OEG-4-6-061308-0571. 89 pp.

Watzlawick, P. (1978). *The Language of Change: Elements of Therapeutic Communication*. NY: Basic Books, Inc.

Watzlawick, P. (1983). *The Situation Is Hopeless, But Not Serious. The Pursuit of Unhappiness*. NY: W.W. Norton.

Wenger, W. (1974) *How to Increase Your Intelligence*. New York: Bobbs-Merrill.

Young, D. R. & Belleza, F. S. (1982) Encoding variability, memory organization and the repetition effect. *Journal of Experimental Psychology: Learning, Memory and Cognition*, 8 (6), 545–559.

Zajonc, R. B. (1980) Cognition and social cognition: A social perspective. In Festinger (ed.), *Retrospection on Social Psychology*. New York: Oxford.

Zeig, J. (1982). *Ericksonian Approaches to Hypnosis and Psychotherapy*. NY: Brunner/Mazel.

Zeiss, P. A. (1984) A comparison of the effects of SuperLearning (TM) techniques on the learning of English as a second language. *Journal of the Society for Accelerative Learning and Teaching*, 9 (2), 93–102.

Zigler, Z. (1975). *See You at the Top*. Gretna, Louisiana: Pelican Publ.

Zukaw, G. (1979). *The Dancing WU LI Masters: An Overview of the New Physics*. NY: William Morrow & Co.

*   *   *   *   *   *   *   *   *   *   *

An organization for newsletters, journals, conferences, casette tapes and video tapes of past meetings:

S.A.L.T. Society
P.O. Box 1216 Welch Station
Ames, Iowa 50010

Here is a useful little pamphlet of good ideas:

100 WAYS TO SAY "VERY GOOD"

Distributed by:
Iowa Council For Children
523 East 12th Street,
Des Moines, Iowa 50319

APPENDIX

Complete classroom examples

A. Spanish Lesson
B. Science lesson
C. Lecture demonstration of method

SPANISH LESSON

(Author's note: The magic of a SALT lesson in increasing learning lies the suggestive-accelerative atmosphere and whole brain learning techniques. This atmosphere is largely non-verbal and the reader will have to generate it in his/her mind in the following account synthesized from several demonstrations of Spanish lasting 3–4 hours each. I have attempted to give "stage" directions in parentheses to help the reader, but you, the reader, will have to generate the rest of the atmosphere yourself, the Spanish wall posters, the Spanish background music, the semi-circular room arrangement, the teacher's supportive enthusiastic style, along with the other aspects of a SALT lesson described earlier in this book. Use your imagination actively!)

¡Ahora vamos a tener nuestra lección en español! Now we're going to have our lesson in Spanish! But first, stand up! ¡Estén de pie! (Instructor motions for students to stand up.) Vamos a hacer unos ejercicios. We're going to do some exercises. First, some stretching, one arm up, the other down. (Instructor demonstrates.) Primeramente, estirándose, un brazo arriba, el otro abajo. Figúrense que escogimos unas manzanas de un árbol. Imagine you're picking apples from a tree. (Instructor stretches one hand up appropriately.) Pick one up high. Escogen una de arriba. Pónganla en la otra mano y

177

luego en la cesta. Put it in the other hand and then in the basket. (Instructor does these motions.) Now there's a ten dollar bill on a higher branch, so stretch higher to get it. Ahora hay diez dólares en un ramo mas alto, así estiren mas alto para ganarlos. Encima del árbol hay un billete de cien dólares, ¡Obténganlo! On top of the tree is a $100 bill, get it! Stretch up as high as you can, then put it down in the basket. Estiren al máximo, luego pónganlo en la cesta. Bastante, siéntense. Enough, sit down please. (Instructor gestures.)

For the next several hours we are going to be having a Spanish lesson. Before we start I'd like to tell you about something that actually happened to me many years ago that shows why speaking Spanish is so much fun. As you'll see, speaking Spanish will be fun for you too here today as we go along. Spanish is a pretty language to listen to, it sounds so musical. I was fascinated with the language after I took a year of it in high school, and later took another year and a half in college. But to get on with my story. . . .

Shortly after my wife and I were married years ago, her folks made us an interesting offer. Would we like to go on a vacation to Mexico with them? Would we do the driving and arranging, if they would pay for it? Since I was struggling along financially while going to graduate school, we accepted with alacrity. Soon we were south of the border, alternating the driving on the Pan American highway to Mexico City.

My wife Locky is an artist and photographer, so that it was only natural that we stopped from time to time to take pictures. It was washday: on the rocks in the river bottom flats we occasionally saw women doing the laundry. Locky requested, "Stop the next time we see women doing the laundry, so I can take pictures." So the next river we crossed, we stopped on the far side for photography. Locky busied herself with taking pictures.

Some kids were playing on the opposite side of the bridge from where we had parked the car; I walked over to them to talk. As the children approached, I started chatting with them in Spanish, asking them their names, how old they were, how they liked school and so forth. This continued for awhile, as Locky was yet taking pictures. After several minutes of this, the kids' mothers came up to see what was going on; I suppose they thought I was going to do something to their kids. I promptly engaged the mothers in the conversation, which they also enjoyed. Apparently not too many American tourists in the 1950's stopped on a bridge out in the middle of nowhere along the Pan American highway in Mexico to talk to the rural people in their native Spanish.

One of the highlights of our trip started innocently enough when one of the laundry ladies asked me, "How would you like to see my house?" By this time, my wife had finished her camera work, and had joined our group. I looked at Locky and shrugged, "Why not? ¿Cómo no?" Locky's parents joined us, and we walked back to a modest thatched house just past the bridge. The woman proudly showed us her small dwelling, reed walls, thatched roof, dirt floor, but cleanly swept and neat. We expressed our appreciation to her for having shown us her home, and were getting ready to leave.

At that point a lady in blue uniform appeared and started the next episode in that memorable day. She inquired, "How would you like to see my house?" "¿Cómo no, why not?" was my reply.

Maria T, the village public health nurse, squeezed herself into the front seat of the car, and we were off to visit her house. Some distance off and away from the Pan American highway, I stopped the car on a sandy street in front of a modern-looking brick house surrounded by a stone wall. We entered the house, chattering away in mixed Spanish and English, saying everything twice regardless of who had talked first. It was with considerable pride that Maria showed us her kitchen, neat as a pin, and clean. She demonstrated her autoclave, a steam oven for sterilizing her hypodermic needles and surgical scissors. Of course we expressed our pleasure and appreciation for having been allowed to visit inside her home. We were getting ready to get on our way again, when she said, "¿Cómo le gustraia visitar a nuestra escuela? How would you like to visit our school?" My immediate answer as before was, "¿Cómo no? Why not?"

We climbed and squeezed back into the car again, and with Maria guiding, we went back across the highway to the village school. Once there, we found it to be a large one room school with about 50–60 students in attendance that sunny day. The five of us tried to enter the back of the room quietly and take pictures unobstrusively. That attempt failed as miserably as bringing an elephant into the classroom and expecting the students to study. As Locky started to take pictures, the teacher protested, "!No, espere! No, wait!" The instructor dismissed class, and had the pupils line up outside the building in the hazy sunshine to get their pictures taken. Locky waited patiently until the students were lined up in several rows to resume her photographic preparations. But again there was protest, this time from the boys and girls, who cried to the photographer, "!No fotos todavía, espere! No photos yet, please wait!"

Puzzled, we waited, not knowing the reason for the delay. We found out in a few minutes. A number of boys and girls had run home, and came panting back with shoes, shoes for themselves and their siblings. They wanted their picture taken with shoes on! Again we were quite profuse in our thanks to the teacher, the students and our blue-uniformed guide. We started to get on our way to Mexico city again, when the public health nurse said, "Cómo le gustaría ver la casa de una estrella del cine? How would you like to see a movie star's home?" Startled, I said, "¿Cómo no? Nos gustaría verla. ¿Pero aquí en el centro de ninguna parte? Why not, we would like to see it! But here in the middle of nowhere?"

After considerable discussion and arguing among ourselves, we clambered into the car with our nurse guide and started for the "movie star's home". We immediately left the Pan American paved highway on a gravel road; that wasn't so bad. Shortly however the stone road turned into a dirt road and our trepidations increased. What were we getting into? After 10 miles or so, the dirt road itself disappeared completely at the edge of a river, and no bridge! Our fears intensified, and our imagination peopled the environment with bandits waiting to jump out and rob us. Our nurse-guide calmly pointed out there was a steel cable going across the river, and that the ferry boat simply was on the other side. Upon seeing us, the ferryman already had started inching the boat manually back to our side, laboriously working the flat ferry toward us with a handle clamped and unclamped to the steel cable repetitively. Five minutes later the ferry docked just in front of the car.

Considerable argument again erupted over the adviseability of continuing. However, we could see that the road obviously did continue on the other side of the river, a fact pointed out by our calm and confident guide. Curious, but with misgivings, I drove the car down onto the flat-bottomed ferryboat. What a strange way to cross a river! The boatman inched us slowly and laboriously across the river, hitching and unhitching to the steel restraining cable as we had seen him do before. Docked on the far side, I drove the car up out of the flat boat wobbily onto dry land once more. The road beckoned, and soon we did arrive at a movie star's home, complete with swimming pool and big stable. The movie star was not home, but the estate was the winter home of Cantinflas, the famous comic Mexican movie star equivalent to our American Bob Hope. Later in Mexico City, we deliberately went to see a movie by Cantinflas, and it was good!

We piled back into the car, retraced our path to the small town on the Pan American highway, thanked our guide enthusiastically, tipped her generously, started again toward Mexico City, and heaved a big sigh of relief. What a day! This was one of the highlights of our month in Mexico! And it all happened because one of us could speak Spanish fluently.

Now why have I just told you this long story? Because I want you to get the feeling that speaking Spanish is fun, exciting and easy. When you can speak even a few words, you will find that the Mexicans, as do people everywhere, really like the fact that you are trying to communicate in their language. They open up, smile and come back at you eagerly when you talk their language. Let's apply the George concept right now to our Spanish lesson coming up, okay? So imagine yourself down south of the border, taking a vacation and enjoying yourself. See yourself saying a few words of Spanish to some of the local people, possibly in a hotel lobby or store. Imagine that the people are pleasantly surprised that you are speaking Spanish; watch their reactions.... Hear them musically answer you in Spanish.... Feel your startled elation, "They understood me!".... Continue for a few seconds in your imagination to enjoy this pleasant phantasy.... Tell yourself that knowing how to speak even a few words of Spanish would make your trip much more fun.... Imagine that you are just going to soak up Spanish like a sponge in the Spanish lesson starting now.... We're going to work with the sheet of paper that I just passed out, entitled, "Introducciones — Nombres y Ocupaciones". What do you think that means? Does it look like anything you know in English?

A student murmurs cautiously, "It looks like 'Introductions', maybe 'Occupations', but the word in the middle?"

"Sure, that's right," the teacher exclaims, "Introductions.... Occupations. Now what goes with introductions? What's the first thing you want to know about a person?"

A student rejoins, "Why the first thing I want to know when I met someone is their name."

"Of course," teacher comes back, "names are what you want to know when you meet someone, and their occupation. What's more important to a person than his/her name? But see how simple it is? 'Introducciones' is 'Introductions', 'Nombres' is 'names' and 'Ocupaciones' is 'occupations'. Change the spelling slightly and pronounce it a little differently, and you can read half of Spanish text right now. About half of all the words in Spanish are cognates; that is you can recognize them from the root of the word which looks about the same and almost always has the same basic meaning. On the next line, what do you think 'modelo' means?"

A student guesses, "It looks like an odd way to spell 'model' ".

Table A-1. Introducciones — Nombres y ocupaciones

MODELO:

¿Cómo se llama Usted (Ud.)?
Me llamo Roberto Bordón. ¿Y Ud.?
Me llamo Marta Silva, mucho gusto en conocerle, Roberto. ¿Quién es Ud.?
Soy un estudiante aquí en la clase de SALT para maestros. Quiero usar este método magnífico en el enseñar en mis clases el otoño que viene. Pero Ud., ¿Quién es Ud.?
!Qué sorpresa! Yo soy maestra también. Trabajo con niños en los tres grados primeros en la escuela pública.
Mucho gusto en conocerle a Ud. Pues, adiós.

OTROS NOMBRES Y OCUPACIONES DE MIEMBROS DE LA CLASE:

Jorge Washington, padre de los Estado Unidos, presidente del país.
Vive en Virginia en su rancho grande con muchos campos y árboles.

Isabel Girones, interpretador, traductor en las Naciones Unidas en Nueva York. Habla el inglés, el francés y el alemán.

Guillermo Acevedo, maestro, enseñador de inglés en Los Angeles en la escuela superior. Casado y con dos niños.

Eva Ortega de Granjas, maestra en escuela primera más ama de casa. Enseña el leer, el escribir y aritmética.

Pacheco Ortiz, astrónomo en la Universidad de Arizona. Descubridor de un cometa nuevo recientemente con el nombre — Esperanza.

Margarita Marín, contadora, tenedora de libros en Nueva Orleans. Obra en la oficina de una compañia grande de petróleos.

Alberto Unser, famoso conductor de autos rápidos, campeón tres veces en La Carrera de Indy 500 (quinientos).

Sara Juarez, danzadora, bailadora con La Nueva Opera Co, Ciudad de México. Baila en la danza clásica y folklórica en América Latina.

Ricardo Navarro, profesor de botánica en la Universidad de Estocolmo. Crece plantas raras de todo el mundo.

Maria Hernandez, compradora de ropa de moda en un gran almacén en San Francisco. Casada y tiene un hijo.

Ana Camacho, bibliotecaria en la Universidad de Mendellín, Colombia. Sabe mucha cosas interesantes de libros.

Tomas Felipe, médico de práctica general en Buenos Aires, Argentina. Ayuda much gente tener la salud buena.

Isabel Pinturón, jefe de una cadena de joyerias "Belleza" en Chile. Tiene muchos empleados y cuatro casas.

Catarina Ángula, profesora de antropología en la Universidad de Florida. Ha escrito tres libros y es muy famosa.

"Exactly," the teacher encourages. "Now on the next line, 'Cómo se llama Usted (Ud.)?' is different; no cognates here, no look alikes. It means, 'How do you call yourself?' or we would say, 'What is your name?' 'Cómo' is 'how', 'se' is 'yourself', 'llama' is 'call', 'Usted' is 'you', and 'Ud.' is the abbreviation for 'Usted' or 'you'."

Let's look at pronunciation. Most of the letters have the same sound (phonemes) in Spanish as they do in English, but "ll" in Mexico is pronounced "y", so "llama" is spoken "YAH-mah". The vowels are somewhat different also. "a" is spoken "ah", "e" as the "a" in "hay", "i" comes out "e" when spoken in Spanish, "o" stays the same as our English "oh", while "u" in Spanish lacks the initial "y" so that "u" is pronounced "ooh", the "ou" in our English "you".

Let's tackle the next line, "Me llamo Roberto Bordón. Y Ud.?" The "Me" in front obviously means "me" in English, so it means ... that's right, "I call me (or myself) Robert Bordon." The letter "Y" (pronounced "e") by itself in Spanish means "and", so the last part is "And you?" Simple, isn't it?

The first part of the next line, "Me llamo Marta Silva," thus would mean.... that's right, "I call myself Martha Silva". Then "mucho gusto" is "much pleasure"; "gusto" is like our work "gustatory" for "tasty". What do you think the rest of that line is, when you meet someone you say, "much pleasure in...." Great, "much pleasure in meeting you." "Conocer" means to know somebody, and the "le" on the end is "you". We would say, "My name is Martha Silva, pleased to meet you, Robert." The question at the end, "Quién es Ud.?" literally is "Who are you?" or really, "What do you do for a job?"

Let's take the next line, "Soy un estudiante aquí en la clase de SALT para maestros." "Soy" means "I am", and the next "estudiante" looks like.... Good, "student" is correct. "Aquí" means "here". "Clase" looks like.... right, "class". "Para" means "for" and "maestros" is probably.... "masters", right. Here, however, they mean a "master of the classroom" or a teacher. The whole sentence thus comes out as, "I am a student here in the SALT class for teachers."

"Quiero usar este método magnífico en el enseñar en mis clases el otoño que viene." Similar to our word "query", "Quiero" means "I want"; "usar" looks like "use", so it means "to use", the infinitive form of the verb. "Enseñar" means "to teach" or "teaching" here. "Clases" you already recognize as .... "classes". "Otoño" is the

Spanish word for "fall" or "autumn". "Que viene" is an idiom meaning "that comes" or we would say "next". The whole sentence comes out "I want to use this great (magnificient) method in teaching in my classes this fall."

The first word "Pero" in the next line means "but", and I'll bet you can puzzle out the rest of the line from what you already know. "Pero Ud., ¿Quién es Ud.?" translates, "But you, who are you (what do you do)?"

The next line "¡Qué sorpresa! Yo soy maestra también," you can guess means.... "What a surprise! I am a teacher also." "también" ... "also". Next come some new words: "trabajo" ... "work", "con" ... "with", "niños" ... "children". Notice that the "j" in "trabajo" is pronounced "h". The rest of the sentence you can probably guess means ... "in the first three grades primary in the school public." The whole sentence is, "I work with children in the first three primary grades in public school.

You should be able to guess most of the last line in the first paragraph: "Mucho gusto en conocerle a Ud. Pues, adiós." .... Yes, it translates, "Much pleasure in meeting you." "Pues" is "Well", and "adiós" is "goodbye". Literally, "adiós" means "to God" in the same sense our "Goodbye" is a shortened form of the old English "God be with you" at leavetaking.

Now that we've been through that list of names and biographies once, you can see how many words of Spanish you already know — lots of them! And the rest are easy to learn also.

For a quick break, let's take a look on the reverse of your sheet, Table A-2, Spanish Songs, at the top of the page, where you see "Frey Felipe". This is an old folk song or nursery rhyme that you will recognize as soon as I sing it. (Instructor sings:)

Frey Felipe, Frey Felipe; ¿Duermes tú, duermes tú?

Toca la campana, toca la campana; Ton, ton, ton; ton, ton, ton.

That is obviously ... "Brother John" in Spanish, right. Let's figure out what it says. "Frey" is like our word "friar" or an old English word for "brother". "Felipe" doesn't sound at all like "John", but it does sound and look like our "Phillip". So the first phrase is "Brother Phillip" ... repeated. "Duermes" has the same root as our word "dormitory", a place to sleep; "duermes" means "Are you sleeping?"

The last line "Toca la campana," is different than our "Morning bells are ringing." It means "Touch (or strike) the bell." "Toca" obviously is similar to our "touch". The last part corresponds to our "Ding, dong, ding," or "Ton, ton, ton."

Now that you know what it means, try singing it with me. I'll sing a little louder than you do, but try it. (Instructor sings, and encourages class to sing along also.)

Table A-2 Spanish songs

FREY FELIPE

Frey Felipe, Frey Felipe, ¿Duermes tú, duermes tú?
Toca la campana, toca la campana; Ton, ton, ton; ton, ton, ton.

LAS MAÑANITAS

Estas son las mañanitas que cantaba el rey David,
Y a las muchachas bonitas estas cantaban así.

Coro:
Despierta, despierta, despierta mi bien,
Ya los pajarillos cantan; ya la luna se ocultó.

LA CUCARACHA

Una cosa me da risa, Pancho Villa sin camisa,
Ya se van los Carrancistas, porque vienen los Villistas!

Coro:
La cucaracha, la cucaracha, ya no puede caminar,
Porque no tiene, porque le falta, mariguana que fumar.

Una cucaracha pinta, le dijo a una colorada,
Vamos a mi tierra, a pasar la temporada.

CIELITO LINDO

De la Sierra Morena, Cielito Lindo viene bajando
Un par de ojitos negros, Cielito Lindo, de contrabando.

Coro:
Ay, ay, ay, ay! Canta y no llores,
Porque cantando se alegran, Cielito Lindo, los corazones.

Good, are you ready to try out for the opera now? You're singing well enough already, would you like to try singing it as a round? Let's have this group start off — I'll help you. (Instructor divides class into roughly 4 equal-sized groups.) This group can be second group, third ... this group fourth. Good, let's get started, (Starts singing and encourages first group. Then gets second group going, third, and last. The round continues two or three times, then stops.)

Great, now that you're alert and refreshed from singing, let's tackle the other names and occupations on the reverse of the sheet after the first paragraph we have gone through already. Here is a list of a dozen names, half men and half women, with a short biographical sketch for each. As we go through these, pick out your favorite person. Pay particular attention to your favorite, as later you are going to pretend to be that person, and go around introducing yourself as that person. Sounds like fun, doesn't it? It will be.

Let's look at the heading itself, "Otros nombres y ocupaciones de miembros de la clase." I'll bet you can figure out what it means, can't you? I'll help you a little, the first word "Otros" means "other", and the rest is easy. It means ... "Other names and occupations of members of the class." Easy, isn't it?

The first person is "Jorge Washington". Notice that the letter "j" in Spanish is pronounced like our "h" and that the "w" comes out like our "v". Who was George Washington, but the "father" ("padre") of the ... United States. The Spanish typically put the adjective after the noun it modifies, so "Estados Unidos" translates as "States United". "Presidente" obviously is "president". George Washington was the father of the US and president of ... the country ("país"). "País" has the same root as "peasant", a poor country worker. The first word "Vive" in the next sentence is like our "vivid", something that is very "lively", so the word means "lives". The Spanish frequently will omit the pronoun subject at the start of a sentence like this, so that "Vive" not only means "lives" (the verb), but "He lives", referring to George Washington previously. He lives in Virginia, same spelling as English, but pronounced a little differently. The "gi" in "Virginia" is pronounced as "he" as in "He is a tall man." "Rancho grande" looks like "grand or big ranch", which indeed is its meaning. The little word "su" means "his". "Con" means "with". "Muchos campos" means ... "many camps", but you camp in a "field", so a better translation is "many fields". "Árboles" is similar to our "arboretum", a tree nursery; so it means "trees". The complete translation thus is "George Washington, father of the United States, president of the country. (He) lives in Virginia on his big ranch with many fields and trees."

Let's try the next person, Isabel Girones. She is an ... interpreter ("interpretadora") and another word for interpreter is "translator" or "traductor" in Spanish. She is at the ... Nations United ("Naciones Unidas") or UN, in ... New York, that's right. The first word "Habla" in the next sentence means "speaks" or better, "She speaks". Since she is a translator in the UN, what languages do you think she speaks? "Inglés" looks like our ... "English", "francés" like ... "French", and you might guess the next most common language is ... "German" for the Spanish "alemán". This whole paragraph translates as "Isabel Girones, interpreter, translator at the UN in New York. She speaks English, French, and German." The little word "el" in front of these languages means "the"; the Spanish say, "the English", "the French", for languages.

Next is "Guillermo Acevedo", or "William Acevedo". He is a teacher ("maestro"), or "enseñador", another way to say "teacher" also. He is a teacher of ... English in ... Los Angeles in ... high school. "Escuela" looks like "scholastic" or "school" here. "Superior" means the same in both languages. In the next sentence "Casado" means "married", and with two children. "Dos" means "two" and "niños" means "children". This paragraph translates, "William Acevedo, teacher, instructor of English in Los Angeles in high school. Married and with two children."

The next person is another lady, "Eva Ortega de Granjas". She is a "maestra" or ... teacher in "escuela primera" ... primary school. The word "más" means "and also". "Ama de casa" means "boss of the house" or "housewife". In the next sentence, you already know that "enseña" means "teaches" or "she teaches". She teaches the three R's, or reading, writing and arithmetic. "El leer" is "the reading" or literally the infinitive "the to read". "Escribir" looks something like "scribble", meaning "to write". The last word "aritmética" is just what it looks like. The whole thing means, "Eve Ortega de Granjas, teacher in primary school and also housewife. She teaches reading, writing and arithmetic."

Now we come to "Pacheco Ortiz". "Pacheco" or "Pacho" is "Frank" in English. He is an ... astronomer ("astrónomo") at the ... University ("Universidad") of Arizona. "Descubridor" means "discoverer" of a .... comet ("cometa") new, or new comet. The long word "recientemente" simply means ... "recently"; the "-mente" ending corresponds to our "-ly" to make an adverb of an adjective. You know that "con el nombre" means ... "with the name". "Esperanza" means "hope" in English. This sketch translates, "Frank Ortiz, astronomer at the University of Arizona. Discoverer of a new comet recently with the name 'Hope' ".

Coming up next is, "Margarita Marin" or Margaret Marin. She is a "contadora" or "accountant" in English. "Tenedora de libros" or "holder of books" is better said as "bookkeeper" in English. "Obra" is another way to say "works" or "she works" in English. She works in the ... office ("oficina") of a ... company ("compañia") big in .... petroleum ("petróleos"). Her short sketch translates, "Margaret

Marin, accountant, bookkeeper in New Orleans. She works in the office of a big oil company.''

Let's liven things up a bit for a minute. Turn to the back of the sheet and find the song, ''Las Mañanitas'', in Table A-2, Spanish songs. Some of you already know that ''mañana'' in Spanish means ''tomorrow'' or ''morning''. Here the title ''Las Mañanitas'' means ''The little morning songs''. But let me sing it for you, and see if you recognize the tune. (Proceeds to sing:)

Estas son las mañanitas que cantaba__el rey David,
Y__a las muchachas bonitas estas cantaban así.

Despierta, despierta, despierta mi bien,
Ya los pajarillos cantan, ya la luna se__ocultó.

Anyone recognize the tune as ... ''Clementine''? Let me sing it again for you. Notice that where I have put an underline ''__'' between two syllables, that the Spanish sing both syllables in one count of the music so as to end the words at the end of the tune. (Instructor sings the songs again.)

Okay, are you ready to try it with me? It's a pretty little tune, so sing along with me this time. (Instructor sings it again.)

Hey, you're starting to sing great in Spanish! That's fun, isn't it? Let's translate it now. ''Estas'' is the pronoun ''these''; ''son'' means ''are'', ''las'' means ''the''. So the first four words are ''These are the little morning songs''. ''Que'' means ''that''. ''Cantaba'' maybe looks a little like ''chant'' or ''canticle'', so the root means ''sing''. However, the ''-ba'' ending on ''cantaba'' makes it past tense, so it means ''was singing'' or ''used to sing''. ''Rey'' looks somewhat like ''royal'', so it means ''king''. The first line comes out ''These are the little morning songs that King David used to sing.'' The second line of the verse continues, ''And to the pretty girls (''muchachas bonitas'') they were sung thus (''así'').

''Coro'' obviously looks like ''chorus'', which it is. ''Despierta'' simply means ''Wake up''; at the end ''mi bien'' comes out ''my love''. ''Bien'' is like ''ben'' in ''beneficial'' which means ''good'' or ''helpful''. In the last line of the chorus, ''ya'' means ''already''. ''Pajarillos'' means ''little birds'', which are ... singing (''Cantan''). In the last phrase, ''luna'' means ... ''moon'' as it looks like our word ''lunar'' from Latin. The last word ''ocultó'' looks like our word ''occult'' or ''hidden''; the previous ''se'' is the reflexive ''itself''. The last two words ''se ocultó'' mean ''hid itself'' in the past tense. The entire chorus thus translates, "Wake up, wake up, wake up my love. Already the little birds are singing, already the moon has set (gone down or hid itself)."

Sing it with me this time. (Instructor sings it again.) That's good, sing it a little louder this time. (Repeats song.) Fine, let's get back to Names and Occupations again on the reverse.

That's great! Let's tackle "Alberto Unser". "Famoso conductor" looks like "famous conductor" or "famous driver" of ... fast cars ("autos rápidos"). "Campeón" resembles "champion" which is its translation. "Tres veces" means "three times". Who was Albert Unser? The three times winner of the ... Indy 500 Race ("La Carrera de Indy 500"). The entire sentence is, "Albert Unser, famous driver of fast cars, three times champion of the Indy 500 Race".

Next is "Sara Juarez". Notice the slight difference in the way her name is pronounced. She is a ... dancer ("danzadora") or the next word ... ballerina ("bailadora") with the ... New Opera Company ("Nueva Opera Compañia"). "Ciudad" means "city", so "Ciudad de México" is "City of Mexico" or "Mexico City". You probably can guess that the next sentence is .... She dances in the dance classical and folkloric in ... America Latin. The whole paragraph comes out, "Sarah Juarez, dancer, ballerina with the New Opera Company, Mexico City. She dances in classical and folklore dances in Latin America."

Then we come to "Ricardo Navarro"; notice how the double r in his last name is trilled; say it "errr", "Navarro". He is a ... professor of ... botany at the ... University of ... Stockholm. The next sentence is, "He grows (crece) ... plants ... rare (plantas raras). The last 4 words "de todo el mundo" mean "from all the world". This entire sketch translates, "Richard Navarre, botany professor at Stockholm University. He grows rare plants from all over the world."

Next is Maria Hernandez. She is a buyer ("compradora" from "comprar" meaning "to buy") of clothes ("ropa" which does not mean rope!) "Moda" looks like our word ... "mode" or "fashion". "Almacén" is "store", so "gran almacén" is a "big store". The last sentence starting out with "Casada" which you probably remember from before means ... "married". "Tiene" means "she has" from "tener" to have or to hold. "Hijo" you notice is pronounced like "eeh-hoe" in English, not "Hi Joe"! The complete paragraph is, "Maria Hernandez, fashion clothes buyer at a big store in San Francisco. She's married and has one son."

Next is another lady, Ana Camacho. The next word "bibliotecaria" looks like "Bible . . . care"; actually it means a "carer of books" or "librarian". She's at the . . . University of Mendellin, Columbia, South America. The second sentence starts with "Sabe", which means "She knows", coming from "saber", "to know." "Muchas" means . . . "much" or "many"; "cosas" means "things". The last word "libros" means "book" similar to our word "library", a collection of books. Her biographical sketch says, "Anne Camacho, librarian at Mendellin University, Columbia. She know many interesting things about books."

Now we come to a medically helpful person, Tomás Felipe. He is a doctor ("médico") of . . . general practice ("práctica general") en Buenos Aires, Argentina. "Ayuda" means "he helps", from the verb "ayudar", to help. "Gente" looks a little like "gentleman", and means "people". "Tener" you remember means "to have" or "to hold". "Salud" means "health" as does our "salubrious" which it resembles; it does not mean "salad"! Let's put this all together, "Thomas Phillip, medical doctor of general practice in Buenos Aires, Argentina. He helps many people to have good health."

We next have rich Isabel Pinturón, who is "jefe" ("boss" or "head") of a "cadena de joyerias" ("chain of jewelry stores") called "Belleza" ("Beauty" in English) in Chile, South America. The next you can guess is . . . . She has ("tiene") many . . . employees ("empleados") and four houses ("cuatro casas"). Stringing this all together, we get, "Isabel Pinturon, head of a chain of jewelry stores named 'Beauty' in Chile. She has many employees and four houses."

Last is famous Catarina Ángula, who is a . . . professor of . . . anthropology at the . . . University of Miami. In the next sentence, "ha escrito" means "she has written", the present perfect of the verb "escribir" to write. "Tres" is the number "three", so she has written three . . . books and is . . . very famous. Her complete sketch thus is, "Catharine Angula, professor of anthropology at Miami University. She has written 3 books and is very famous."

That wasn't so bad, was it? But let's try another song. Turn your Spanish sheet over to "La Cucaracha". This word can mean either a "cockroach", which it looks like, or a "foot soldier" in the Mexican Army. Guess which it means in this song. (Instructor sings:)

Una cosa me da risa, Pancho Villa sin camisa,
Ya se van los Carrancistas, porque vienen los Villistas!

Coro:
La cucaracha, la cucaracha, ya no puede caminar,

Porque no tiene, porque le falta, mariguana que fumar.

Una cucaracha pinta, le dijo__a una colorada,
Vamos a mi tierra, a pasar la temporada.

Let's translate the first line: "Una cosa" is "one thing" in English; "me da risa" is an idiom meaning "makes me laugh". Pancho Villa was a famous Mexican bandit who had his own private army called "Villistas". "Sin camisa" means "without (his) shirt (on)". The next line is, "Now running away ('se van' in Spanish) are the Carrancistas", the soldiers of the regular Mexican army under the direction of then President Carranza. "Porque" means "because" and "vienen" means "are coming". Thus this first verse comes out, "One thing makes me laugh, Pancho Villa without his shirt on. Now the Carrancistas are running away because the Villistas are coming!"

Next is the chorus ("coro"), which starts, "The cockroach, the cockroach, now he can't travel ("puede caminar" means "he is able to travel.") Why can't he travel? "Porque no tiene" you might guess as, "because he hasn't," which is right. "Le falta" means "missing to him" or when you are "faulty" about something, you are "missing it". What do you think he's missing? "Mariguana que fumar" means just what you think it does, "pot to smoke (marijuana)". The whole chorus translates, "The cockroach, the cockroach, now he can't travel; Because he hasn't, because he's lacking, pot to smoke."

The second verse starts with, "Una cucaracha pinta" which looks like it might mean "a painted cockroach". "Le dijo" means "told her", the past tense of the verb "decir" to say or tell. "Colorada" like our state of Colorado means "colored" or "colorful", but in this case referring to another cockroach. "Vamos" means "let's go" from the irregular verb "ir" meaning "to go". "Tierra" means "land" as in the Latin "terra firma"; here however it is better translated as "my place" or "my ranch". "Pasar" is a verb meaning . . . "to pass". The last word "temporada" means the "hot season" or "hot time"; it is similar to our word "temporary". The whole second verse is, "A painted cockroach told a colored one, Let's go to my place to spend the hot season."

Ok, folks, what we just went through was a "preview" or "decoding" of the material we are going to learn in the next few hours. As you can see, really about half of all the words in Spanish are cognates of similar words in English that mean about the same thing. Of course the ending may be different and the words may be spelled a little differently, but the root or basic part of the word is quite recognizable. So you already know quite a few words of Spanish; how about that! Let's take a 15 minute break before continuing. (A short break is next.)

FIRST CONCERT WITH CLASSICAL MUSIC

(As the students return from the break, the instructor has lively Spanish guitar music playing.) All right people we're going to go through the Spanish material in a special way with the classical Spanish music playing in the background. The music is Albeniz' Classical Spanish Music. First, I'm going to say the Spanish word or phrase slowly in Spanish, then I'll give its English translation, and last I'll repeat the word or phrase at normal speaking speed in Spanish. Then I'll pause for a few seconds, and go on to the next phrase or sentence. While I'm talking and during the pause, make the words and their meaning come alive for you. For instance, you can imagine that you're watching a movie with scenes that you make up, or you can think of linking the Spanish word with its English cognate, or you can project yourself into the action you visualize along with the words; feel yourself taking part in the action; it is happening to you. Use your imagination to get yourself dramatically involved in the words. Ready, any questions? Fine, let's try it. Make sure you have the side of the sheet labeled "Introducciones — Nombres y Ocupaciones." Think of yourself down south of the border again; here we go.

(Instructor reads a Spanish phrase slowly, gives its English translation, and repeats the Spanish at a normal rate of speaking. He pauses, and continues similarly.) Introducciones — Nombres y ocupaciones. Introductions — names and occupations. Introducciones — Nombres y ocupaciones. (pause 3–4 seconds.) Modelo — model — modelo. (pause) ¿Cómo se llama Usted? What do you call yourself, or what is your name? ¿Cómo se llama Usted? ... Me llamo Roberto Bordón. ¿Y Ud.? I call myself Robert Bordon. And you? Me llamo Roberto Bordón. ¿Y Ud.? ... Me llamo Marta Silva, mucho gusto en conocerle, Roberto. I call myself Martha Silva, pleased to meet you Robert. Me llamo Marta Silva, mucho gusto en conocerle, Roberto. ...¿Quién es Ud.? Who are you, or what do you do? ¿Quién es Ud.?

Soy un estudiante aquí en la clase de SALT para maestros. I am a student here in the SALT class for teachers. Soy un estudiante aquí en la clase de SALT para maestors.... Quiero usar este método magnífico en el enseñar en mis clases el otoño que vience. I want to use this great method in teaching in my classes this fall. Quiero usar este método magnífico en el enseñar en mis clases el otoño que viene.... Pero Ud., ¿Quién es Ud.? But you, who are you? Pero Ud., ¿Quién es Ud.?

¡Qué sorpresa! Yo soy maestra también. What a surprise! I am a teacher also! ¡Qué sorpresa! Yo soy maestra también.... Trabajo con niños en los tres grados primeros cn la escuela pública. I work with children in the first 3 primary grades in public school. Trabajo con niños en los tres grados primeros en la escuela pública.... Mucho gusto en conocerle a Ud. Pues, adiós. Pleased to meet you. Well, goodby. Mucho gusto en conocerle a Ud. Pues, adiós.... Remember to keep making images about the words, or imagine feeling yourself taking part in the dialog.

(Instructor continues in the same fashion for the remaining 14 biographical sketches that make up most of Table A-1. He follows along with the music, going faster when it does, reading more softly when the music volume drops, etc. He also raises his voice occasionally to emphasize certain lines dramatically, others he reads in a whisper to heighten interest, but always in keeping with the content. This procedure takes another 20 minutes.)

Well, how did you like that? That was our first musical concert, reading along with classical music. Let's make some more music of our own. Turn the sheet over to the last song, Cielito Lindo. (Instructor proceeds to sing the song.)

De la Sierra Morena, Cielito Lindo viene bajando,
Un par de ojitos negros, Cielito Lindo, de contrabando.

Coro:
Ay, ay, ay, ay! Canta_y no llores,
Porque cantando se_alegran, Cielito Lindo, los corazones.

Isn't that a beautiful song just to listen to? Let's translate it. Anybody know the name in English? ... Yep, "My Blue Heaven". In the first line "Sierra" means "mountain" because it looks like a "saw", its second definition. "Morena" simply is "brown". "Viene bajando" means "is coming down"; "bajando" comes from "bajar" meaning "to lower". What is coming down is told in the next line. "Un par" looks like ... " a pair", which it is. "Ojitos" means "little eyes" that are "negros" or black. After repeating the title, "contrabando" means just what it looks like, "contraband". The verse translates, "Down from the brown mountain, My Blue Heaven, is coming. A pair of little back eyes, My Blue Heaven, that are forbidden."

What is he talking about? ... The pair of black eyes probably belongs to the boss' daughter, and her old man won't let our male singer see her for a date. So he consoles himself in the chorus by venting his feelings with "ay, ay, ay, ay" which says about as much as "Boy oh boy" in English. "Canta" as you can guess means ... "sing". "No llores" means "don't cry". "Cantando" is "singing". "Se alegran" translates "make happy" from the verb "alegrarse" to make oneself happy. After repeating the title Beautiful Little Heaven, you discover what is gladdened is "los corazones" or the "hearts" of the singers. The chorus in its entirety is, "Ay, ay, ay, ay! Sing and don't cry, for singing, My Beautiful Blue Heaven, will gladden your heart." Personally I think this is one of the prettiest songs I know, both for its words and its tune. Sing it along with me, will you? (The instructor and class sing the song several times.)

SECOND MUSIC PRESENTATION, REVIEW WITH BAROQUE MUSIC

That was fun, wasn't it? For a quick change of pace, which one of the four songs on the reverse of the sheet would you like to sing? Las Mañanitas? Ok, let's sing it. (Instructor and class sing it.) Fine, now I want you to listen to some different music. We're going to review our "introducciones — nombres y ocupaciones" with baroque music. The music you hear now is Vivaldi's Four Seasons. Listen to it for a minute; try to get the feel of it and let yourself flow with the music. Relax and just let yourself flow with the music. (A minute goes by.) This time, just relax and focus on the sound of my voice saying the words; listen to them. I suggest you close your eyes, or if you keep your eyes open, pick a point up on the wall and stare at it. The purpose is to keep your attention focused on the words. Don't worry this time about making images; if any images or thoughts or feeling show up in connection with the words and their meanings, just enjoy them. The goal this time is to let the words and music flow without effort through your mind; just relax and enjoy it. As before, I'm going to say the words once in Spanish, give the meaning in English, then repeat the words in Spanish and pause. First listen to the music a little, and then I will start the review.... (Instructor then reads a short sentence or phrase in Spanish with an even, monotonous tone of voice, gives the English translation, repeats the Spanish, then pauses before going on. This procedure continues for the next 20 some minutes to review the entire Table A-1, Introducciones — Nombres y ocupaciones. At the end, the instructor plays the music for a minute without any words, then says:) That's the end of the passive review, open your eyes, stretch, get up, and we'll take another break.

PRACTICE PHASE — ELABORATION

(After the break and class resumes again:) We're now halfway through our Spanish lesson today. First, you need some practice speaking Spanish. Read the first paragraph or Model aloud along with me. (Instructor reads the first paragraph with the class reading along in chorus.)

What I want you to do now is to pick a partner, and go through the Model in the first paragraph taking turns. One of you read the first line, and the other person answer. I'll walk around and help you with the pronunciation. (This takes about 10 minutes; instructor walks around the room, visiting each group. He encourages the students, and occasionally will pronounce a word or sentence correctly to help them.)

Now comes the fun part. Pick one of the short biographical sketches that appeals to you. Pick someone you haven't introduced yourself to yet, and introduce yourself. Ham it up, be that person! Use as much of the model from the first paragraph as needed, but be sure to include most of the information from your sketch. When you have finished meeting one person, move on to the next. Introduce yourself to 4 or 5 different people this way. (Instructor moves about the room helping students and encouraging them. This part takes about 15 minutes.)

You people are great! Sure you're making some mistakes in pronunciation and grammar, but if you were in Mexico, people would understand you! Did you take time to understand your partner?

Now let's read all the other biographical sketches together so you get more practice speaking Spanish. Just let it roll off your tongue.

Ok, the first is ... Jorge Washington.... (The class reads the rest of Table 1 slowly with the teacher in another 15 minutes.)

Now for 1 more time, pick a different biographical sketch. Go and introduce yourself to yet some different people. (Instructor allows about 10 minutes for this, helping people as before.)

Wonderful! Let's take one more pass through the songs. (Class proceeds to go one more time through all the songs.) You people are really coming along with getting to know your Spanish! Now let's play charades for a few minutes. Just to get you started, I'm going to act out a person, and you've got to tell me in Spanish who I am and what I do. (Instructor proceeds to act out being an astronomer, looking up into the sky with an imaginary telescope.)

¿Quién soy yo? Who am I? The class answers. "Pacho Ortiz, astrónomo, descubridor de un cometa."

Bueno, exactemente! ¿Cómo se llama el cometa? Someone ventures, "Hope, Esperanza."

Fine, now break up into groups of 3 or 4 persons. Discuss some similar charade that you can do. Use all the action and descriptive phrases that you can think of in Spanish. Write down these key words and phrases in Spanish, so that you have a script of sorts. I'll give you 5 minutes, then we'll have you get up here in the center, and act out your action. Then we'll take turns guessing what you're doing and who you are. You can combine names and actions in the list, or you can be creative, and make up your own charade for a completely different character. Any questions? (Group takes 5 minutes for planning charades.)

All right, who wants to be first? Anybody eager to show how good you are? ... Fine, come out here in the middle, and do your thing. (Some one volunteers. People guess rather easily who and what is being acted out.) That's the way to go! Who wants to be next? (This process continues until all groups are finished.) I can see Hollywood needs to get ready from some competition from you people!

UNGRADED QUIZ

Now that you're all steamed up with acting, thinking and talking in Spanish, let's take a short ungraded quiz on how much you know. Take out a sheet of paper and number from 1 to 10. Don't put your name on it. (Instructor plays baroque Spanish music again.) The first five questions that I'm going to put here on the board are to translate from Spanish to English. The next five will be to write the corresponding Spanish for the English I give you.

1. ¿Cómo se llama Usted?
2. Soy un estudiante aquí en la clase de SALT.
3. Sara Juarez, danzadora, bailadora con La Nueva Opera Co.
4. Frey Felipe, ¿Duermes tú?
5. Porque no tiene mariguana que fumar.
6. I am a teacher also.
7. I call myself (First name, Last name).
8. Albert Unser, famous driver of fast cars.
9. The cockroach, now he can't travel.
10. Ring (or touch) the bell.

(Instructor moves around through the students while administering the 10 questions. He looks to see if students are finished writing and then asks:) Anybody want more time? No? Let's score these now. The first one is, "¿Cómo se llama Usted?" This means ... "How do you call yourself?" Or, "What is your name?" There are about 3 words there that are important, "Como, llama, Usted" that you should have translated for full credit; give yourself part credit as you think you deserve. (Instructor walks around room checking. The correction process continues until all 10 items have been discussed and corrected.)

Count up your score, and see how well you did. How many got at least 5 out of 10 right? (A considerable show of hands goes up.) How many got at least 6? ... 7? ... 8? ... 9? ... 10? Hm, it looks as if an average score is about 7! That is an excellent score for your first lesson with SALT. Of course, it would pick up slowly as we went along. But, let me interpret that 70% for you. There are about 180 words here in this Spanish lesson, and 70% of that is 126 words. I'll bet you didn't know you knew that many words already in Spanish, did you? (End of Spanish lesson.)

B. NINTH GRADE SCIENCE LECTURE

This lecture period started with five minutes of mild physical exercises, such as diagonal stretching, etc., and mind-calming exercises. The lecture material which follows was accompanied by background music.

Now your body is relaxed and your mind is calm. Return to that day, you were very young, and you learned something you were excited about. Maybe it was the day you learned to ride your bicycle or you learned about Halloween or Santa Claus or the tooth fairy. Think about that day for a while. Can you remember where you were? What room were you in? ... Can you recall who was there sharing that excitement with you? ... Can you remember the name of the person or teacher showing you, helping you? ... How did you feel? ... Put that feeling in your hands.... Return there right now. Think about how your hands felt that day.... Let that feeling spread up your arms.... Let that feeling go to the top of your head.... Spread clear down to the soles of your feet.... How did your stomach feel that day? ... Remember our stomach shows our excitement most of all. ... What were the thoughts and attitudes you had as a child when you were eager and excited about learning? They helped you remember all these years.... They'll help you just as much today. Your mind is just as good a mind yet. Thank you. (The background music stopped here.)

May I ask you to take out a piece of paper for us and write ten little questions and answers. You write the answers, I have the questions here.

Tim, take out a piece of paper. Tim, where's your pencil? All he's got is his arm. What am I going to do with his arm?

Bob, are you ready?

I'm going to ask ten little questions, right?

Remember the other day we talked about the symbols, the abbreviations for the elements. What was the abbreviation of the symbol for hydrogen? How do we say "hydrogen" in abbreviated or symbolic form? Hydrogen. There was a shortcut, shorthand way of writing hydrogen. I forgot, did you?

Let's go on to the next one then. What's the symbol or abbreviation for oxygen? Oh boy! You wouldn't ask another one of them, would you? What's the symbol or abbreviation for carbon?

I've asked three: hydrogen, oxygen and carbon. How do we

abbreviate them? How do we symbolize them so we don't have to spell them?

How do we write "water" in this class? We said water could be symbolized by using these symbols, how? How do we write the representation for water symbolically? How do we symbolize that? That's number four.

Okay, number five then. We were just talking about a rule or explanation that explains why molecules move. What was the name that was given to this formalized name for the rule about molecules and their movement, and what rules are included in this rule? What was the name we gave to the explanation of the motion of molecules. Did I erase it off the board? I guess I erased it. Son of a gun. What was the name we were just talking about the last several days? I didn't ask you to explain it now. When you see the name in the book, I want you to understand what the author is talking about. When you see this name, it is supposed to mean motion of molecules. We're supposed to explain these things to you, but we can't show you because the molecules are invisible.

Hey, how about number six? Somebody asked me the other day about air. I said air is not a molecule, I can't use it. I said air was an example of something else. Air was an example of some other kind of thing, not a molecule. What was it an example of?

What's something you like then? All right, let's go to spelling words, then. We're all such good spellers in here. How do you spell the word "liquid"? "Liquid"?

How do you spell "celsius"? A kind of temperature scale we're talking about. You know it, Jim? Beautiful! We'll have some new words for you next week, Jim! Okay? You want to see them ahead of time, or you want to just wait and come on into class? Okay, you're going to — yes, honey, you go ahead. But the rest of us are going to be spelling the word "thermal," that's a fancy way to say heat. That should be number nine, right? Now I looked at the list we had the other day, and I decided I was going to pick the hardest word in it, and the longest one. And the kids all laughed at me. The longest word was "temperature." And they said, "We know how to spell temperature already." So I guess I was wrong. Don't tell me how.

Okay, anybody got any questions over the ten I've already asked? One was hydrogen, oxygen and carbon. Then the name for water in the symbolic form. After that, the name for the explanation for the motion of molecules. Then, what's "air" an example of? If it's not a molecule, what is it? Then spell "liquid," spell "celsius," spell "thermal,'' and spell lastly "temperature." Any questions?

Out of curiosity, let's go back and see how you did. Number one, for the symbol of hydrogen, I have "H". "H". The symbol I have for oxygen, "O". The symbol I have for carbon is "C". What do we say is the symbol for water, then? "H_2O". What was the name? The name was the "molecular kinetic theory." That's too long? Oh, no, no, no. Some books call it the "molecular theory," and some call it the "kinetic theory". My book calls it the "molecular kinetic theory." And I had all three of those words in the spelling list, didn't I? What's air? It is a mixture of gases. It is an example of a mixture because it is more than one gas mixed together. It is mixed together. Gas should mean just one kind of element, not a mixture. How to spell "liquid"? L-i-q-u-i-d. How do you spell "celsius"? C-e-l-s-i-u-s. "Thermal"? T-h-e-r-m-a-l. And lastly then, "temperature"? T-e-m-p-e-r-a-t-u-r-e.

How many got all ten right? Anybody get all ten right? How many got nine right, then? There's a couple of people. How many got eight right? Look at all them hands come up! Okay, seven should do most of us. Seven or better, should be better than half of the class. That's not good. Somebody else is dragging up a few more over there. Six? Anybody want to brag about six? Anybody want to brag they got them all wrong? Lonnie? I guess I'll have to have a long talk with you. Bob, you run around and pick up the papers while I talk with Lonnie. Lonnie, you haven't been here, dude. Nine weeks of school are over, and this is the second time you've been to class. And you're late today. Now I have to give you a card, with your grade on it, next Friday, do you understand that? Well, I haven't got any work from you, so I have a problem. Now, do you understand these things we do at the beginning of class? Do you have any questions over those? Jim was just saying he'd better come to school. He can't learn these things if he's not here. Now I use Jim for my example because you know Jim.

Jim, can you learn when you sit here and do the things we say? Yeah! There's a chance, you see, when you're *here*. I don't know what you're expecting out of school, Lonnie, but not being here, you're not getting it.

Now let me tell a story to Jim and Lonnie, folks, and I want the rest of you to hear. A story. You don't want to hear my story? Girls, girls! Now Lonnie, I want you to imagine something. You're going to go to the grocery store. I want you to visualize yourself going grocery shopping. You have a cart, you go down the first row. What do you pick up? Some fresh fruit, what kind of fruit do you like? Put it in your cart. Do you want some milk, put in your cart. Do you want some hamburger, put it in. Steak? Would you go up and down the aisles and pick out all the things you like to eat: some cake, some ice cream, put it in the cart. Now you have your basket full, right? Full of goodies. You're ready to go to the check-out counter. You're at the check-out counter. Now, in your imagination: set your groceries up; the check-out clerk punches it on the cash register, the bill comes up to $40. You lay the money down. You get your receipt. There's your groceries all sacked up in the basket. Now imagine yourself turning and walking out of the grocery store and leaving all the groceries there. You just paid for all the things you wanted and you leave them there. And you try to walk away. That isn't smart, is it?

Lonnie, somebody is paying for our supermarket shopping here in school. Now maybe you don't understand how good the stuff is in this "can" called physical science. Maybe you never sampled our kind of cake called "English," and somebody is paying. You're walking away from the supermarket school leaving behind all the goodies. Like Jim says here, "I can do it." He's showing that he has learned something this year. Very important. You wouldn't leave your grocery sacks at the supermarket. I don't think it's smart for you to do it here either. So, if you'll excuse me, I'm going to take that attitude. You are buying — and paying — for goodies. And you let them go.

Now the only regrettable thing I see is there is no provision for you ever to come by this grocery store again. You only get to go through this "grocery store" school once. If you don't get the goodies while you are here, you are going to go to another grocery store which requires you to have these goodies, so you will just end up compounding the problem. The same is true with grade school. Now, not too many teachers want to go back and spell "cat" for you, do they?

Your school is all paid for. Tell me, I want you to understand how I look at things. You only come here once. Now some kids get held back one year, maybe they get to go back through, but I don't think they get to go through the same way the second time. Now anybody got any questions? The example I used to use for the kids in high school was going to the movies. We didn't have so much money back then. You go up and pay for two tickets to go to the movies and then throw the tickets down and walk away. Well, that's the way some people approach school. Jim, the way you're approaching school, you'd think school was for fooling around. That's not what school is about. When you're not here pushing. "Teacher, answer this question for me; think on this thing, teacher; give me an explanation; let me read another book; give me another idea," you're wasting time and money.

Somebody is paying for your school. The cost for each one of you per school year is about one thousand dollars. Somebody is paying $1000.00. The taxpayers are doing that. Hey, dude, nobody is ever going to pay for it again for you. You kids see that. That's the end of my example, okay?

We want to try to do a number of things again this morning. I was talking to you the other day about the kinetic molecular theory. I want to make sure we have the picture and models of atoms in our mind, and that the atoms may join together. What do they make when they join together? They make a molecule. Who was in the molecule? I forget. Who was in the molecule? Didn't they make a molecule? Laurie? Delana? They're both not here. Both my molecules are gone. What do I do now? All right, we made a molecule, right? And our big point was that they're always in motion. We talked to you about the temperature. Did I get into the discussion of gas with you? Did we make that chart on the board? We said what? Water is one of the molecules we were talking about, right? Water is a solid when it is 0° Centigrade or Celsius, and it's a gas when you get it to 100°; in between it's a liquid. As the temperature goes up, the speed went up, right? I said the temperature and speed were related and this gives a good explanation of why things melt, why things boil and turn into a gas. The speed goes up.

There's a point I think I missed the other day, and I want to make sure I've said it. We're talking about molecules moving now, and explaining temperature and gases and liquids and so forth. They're moving, we're speeding them up or slowing them down. Would it be possible ever to get them to be absolutely stationary, still, stop them? We're thinking and visualizing a moving molecule now, Laurie and I and Delana, would it ever be possible for us to stop? The scientists have contemplated this one and they came up with an explanation. Yes. Yes, it could stop. It would stop at a temperature on the Celsius scale at a minus 273°. There is absolutely no motion at this time. And guess what? They call that temperature, the absolute motionless temperature and they made a temperature scale of it. They called it the Absolute Temperature scale and 0 (zero) was here, 273° matches zero on the Celsius scale. Up here they have to have boiling at 373°. These are the two temperature scales we're going to see and use. In the book, you'll see "absolute" jump out at you once in a while. In reality, have we ever got down to absolute 0° temperature? Have we ever got all the motion stopped? No. We've got close, clear down to less than half of a degree, clear down to less than 272° below zero. On a Fahrenheit scale that's close to 500° below zero. How long would you last if it was 500° below zero? Not too long. That's awfully cold. The air in this room would have turned into a solid. What are you going to breathe? There's going to be no gases. Tammy, would I do a thing like that to you?

Did I talk about absolute zero and absolute motionlessness the other day, the last day we were here? Wednesday? I don't think so. Did I talk about it? We froze molecules only, but we said frozen water still did what? It still moved; somehow there's still some motion in it. The tape, the chair; you're a solid right? You are made up of molecules. Are you moving right now? Yes, if you are not this cold, 273° below zero Celsius. But you and I don't feel this motion, do we? It's very, very small or slight and as I say, most of us say, "I'm not moving, the molecules in my finger aren't moving." Of course not. We're talking about motions so small that under normal conditions we can't feel them, or see them, or talk about them. We all agree and this is also what the books say and this is what I think.

I don't want you coming in here and saying, "Mr. Gritton, you never saw it." I admit it. "Mr. Gritton, you never saw a molecule." I admit this. But from other evidence, we believe in the existence of atoms. From other evidence we believe that atoms are put together to make molecules. From other evidence these invisible things move. I don't have any way to show you these invisible things. No human has ever seen them. I could make drawings on the blackboard, I could show you motion pictures. We could make a model with Laurie and me. Didn't you fellows help me to be water molecules? We froze and moved slower. We talked about motion. Would you rather have it yourselves or rather have it on film? To me it doesn't make any difference. Do we agree that this is the basis your teacher is talking about, this is the basis your book has? You have to agree with it? No, but when you talk to me, or read the book or listen to a film, you need to know what scientists are saying. Background, right? Our book does this in only two or three pages. I'll take a little more time with you than the book does and make sure we agree.

Temperature — two scales. Notice I didn't include the Fahrenheit temperatures scale. If I asked you how hot it was in this room, you'd probably tell me 65 or 70 degrees Fahrenheit. We don't use this scale here because it's on its way out; it is old-fashioned. It's worn out — bye-bye. If you're young, you're going to live tomorrow, you're going to live next year, you're going to live the next 50 years; the Celsius scale will be the major temperature scale in your life. That's all I was going to talk about.

So, let's talk about the absolute temperature scale. We won't do much to it. All we have to do is take our Celsius temperature and change it to this one, we subtract 273° for each number. So if we want to change, all we have to do is remember 273° and add or subtract it.

One other point, I want to make sure that I've said is this: This, I said, was a theory, a possible explanation — molecules' moving. It implies certain things. For example, if things increase their temperature, they move faster, they get bigger. And vice versa, if things get colder, they stop moving as such, they contract. That's a pretty good statement. It fits in with the theory just right. Things move faster, they take more space, they get bigger. As things get colder they stop moving as such, they get smaller. As things get colder they stop moving as such, they get smaller. As things get smaller, they contract, another necessary statement. As water gets colder it turns into ice.

If water turned into ice and got smaller in size, water-ice cubes would sink to the bottom of the glass. Anybody ever see an ice cube sink to the bottom of the glass? What happens to that ice cube? When you put an ice cube in a glass of pop, where is it, on the bottom? Not unless something is on top to hold it down. What do ice cubes do? They float. This is another way of saying they get bigger and they didn't go according to my rules about getting smaller as they got colder. If ice cubes float, my theory is wrong.

Here is an example where my theory is wrong. I know ice cubes float; you know ice cubes float. My theory says ice cubes should sink. Something is wrong. Either the ice cube doesn't know what the world is doing or we don't. To tell you the truth, I don't think the ice cube does any thinking. It's part of nature. I think we're the ones doing the thinking and I think we got a bad theory. I think it's got some flaws in it. It explains an awful lot of things nicely for us. Solids, liquids, gases, expansion, contraction, why highways buckle in the summer time, why you shiver and shake in the winter time because you're cold. Sure, it explains a lot of real nice things for us, but did I say it was perfect? The point is, no, it is not. We're waiting for one of you; you're going to be the walking genius, right? You're going to be the man who is going to do it for us, we're waiting for you to come along and be the genius and say, "Hey, I've got a new idea stuck in my head and I'm going to show you why ice cubes float."

C. LECTURE-DEMONSTRATION ON THE LOZANOV METHOD

(Note: a video tape of a lecture-demonstration similar to this is available from: Media Center, Iowa State University, Ames, Iowa 50011.)

In all sincerity, by the time you walk out of here two hours from now, I hope you will have had one of the most creative learning experiences that you ever had in your life. I'm willing to bet right now that you won't believe you can learn so easily. I know I didn't when I started this research business several years ago. Nevertheless, there are a number of techniques, psychological, mental, practical things that you can do to help people to learn. What I plan on doing today is tell you about some of the revolutionary, very recent things that are occurring in education that help people learn in such fantastic ways as this. I happen to be a college professor at Iowa State University in Ames, Iowa. I spend a lot of time doing research in educational technology. Several years ago, I taught Spanish for one whole year at ISU. Getting permission to teach Spanish in itself was no small feat; it included two weeks' arguing with the Spanish people, mostly to convince them I knew what I was talking about. Essentially, the people in the experimental Lozanov section learned Spanish about three times faster than the students in the regular comparison section.

Much more interesting, a friend of mine at the University of Iowa this past summer taught Spanish twice with this special method. What he was trying to do was to teach two years of Spanish in two weeks. Now that's approximately a 10 to 1 compression. What he was doing was compressing a normal year-long course of Spanish, one hour a day, five days a week, for an entire year. He was trying to collapse that into five days a week, four hours a day, for two weeks, roughly a 10:1 speed-up. He was teaching Spanish about seven times faster than you or I learned it. This starts to get very interesting!

George Lozanov, the man at the University of Sofia, Bulgaria, the brains behind this educational discovery, claims that you can teach any school subject, not just foreign languages, from 5 to 50 times faster than presently done. While we can't verify his claim of teaching school subjects 50 times faster than normal, at least I am going to sit here and tell you we can do it three to seven times faster than the normal or the conventional way of teaching. I'm sure you don't believe me when I say that. You will by the time you get out of here. The reason I say this, is that it took me something like two years before I was ready to believe that I was seeing with my own eyes. I fiddled with this method for several years before I got nerve enough to teach Spanish this way. In teaching Spanish this way three years ago, I knew only about half of how to do it correctly. We found a few other things since then about doing it better. I'm sure we don't have all the answers yet. But we do know enough that we can do just what I said, teach most school subjects much faster than normal for the same achievement and the same comprehension.

And the kids love it! It's very interesting. I talked to one of the school teachers in Des Moines recently about the method. The reaction of his eighth grade science class is generally very favorable. We have approximately half a dozen teacher's at this Junior High School in Des Moines using the Lozanov method now. This school in Des Moines is located in one of the poorer, low socio- economic districts. To give you an indication of the background of the neighborhood, this description, I think, is appropriate: When a police siren goes down the street, there are half a dozen kids in a class of 50 that look nervously around. If there's a knock on the door and a policeman comes in that door, three kids go out the window. Every so often, kids don't show up in class: "Where've you been?" "Oh, I spent a couple days in jail." This is the neighborhood this school is in.

Well, this is interesting to show you the effect of the Lozanov method on such kids. The other day my friend there, the eighth grade science teacher, had reprimanded a young man because he was bugging the girl next to him, hitting her and pestering her. Finally, the teacher said, "Come on now, Joe, go out into the hall; the rest of us want to learn, you go on out in the hall." Normally that would be a license for the boy to cut school for the rest of the day, to cut classes, to misbehave, and do all sorts of other interesting things rather than going back to class. Do you know what happened? That kid spent his entire five minutes outside of class like this: He had the door open and was peeking in so he wouldn't miss a word of what was going on in class!

I would like to do several things here this afternoon. First, I'd like to say a little on the subject of learning. That'll take me about ten to fifteen minutes. Then I'd like to give you the entire Lozanov method, with you people participating. That will take about an hour to go over the entire method, to let you people have a feel about what this creative learning method is all about. Then I'll be asking you to learn some rare English words, words you've probably never seen before in your life, and won't, unless you look them up in the unabridged dictionary. Several years ago I didn't know what they meant myself.

The reason I'm doing this is that I don't want words you people already know. I'm going to show you how easy it is to learn these words. Then there will be a time for discussion. All right? That's what is going to happen this afternoon.

Well, let me describe first what this method is, then I'll show you how it applies in practice. I'm sure most of you know that you can do some rather startling things with hypnosis. For instance, I could hypnotize you and have you remember long-forgotten things. If you're hypnotized, you can do what is called age regression. Take you hypnotically back to your fourth birthday, and you'll be able to tell me with perfect clarity what flavor the cake was, the color of the frosting, how it tasted, how many people were there, how you felt, what the room was like, what color of carpet was on the floor. You'd be able to tell me with essentially something approaching perfect memory, what happened at the time of your fourth birthday. The Lozanov method achieves results like this, but *without* hypnosis. There is one similarity. There is a lot of suggestion going on, but it isn't hypnosis. Nobody is going to zap you and all of a sudden you've got a perfect memory. There is a lot of suggestion, but there are many other things going on, too. There's a lot of fun, there's a lot of game playing, pretending to be a kid again, learning, and exercises, both physical and mental. As a matter of fact, the method itself can be broken down into three phases: a preliminary phase for both the students and teacher, a presentation phase where the material is gone over in certain, rather interesting and novel ways, and finally, a practice phase where students put into use the material they have just heard. That is a quick description of the method.

At this point, I would like to start in with some of the preparations. One of the important elements of this is what I have been attempting to set up here so far if you have been listening and trying to analyze what I have been saying. You noticed I told you that by the time you get out of here you will change your opinion on how well you learn, how easily it's done, how easy it is to learn. You also noticed I said that you probably don't believe me, and I'm sure that you don't. Nevertheless, I'm setting the stage for this. This suggestive positive atmosphere means for one thing, that you don't tell a kid he's dumb, you don't even imply that he's stupid, or that he made a mistake, or that he can't learn, that he's retarded. You don't do any of these things. You support the kid in this learning. If he makes a mistake, you don't label him as stupid to his face, as "Jim, that was not a very bright thing to do, that was a bad way to do it." You don't do this in the Lozanov classroom. What happens instead is that the instructor glosses over this error and Jim would get corrected in passing, or he would correct his own papers. But so doing isn't directly pointing an accusing finger at Jim and embarrassing him. There are frequent tests, but they are ungraded and I'll say more about those in a little bit.

Let's continue with the prepresentation phase; the suggestive positive atmosphere is one of the most critical elements. This is difficult to do in practice. How do you be positive when you've got kids coming up in class where you would like to take them and knock their heads together? Well, you don't even think about knocking their heads together. What you do is inspire them with your own teaching, your own manner, to want to learn. You remember the example I just gave you about the kid that had to be reprimanded and sent out of class as a discipline problem. That is the way you handle the kid, with a positive approach. You remember he wanted to keep on learning, he did not want to be excluded from the fun. This is one of the effects of this pervasive positive atmosphere.

One of the hardest parts of teacher training to use this method is being suggestively positive. How do you convert a teacher who is stuck in the groove like me after ten to twenty years of teaching? How do you convert them? How do you get them out of this groove of being a disciplinarian and correcting kids? How do you do it? It's not easy, but it can be done. There are a number of techniques. The instructor speaks with authority. The kids are reminded of sometime in their life when learning was fun and easy, what you call infantilization. This is a very interesting process, but there are other and different techniques as well.

In starting a language class, infantilization as a game runs like this. Everybody, when they come into class is given a fake name and a fictitious biography. Mr. Houston, over here, might turn out to be Mr. Smith who wants to learn Spanish because he is going to South America as an engineer for an oil company next year. When you take part in all this, you take part as Mr. Smith. If Mr. Smith makes a mistake, that's not bad because that really isn't me, Mr. Houston, it's Mr. Smith. This is one of the ways of making the positive atmosphere, you make a game out of it. At the same time, you get rid of the embarrassment of that person's mistakes. If somebody goofs, it really isn't me, it's somebody else. Adults are quite concerned about making mistakes and being embarrassed in front of their friends. They don't like this. They go to great lengths to avoid this. They will not take refresher courses because they don't want to appear foolish or stupid or dumb or ignorant in their own eyes. They don't like that. Kids don't either.

In terms of preparation, there are essentially three steps: physical relaxation exercises, the mind-calming exercises and finally, pleasant learning recall. First, there are a number of physically relaxing exercises. I suspect that this is as good a time as any to show you what these are. Since this is part of the workshop, put down your paper and pencils and stand up, please. (Five minutes of exercises followed; bendovers, diagonal stretching, side bends and waves of tension relaxation.)

After the physical relaxation, there is mind-calming. Please note there is a definite sequence here. Before a person can concentrate, you have to have your mind calm, your mind clear. Kids in school are particularly worried about pulling the pigtails of the girl next to them, and poking her in the ribs. If a girl, her typical worry is what sort of date she is going to have tonight. Things like this are on their minds, so before a person can learn, before they can concentrate, they have to get their minds calm; clear their minds. Before a person is willing to attend to his or her mental life, such as concentrating on a lesson, the person has to relax physically. Now you people should be as limp as rag dolls, relaxed physically. That's the reason behind the sequence.

Mind-calming exercises, well, let's try it. Wiggle yourself into your seat at this point. Get yourself comfortable. Put both of your feet on the floor. Get comfortable because you are going to be sitting quietly and sitting still for five minutes. If you have to wiggle or change position because you have a cramp or something, please do so, but do so quietly and then go back to sitting still. Wiggle yourself into your seat, and close your eyes.

Imagine now, if you will, that you are walking up a hill or mountain just before sunrise. It's a clear, beautiful sky. The sun is about ready to come up, and you are walking up this hill to the top of the mountain, very relaxed, calm, eager, and you are waiting for the sunrise. You've been walking through woods and the trees are on both sides of you. And now you are just about to the top of the hill. Very relaxed, eager. Now the sun is finally coming up, and now it is day. A very beautiful situation. The sun is just peeking over the hill. It is an extremely beautiful scene. You are very relaxed. The sun is now causing long shadows in the valley. But even then it is very beautiful. It is a dramatic situation. You are very relaxed and very comfortable, very much at peace with yourself, very calm. Very calm.

Open your eyes. Listen to me. Isn't that a nice experience? The mind-calming part of this, then, as you have just seen, is a way to get your mind off all other nit-picking things that are bugging you, so that you can calm down and concentrate on learning.

Now the last part of the preparation has to do with what's called "early, pleasant learning restimulation." I'll take you through this, too. Again I'll ask you to experience this. Restimulation is an interesting psychological technique where you get people to remember by the back door. You concentrate on a person's body sensations and feelings; a person can remember these easily. If you remember a pleasant situation, for instance, it's very easy to remember how you felt, what you were doing, where you were. And once a person starts remembering a situation this way, then the rest of the memory starts flooding back automatically. The technique here is to focus on the way the person feels and the person's thoughts. Have you ever had the experience of trying to remember a person's name and after a while it just jumped up in your mind? Well, this is a way of facilitating that process.

All right, enough said about it, let's do it. I'd like to have you close your eyes again. This time I ask you to pick some pleasant, early learning experience. Now it could be as recently as the best novel you read within the last year where you were so absorbed in reading it that you couldn't put it down, you were so eager to learn how the story came out. Or this learning experience could be very early, and preferably, the earlier, the better. This is why I'm taking this much trouble to explain it. The earlier, the better. Most people have extremely good memories when they were kids. For instance, it would be nice if you could pick your mother or somebody's reading you a bedtime story. What I'm trying to do is to get your memory restimulated about sometime when learning was fun, you enjoyed it and your memory was tops. For instance, suppose your mother was reading you the story of Goldilocks and the Three Bears. You want to catch that eager feeling to learn to know how the story turned out. Once your mother read you the story of Goldilocks and the Three Bears, from then on you knew how the story turned out. You didn't have to go back and read it for that purpose. You might reread it and enjoy it, but not to know how the story came out.

Have you all picked some instance in your life when learning was fun? Everybody got some instance? The earlier, the better. It could be as recent as a year ago, or back as far in your life as you can to some instance, hopefully in childhood. All right, everybody got some situation? Close your eyes. Recall where you were. Use your imagination, if you have to. If you have to, put in something that appears logical on the basis of what you remember about this situation. Whom were you with? How did you feel about the situation? Take a look at how your mouth and throat felt. What sort of thoughts were you thinking? Take a look at the way your stomach felt. Then see about your hands and feet. Then take a look at your thoughts again. What were you thinking? Were there any sounds in the background? Was somebody talking, playing music? Now take a look at your emotions, your attitude. Now then, hang onto that eagerness to learn and knowing that you had a top memory skill; open your eyes and listen again.

That is the third part of the preliminary preparations. Normally at this point, you would go directly on to the material to be learned. At this point, however, I would like to read to you some of the things Edgar Cayce (ARE, 1970) had to say about learning and memory. Dr. George Lozanov has been developing this method at the University of Sofia, Bulgaria in Europe for the last twenty years. As you may know, Edgar Cayce was this country's most famous lay psychologist. People were always asking him questions for advice. What I want to do here is to take a look in some detail at his answers to questions about learning. People would ask him, "What about my memory? What about my ability to remember or concentrate?" The answers fit right in with what George Lozanov has said.

For instance, someone would ask Edgar Cayce, "What do I do for my loss of memory?" What did Cayce say? "You need to bring an individual awareness back into your mind. You stimulate the sensory nerves between shoulders, neck, and head by massage." Remember just a few minutes ago when we spent a minute or so working on turtle exercises? That's one way to do it.

Another person asked, "What's affecting my memory?" Cayce said, "Well, it's the vibrations not being in harmony between the sensory nervous system and the somatic nervous system. You should train your memory by constant usage just before going to sleep." This is similar to the mind-calming exercise we just went through, the mountain-top sunrise, typical of the way you feel just before you go to sleep. Cayce went on to say, "Get set to remember and repeat this when you awake."

Another person asked him, "What' causing my inability to remember?" Cayce replied, "You need to balance the mental and active portions of the physical body. You have to coordinate and harmonize the activities." This again is what we're doing with the physical relaxation exercises and the mind-calming exercises. Be relaxed, feel your body coordinated and harmonized.

Another person asked him, "Why is it hard for me to remember names?" Part of Cayce's answer was, "The energy in your nerves was being exhausted. You're working too hard at it." One of the emphases in the Lozanov method is that learning is easy. As a matter of fact, Dr. Jane Bancroft (1975) at the University of Ontario in Canada, calls this whole business, "Learning Without Stress."

Another person asked Cayce, "How do I strengthen my memory?" He said, "Reduce your high nervous tension. Massage the areas that are tense along your spine and coordinate the activities of your mental and spiritual bodies." Very interesting; I hope you are beginning to see the pattern.

Here's a boy who was rebelling and his parents asked Cayce, "Why is our son rebelling against school? Are we too strict with him?" Here's Cayce's answer, "From incoordination of the body and suggestions to the same, the body has come to be rebellious and his mind forgets." Then Cayce went on to say this key statement, "When people forget, their inner consciousness has rebelled and they prepare to forget."

"How do you improve your memory?" was again another question. Cayce counselled, "You have to guide and direct the person. You don't condemn." Remember what Lozanov said? You don't tell a person he's stupid, you don't even infer that he is, you don't behave like that in the classroom. You have this pervasive, positive, suggestive atmosphere that learning is easy, it is fun, and that people will do much better at it than they have in anything else they have done previously.

"How can I improve my memory?" yet another person asked Cayce. He admonished, "Better coordination. Concerted effort of body, mind and purpose. You have to be able to coordinate the physical and mental. Take a textbook, read it, then go over it in your mind, your consciousness. Then put it aside and mull over its possible application." What do you mean by mulling it over? You think about it. Notice I have broken the Lozanov method into parts. There are preliminary, presentation and practice parts. The practice part in the Lozanov method is very much its application.

Yet again Cayce was asked, "How do I improve my memory power and concentration?" Cayce responded, "Lose yourself in what you are doing." When we went through the mountaintop exercise, you got your mind off all the rest of your problems. You lost yourself; you prepare to learn.

"What should be done to overcome an unsatisfactory memory?" Cayce responded, "Well, use your mind creatively and concertedly, and you'll find that your memory improves. You also have to apply this and you have to want to remember, instead of wanting to forget." Yet again, "Why is it difficult for me to remember?" Cayce replied, "It is because you have trained yourself to forget."

All of us here in this room have gone through the public school system, some even the universities and colleges. We have come as a result to adopt for ourselves a level of learning that is normal for us. Yet what is normal for us, our present level of learning ability, is much, much less than is possible. Again I say, you'll see this before you leave here this afternoon.

Here's another question to Cayce that I think is interesting. "What causes sleepiness and lack of memory when I read?" Cayce's answer: "Toxic forces, poisons in the body. The flow of the lymph decreases in concentration, this causes drowsiness and this terminates the mind activities." What about all these exercises we did? What they do, among other things, is to cause the lymph to flow back and be recirculated by the heart. Very interesting.

"What is the cause of the blank feeling that comes over me and the corresponding inability to concentrate?" Cayce stated, "Pressure of gastric forces and poisons in your body." He added, "Massage along the spine and especially the cervical vertebrae which are right here in your neck, and the third and fourth dorsal vertebrae which are just above your shoulder blades. Then meditate. Meditative forces are a big help. Spiritual vitalization of your system can raise these forces considerably." Cayce went on, "Relax fully, especially the head and neck. Exercise these during reading. Read, lay aside, meditate, and ponder how you apply what you just read." Here's a final direct quote from him, "The clean, healthy body makes for a better indwelling of a healthy keen mind so that the spirit may manifest better." The statements I just read for you come from an excerpt of the Edgar Cayce readings in the circulating file on Thought, Concentration and Memory (ARE, 1970).

The next part of the Lozanov method has to do with the actual presentation of the material. The material is presented twice. The first presentation phase is called the active presentation phase. The instructor is active, not the kids. The kids are sitting there passively, lapping it up. The instructor is very active in a number of ways. For instance, he can vary the tone of his voice in some rather interesting ways. At times, he may be talking in a normal tone of voice, at other times he may be shouting or whispering. As an example, suppose you were teaching Spanish: you would be presenting vocabulary words in triads. Let's just do it; "Hijo — son — hijo." The word "hijo" (EE-hoh) means "son." Shouting, "Padre — father — padre." You get this sort of dramatic change. If the kids have been asleep, they wake up suddenly and they come back to their lesson. Other times the instructor will be using all sorts of gestures and pantomimes. The instructor can also vary his presentation, such as a very slow suggestive level where he is going along point by point, taking trouble to emphasize things. Other times, he may go along wildly because he has a lot of things to cover before the class is over and wants to get them all said. So there are lots of things that go on in what is called the active presentation phase.

As part of this demonstration-lecture, I've been telling you what's happening and why. Now I'm going to ask you to learn some rare English words. I'm going to pass out two lists of twenty-five words. I'll be very surprised if you've ever seen any of these words before. They are all in the unabridged dictionary. Everyone take a set.

All right, in the active phase, what are the students doing? They have prepared themselves in the preliminary phase by physical relaxation mind calming and the early pleasant learning restimulation. During the active presentation, the students are requested to use imagery. I'll be giving you some word images to go along with this in a little bit. I want you to go along with my suggested images and visualize these things in your mind, so that when I'm giving you the image I want you to see that image, I want you to *be* that image, I want you to smell it, to taste it, to experience it every way possible: you got that? Now we are going to go through these words and I want you to do just that. I want you to go along with the suggested images. I want you actively to do the mental gymnastics in your mind. In addition, I want you to experience the words as fully and completely as you can. By the way, there will be a quiz or a check on this, but have no concern about this because it will be ungraded; you are going to score it yourself. Don't get uptight. Anyone got any questions?

First pick up the list with the word "babracot" on the top. What I want you to do again is to review this early pleasant learning experience. So wiggle yourself into your seat, get comfortable again for a minute, put your feet on the floor, hands in your lap. Go back over this early pleasant learning experience one more time, just so you know how it feels. Take this same early learning experience; think again where you were; whom you were with. Take a look at what your breathing was doing; what were the thoughts in your mind; how did you feel; were there any sounds in the room; how did your stomach feel, your feet, your hands, how were your emotions; how were your thoughts. All right, maximize that feeling of your eagerness to learn,

hang onto it, and that top learning skill; open your eyes. We are going
to go through these lists. Now remember, go along with my suggested
visual images and really feel this image I'm suggesting. All right, here
we go. Does everyone have the list?

Babracot — rack or grate. Picture a baby in a cot in a rack by the
fireplace. Babracot.

Solander — map case. Visualize an explorer looking around at the
land with a map and putting the map away. Solander.

Mackle — a blurred print. A mackerel fish, flopping all over the
paper, blurring it so you can't read it. Mackle.

Kelbuck — a whole cheese. A buck deer eating a whole big cheese
all by himself. Kelbuck.

Rimpled — wrinkled. A person rimpling and wrinkling up his
forehead. Rimpled.

Lutose — mudlike. Two boys ludicrously throwing mud at each
other, having fun. Lutose.

Deforce — withhold by force. Dee police force says, "You can't
have it." Deforce.

Tocher — dowry. A father touching his daughter at her wedding
with a gold dollar. Tocher.

(This continued for fifty such words.)

In the active phase, the instructor is actively involved in presenting
the material in a dramatic way. I think you would all agree for those
fifty words you just went through, that the instructor was doing
something much different that you've probably ever seen in your
classroom.

The instructor goes into the passive stage in a mild, yet authoritative
tone of voice. We'll repeat these words for a second time in just a few
minutes. During this stage, the students are requested to sit quietly
and to re-enact in their mind's eye how the instructor went through the
words. You are to re-enact the images that I asked you all to make.
This second time through the list I'm not going to give you that image,
but I want you to re-enact it, to see it again, to feel it again in your
mind's eye.

We're also going to repeat the list with a variation, with music in the
background. I'm going to pace my presentation with the music. Also
I'm going to ask you to synchronize your breathing with what I'm
saying. I'll give you the same words all over again. I'll say the rare
word, its common synonym and repeat the rare word. While I do this,
I want you to hold your breath. So after I get through with this triad,
these three words, exhale breathe back in, and you should be back
with me for the next triad again holding your breath. Music will be

playing. You can listen to the music if you wish, but really pay attention to what I'm saying. All right? You've all got that?

Let's practice the breathing right now. Everyone take a deep breath, hold it, "hijo — son — hijo," everyone breathe out. Inhale, hold it, "padre — father — padre," exhale. Breathe back hold it, "madre — mother — madre," exhale. Got that? Do you have the idea? So to repeat, while I'm talking this time, hold your breath. Two things I want you to do are: while I am talking hold your breath and review the word images. Then I'll pause for an equal length of time, during which you are supposed to exhale, inhale again, and get ready to hold your breath. All right? This will be a 4-4 count: two counts for inhale, 4 counts to hold your breath, two counts to exhale and another two to inhale again. The second thing I want you to do is to go back over these visual images I have suggested to you. Just go back to what you were doing in your imagination to recreate that image. I won't give you the image this time, but you think about it. All right? Those two things I want you to do; hold your breath and review images while I talk. Any questions before we get started?

To repeat, you hold your breath for a count of four while I say the word; you exhale for a count of two and you inhale for a count of two. Start with inhalation, inhale 1,2; hold your breath for 1,2,3,4, while I say the words; exhale 1,2; that's a total of eight counts. Half of it is spent holding your breath while I'm talking. One quarter is spent inhaling and the remainder is exhaling after I get through talking. Okay?

All right, get settled in your seats. Think how much fun it is to learn. Remember or recall a pleasant early learning experience. Remember how fun it was, how easy it was, how much fun. Hang onto that feeling now as we go through this list again. Inhale. Hold, 1,2,3,4. Exhale. Inhale — hold your breath for four — exhale. Review the images.

Gamot — legislature — gamot. (The list of fifty words was repeated calmly in this fashion with steady background music.)

Now a few words on material organization. The material that you just went through was carefully organized. I very carefully picked these rare words and common cognates for you, and in addition, I had a prepared image for you. I spent a lot of time working this up. I didn't do it in just five minutes or an hour; it took me a while. Consider a typical classroom situation for instance: the material would be organized around one of everyone's favorite themes, food. Isn't that something to talk about? Certainly! All these lessons are organized around different, but central, themes. So when it comes to food, all right, what are the names of foods: peas, carrots, potatoes, meats, all these things. How do you order them? What do you do in a restaurant, you talk about foods, you sit down at a table, you order; there's a waitress at your table. You are going out, you spend money, it's being transacted; it's all around a central theme: food. The organization is one of the keys to this little deal.

The last Lozanov phase is practice. Students in the practice stage then are going to have to practice the material they have just gone over. Typically, this is done in alternate sessions. Now you are in the second day. Ignore what happened just now, that's yesterday. This is now tomorrow for you, practice. The students have to make dialogues, they write plays, they write down things, they have to use the words just learned. This is tomorrow. Please don't write on the word sheets I passed out to you. What I want you to do at this point is to break up into twos. In the next ten minutes use every one of those 50 words in a meaningful sentence. Okay, let's get started. (Ten minutes of animated practice followed.)

Okay, that's ten minutes. That was fun, wasn't it? Please pass in the word lists. Let's see how many of these rare words you know. I'm going to pass out two sheets of paper with the 50 words in a different order. Write the common meaning for each rare word. (The lists were distributed and about five minutes allowed for writing.)

Well, I see everyone has stopped writing. Fine. Let's see how well you did. Correct your own papers by marking in the margin or writing with a different color pen or pencil. (The fifty words were given for the last time along with their common meanings.)

Let's see how well you did. Count up how many you got right. (Pause.) Anyone get less than five? (One or two hands go up.) Between six and 10? (A few hands.) Between 11 and 15? (Some hands up.) Between 16 and 20? (Pause.) 21 to 25? (Pause.) 26 to 30? (Pause.) 31 to 35? (Pause.) 36 to 40? (Pause.) 40 to 45? (Pause.) 46 to 50? (Pause.)

Well, a typical score appears to be 25 out of 50 rare words you never saw before. How about that! That's very good! And one (of 22) got all 50 right. Excellent!

There is a snowball effect in the Lozanov approach. Today you got 50% right, tomorrow you would get 75%. By the next day most of you would be getting 90% right consistently. But even today you did very well, much better than expected. Right? Good! Thanks for your attention; that's all for today.

AUTHOR INDEX

218

TOPIC INDEX